Rosemary Auchmuty was born in Egypt in 1950 to an American mother and an Irish father. She grew up in Australia, and was educated at Newcastle Girls' High School (where she was school captain) and the Australian National University, from which she obtained a Ph.D. in history in 1975. Since 1978 she has lived in London. After several years of teaching history and women's studies in adult and higher education, she took up the study of law part-time as a mature student, and now teaches law and women's studies at the Polytechnic of Central London.

She has published two school textbooks and many articles on women's history. She contributed two chapters to the Lesbian History Group's book, *Not a Passing Phase* (The Women's Press, 1989), and has also published several short stories, including two in the anthology *Girls Next Door* edited by Mary Hemming and Jan Bradshaw (The Women's Press, 1985).

Rosemary Auchmuty has been an avid reader of stories about British girls' boarding schools since she was nine years old, probably because she did not go to one.

THE WORLD OF GIRLS
ROSEMARY AUCHMUTY

First published by The Women's Press Ltd 1992
A member of the Namara Group
34 Great Sutton Street, London EC1V 0DX

Copyright © Rosemary Auchmuty 1992

British Library Cataloguing in Publication Data
A catalogue record for this book is available from the
British Library

ISBN 0 7043 4310 X

Photypeset by Intype, London
Printed and bound in Great Britain by
BPCC Hazells Ltd.
Member of BPCC Ltd.

In memory of my mother
MARGARET WALTERS AUCHMUTY
(1910–1984)
with love

Permissions

The author would like to thank the following:

HarperCollins Publishers for quotations from the *Chalet School* books by Elinor M Brent-Dyer and the *Abbey* books by Elsie J Oxenham.

Reed Book Services for quotations from the *St Clare's* and *Malory Towers* books by Enid Blyton, (Methuen).

The editors of the journal *Trouble and Strife 10* (Spring 1989) for permission to reprint some of the material in chapter 6 in revised form; also from *Not A Passing Phase* by the Lesbian History Group, (The Women's Press, 1989).

A P Watt Ltd for quotations from *You're A Brick, Angela!* by Mary Cadogan and Patricia Craig, (Victor Gollancz, 1976).

Woolnough Bookbinding Ltd for quotations from the *Dimsie* books by Dorita Fairlie Bruce.

Every effort has been made to trace the original copyright holders, but in some instances this has not been possible. It is hoped that any such omission from this list will be excused.

Contents

Acknowledgements

This book has been a long time in the making. My thanks go to Ros de Lanerolle, who commissioned it; to the editors of *Trouble and Strife*, who published my first essay on the subject; and to all the people who have spoken or written to me about their own experiences of girls' school stories. This includes my editor Loulou Brown, who not only edited my manuscript expertly, but shared with me her insights into the subject with tact and enthusiasm. I am grateful to many friends in Australia, Britain and the United States for help and encouragement in writing the book, especially Peter Spearritt, Martha Vicinus, Amanda Baird, Jen Green, Emma Milliken, Lis Whitelaw, Sheila Jeffreys and the members of the Lesbian History Group, Anne Heavey, and Sibyl Grundberg.

Preface

The first girls' school story I ever read was *Gay from China at the Chalet School* by Elinor Mary Brent-Dyer, which I received as a Sunday School prize when I was nine years old.

I grew up in Australia. At that time no one there seemed to think it odd that Australian children should be given books about British boarding schools. This one was a reprint of a novel first published in 1944, set during the Second World War – of which I knew nothing – and therefore totally foreign, with its talk of blackouts and rationing. No one thought it odd that a nine-year-old should be given such a big book – 240 pages of close type – with not even one illustration to leaven the text. Anyway, I read it, and then discovered that there were other books in the series, some of which my Sunday School companions had been given. I borrowed these, and became an addict – not only of Chalet School stories but of girls' school stories in general.

My mother was a great and indiscriminate reader. She borrowed detective novels and thrillers by the armful from the public library, and also bought them second-hand at fêtes and jumble sales. The library was pretty much a dead loss as far as school stories were concerned, the Australian authorities evidently sharing the view of their British counterparts that the genre was bad for children. But the fêtes yielded treasures. Since my mother always read my books as well as her own – she could never get enough to read – she knew which authors and titles to look out for, and it was a great thrill to come home from school and find a 'new' Abbey or Dimsie volume waiting for me. Occasionally I was able to save enough pocket money to afford a brand new school story from the religious bookshop in Sydney which seemed to be the only stockist. And once I won three Chalet School books, signed by Elinor Brent-Dyer herself, in a competition run by the Chalet Club which I had (of course) joined.

It is to my mother that I owe the suggestion that I should write a book about school stories. When I had acquired a degree in history she remarked drily that I might usefully combine my research skills with my by now profound knowledge of the genre. It was not that my mother thought particularly highly of the books herself; she just could not bear to think of those hours of reading and re-reading wasted. But in the early 1970s girls' school stories were hardly considered suitable material for historical research; the book was not to see the light of day in my mother's lifetime.

In the 30-odd years which have passed since I first encountered girls' school stories, many people have asked me (usually with incredulity in their voices) to explain the appeal the books had for me. The books are so British, they point out, so elitist, so patronising about the Empire and so much else. They promote a value system and morality already outmoded in the 1950s and rejected outright in the 1960s. And here was I, growing up in a relatively classless society on the other side of the world, and educated in a state-run day school. What on earth did the books have to say to me? How could I *identify* with anything in them?

The easy answer is to say that I didn't, and that that was precisely why they appealed. I loved the books *because* I didn't live in England and didn't go to boarding school. I have always known that, by and large, women who did attend boarding schools do not enjoy reading girls' school stories. My two English cousins, my contemporaries in age, told me as much. They didn't enjoy boarding school much either. Other women have said the same thing. They loved adventure stories, mystery stories, anything which took them out of the prison-like schools; they read to escape from, not to get into, them, as the rest of us did.

But such a reply would tell only half the truth. For there

were other elements in the girls' school stories that I appreciated, only it took me years to recognise and identify them.
This book is an attempt to say why girls' school stories have
appealed, not only to me personally, but also to many
women of different ages and background, in Britain and
elsewhere, across more than half a century.

It was only when I came to live in England in 1978 –
drawn I am sure by the idealised picture I had gleaned from
school stories – that I met a number of women who, like
myself, had enjoyed the books in their youth. These were
the heady days of the Women's Liberation Movement, when
women were rediscovering the joys of working together in
a common cause as feminists had done in the late nineteenth
and early twentieth centuries. I began to make links between
the ideals of the women's movement, its talk of positive role
models and the benefits of single-sex education, and my
enjoyment of girls' school stories which had promoted similar ideals. In conversation, friends agreed that their ideas
about women's capabilities and roles had been shaped by the
strong adventurous heroines of the school stories they had
read in girlhood.

Throughout the twentieth century there has been an almost
complete reversal of the Victorian notion of separate spheres
for men and women, to the point that at the time my contemporaries and I were growing up in the 1960s, the opportunities for women and girls to have space for themselves without
males being present were becoming very limited. The single-
sex clubs and societies of earlier generations, the segregated
schools and women's colleges, were fast becoming things of
the past. Co-education and the greater sexual freedom of
modern times have proved to be mixed blessings for girls
and women, as they have taken away the advantages as well
as the disadvantages of the old system. For instance, women-
only gatherings, once taken for granted, now frequently
arouse suspicion, since feminism has made people aware that
women without men pose a threat to a society organised in
the interests of male power. This shift from separate spheres

to the compulsory mixing of the sexes has been gradual and uneven but inexorable; and I think it helps to explain the popularity of the girls' school stories, however old-fashioned and open to criticism in so many ways, among women who perceived the world depicted therein as a refuge and an alternative to the real world of patriarchal relations.

The field of schoolgirl literature is vast. One is filled with admiration for Mary Cadogan and Patricia Craig, who not only surveyed the entire range of fiction for girls in *You're a Brick, Angela!* (1976) but subsequently gave us studies of wartime fiction (*Women and Children First*, 1978) and women detectives and spies in fiction (*The Lady Investigates*, 1981). I have not attempted anything so ambitious. To illustrate my theory that girls' school stories owed their continuing popularity to their presentation of a woman-centred world, I have chosen to examine the work of four authors only: Elsie Jeanette Oxenham, Dorita Fairlie Bruce, Elinor Mary Brent-Dyer and Enid Blyton.

Why these four? One reason is that with Angela Brazil they form the 'Big Five' of girls' school story writers: the best-known, most prolific and, generally speaking, the best exponents of the genre. Angela Brazil was the pioneer and perhaps the most famous, at least in the years before the Second World War; but I have not included her in my study for three reasons. First, she belongs to a slightly earlier generation than the others (1869–1947), while the lives of my chosen authors span the years 1885 to 1970. Second, she has already been the subject of a fascinating short study by Gillian Freeman, *The Schoolgirl Ethic* (1976). Third, and most important, she did not write series. Nearly all her books were one-offs, with a new set of characters for each, so with only the occasional exception of a single sequel, there was no opportunity for characters to develop or grow into adulthood.

Oxenham, Bruce and Brent-Dyer all owed a major part of their fame to the fact that they wrote series – the Abbey books, Dimsie books, and Chalet School books, respectively – which followed the same set of characters through their schooldays to marriage and motherhood and subsequently, in the case of the first and last, through the schooldays of their daughters. The advantages of focusing on a sequence of books about the same characters are manifold. We can observe the authors' views on a range of topics about women of all ages, and at most stages of their lives. There is much greater opportunity for authors to develop their characters and ideas across a period of time and in a variety of contexts, not just at school but in the home and at work as well. And there is greater opportunity for the reader to get to *know* the characters, to become involved in their world. Helen McClelland believes that the enduring popularity of the Chalet School books is owing to Brent-Dyer's 'having created at the beginning of the series a set of characters who . . . gradually assumed an independent existence in her eyes and those of her readers'.[1] Her words apply equally to the works of Elsie Oxenham and Dorita Fairlie Bruce, each of whom, if not quite on the same scale, evolved an imaginary world which held generations of devoted fans in thrall.

Between them, these three authors wrote close on 250 novels for girls and I have read them all, the one-off books as well as the series, in an effort to get as comprehensive a view as possible of the authors' ideas.

Enid Blyton is a special case. By far the most prolific children's writer of all time – she wrote over 600 books – she did not specialise in school stories as the other three did. But she did write 16 of them, mostly arranged in series. She was a contemporary of Oxenham, Bruce and Brent-Dyer, and her books were – and are still – immensely popular. She is also the most criticised children's author in the English language. Her works have been banned or rationed in schools, public libraries, and private homes; they are said to be racist, sexist, cosily middle-class, poorly-written, and without educational value. For this reason therefore I have found it a useful exercise to include her in my survey. Did

Blyton, as has been alleged, reduce the components of children's fiction to the lowest common denominator? Are her books so much 'worse' than those of Oxenham, Bruce or Brent-Dyer? If so, in what ways, and on whose terms? And do her books also share their strengths?

The organisation of a book such as this poses a number of problems. Should the material be arranged thematically, chronologically, or by author? I have tried to incorporate all three approaches. Apart from Chapters 1 and 2, which are introductions to the genre and the writers, each chapter concentrates on one theme illustrating my general thesis: the ethos of the school, heroines, friendships, the 'crush' and 'training to be a wife and mother'.

Within each chapter the topic is covered chronologically; it is essential to be historically specific – the 1920s were a very different place for women in comparison to the 1950s or 1960s, for instance – and to note changes over time. Evidence for the discussion on each theme will be drawn from the works of all four authors, but each will be dealt with separately. It would not be fair to the writers concerned, whose differences of opinion and concern were often as great as their similarities, to lump them together into a set of undifferentiated generalisations about the way women were written about in any given period.

I have specifically *not* tried to offer an exhaustive critique of these four authors' works. Indeed, I have eschewed literary criticism altogether; I have neither the expertise nor the desire to enter into any appraisal of the literary merit of the works concerned. In using the works as historical evidence, I have made an effort not to do violence to the authors' achievements. I have tried not to take extracts out of context or to misrepresent the authors' intentions; it is my belief that by placing the writings in a historical context I am less rather than more likely to do this. My usual approach has been to use one or two particularly pertinent scenes or quotations to illustrate each point.

For those readers not conversant with the output of the four authors, I have provided a brief summary of the lives and writings of each in Chapter 2. There are no published biographies of Elsie Oxenham or Dorita Fairlie Bruce, so I have had to piece together what details of their lives I could glean from a small number of secondary references. Much more information is available for Elinor Brent-Dyer, including an enjoyable biography by Helen McClelland called *Behind the Chalet School* (1981) to which I am much indebted, and for Enid Blyton, who has been the subject of an official biography by Barbara Stoney (1974) and an unofficial one by her daughter, Imogen Smallwood (1989), as well as a number of critical studies. (Blyton's own *The Story of My Life* (1952) cannot be considered a reliable source.)

School stories portray what I have called – borrowing the title of the book from a very early exercise in the genre by L T Meade in 1886 – *A World of Girls*. This is a world where authority figures as well as colleagues and comrades are female, where the action is carried on by girls and women, and decisions are made by them. Girls and women rise to the challenges presented by ideals such as honour, loyalty and the team spirit. Women's emotional and social energies are directed towards other women, and women's friendships are seen as positive, not destructive or competitive, and sufficient unto themselves. School stories offer female readers positive role models to set against a reality which is often restrictive or hostile to them.

1 The School Story in Context

Literary critics have never concealed their contempt for the school story. Marcus Crouch wrote of 'assembly-line stories of girls at boarding-school' with 'no literary quality, no originality or point of view. They soon disappear from the publisher's lists, being replaced by others as lacking in creative quality.'[1] The *Junior Bookshelf*, a periodical for children's librarians founded in 1936, never reviewed a school story and rarely accepted advertisements for them. Disparaging references to 'the *Marcia Wins Through to the Fifth Form*, or *Peter Triumphs for the Team* type of book' made plain its attitude when the genre was in its heyday before the Second World War.[2]

The school story was condemned, together with other forms of popular fiction like the light romance or the Biggles-type adventure series, as badly written, full of stereotyped characters and plots, and produced to a formula which made discrimination impossible and 'true critical values' irrelevant.[3] 'How can children distinguish,' demanded a perplexed Margery Fisher, 'between innumerable madcaps of the Fourth recognizable only by the colour of their tunics or the length of their hair? How can they distinguish between one set of ink-stained desks and another?'[4] Settings were narrow, it was claimed, plots monotonous, the possibilities for lifelike characters restricted. A frequently invoked analogy with food gave point to warnings about the dangers of a diet of junk-reading. Q D Leavis, for example, opined in *Fiction and the Reading Public* (1932) that 'a habit of reading poor novels not only destroys the ability to distinguish between literature and trash, it creates a positive taste for a certain kind of writing, if only because it does not demand the effort of a fresh response'.[5] But deplorable as such a perference might be in adults, in children it was tragic, since the 'formative years' were the ones in which people were most impressionable and susceptible to influence.

Leavis' observation was echoed by Janice Dohm in an appraisal of the work of Enid Blyton:

The world created by the mediocre, in any medium and whatever motivates the maker, is small and shoddy, gradually closing the minds and narrowing the interests of the audience until only a few familiar formulas can provide entertainment and escape.[6]

The fact that some children *liked* to read formula books was, according to this view, irrelevant. Their taste was considered to be poorly formed and, as Boris Ford remarked succinctly, 'what adults read is their own affair, but what children read is *our* responsibility.'[7]

An article in the *Junior Bookshelf* in 1937 expanded on this point:

Since we desire our children to grow up useful members of society, with a workable and allowable code of morals and conduct, with some virtues and as few vices as possible, with a reasonable amount of knowledge and with a more or less cultured outlook, surely we cannot leave them, ignorant and inexperienced, to select their mental and spiritual food at random from the confused welter of reading matter which floods the market nowadays?[8]

The school story was singled out for specific criticism because it was 'unrealistic'. George Orwell was the first to voice this objection, against the serials featured in the boys' papers *Magnet* and *Gem*, in a celebrated article in *Horizon* in 1940. 'Needless to say,' Orwell pointed out, 'these stories are fantastically unlike life at a real public school . . . There is all the usual paraphernalia – lock-up, roll call, house matches, fagging, prefects, cosy teas round the study fire, etc etc . . .' What was unreal was that most of the boys in the stories were titled and had never heard of class friction, trade unions, strikes, depression, unemployment, socialism, fascism or civil war. Religion, politics and sex never intruded on their lives; girls were evidently non-existent. These fictional boys and their readers lived in a fantasy world that never changed: 'The year is 1910 – or 1940, but it is all the same.'[9]

A contributor to the *Junior Bookshelf* in 1954 extended his criticism to girls' school stories. Here the schoolgirl code of honour was measured against the problems of contemporary society and found wanting:

> The values are the familiar ones of 'truth will out', loyalty to one's friends, refusal to sneak or inform authority, the importance of games, personal standards and the repu-tation of the school, – not bad values, but perhaps not sufficiently in touch with the dilemmas of the modern school-child in the age of football pools, television and crowded classrooms.

The school story was seen as particularly retrograde at a time when an 'atmosphere of reality' had become 'the aim of the modern children's family story'.[10]

More than 20 years later Mary Cadogan and Patricia Craig in *You're a Brick, Angela!* levelled this charge at Elinor Brent-Dyer's popular Chalet School series:

> The 58th Chalet book (1970) contains its quota of natural and unnatural disasters (a thunderstorm, two floods, and a green dye which falls on someone's head); minor acts of defiance on the part of unruly Middles . . . and problems and worries for the headmistress: 'Then she turned her attention to the list of curtains required for the new dormi-tories that were coming into being next term. This was not an easy matter to decide, for there were so many

dormitories already to take the name of the different flowers that finding new names was something of a puzzle.' For all its flavour of a period piece, this was written in the present decade, in the era of the *Little Red Schoolbook*, the Rupert Bear obscenity trial, teachers' pay disputes, and a great deal of concern over the increasing use of marihuana in schools.[11]

By the 1970s the critics' message was clear. Children could not identify with the characters in school stories, they found the plots 'impossible' and, because the majority did not themselves go to boarding schools, novels set in such a milieu could have little appeal or 'relevance' to them. What children wanted now, Frank Eyre told us in 1971, were 'books about girls with illegitimate children, drunken fathers, and coloured lovers; about pop stars and back street gangs; about punch-ups and other violence; about most of the popular topics of today'.[12] And in 1976, Cadogan and Craig claimed that 'Unlike the situation which existed in the 1920s . . . comprehensive schoolgirls today prefer to read about girls at comprehensive school.'[13] The heyday of the boarding-school story had passed – or had it?

IN DEFENCE OF THE SCHOOL STORY

Popular culture has always had its defenders – principally its creators, distributors, and consumers. When George Orwell launched his broadside against the *Gem* and *Magnet* stories, their author, Charles Hamilton, was quick to respond. The writer's business, he said, was

to entertain his readers, make them as happy as possible, give them a feeling of cheerful security, turn their thoughts to healthy pursuits, and above all to keep them away from unhealthy introspection, which in early youth can do only harm.[14]

At the very least, school stories were seen as good, clean fun.

A larger group of defenders insisted that, whatever its failings, the school story was harmless enough. They argued that people, young and old, lived their lives at many levels. 'The cultured do not spend their whole time in the pursuit of culture . . . normally they can enjoy trivial and vulgar things – such as poor films, variety, jazz, and literature of inferior kinds'.[15] Sometimes people wished for strong mental stimulation, at other times for relaxation. Easy-to-read formula books fulfilled the latter expectation. While helping to pass the time pleasantly, they might also provide a restful change after taxing labour, or an entertaining distraction from everyday troubles or tedium. This was as true for children as for adults. As *New Society* critic Jan Marsh pointed out, '*The Famous Five* can be positively refreshing after *The Weirdstone of Brisingamen*' [a novel by Alan Garner published in 1960].[16]

Teachers asserted that anything that encourages children to read, whether Biggles or even *Red Star Weekly*, was worthwhile. If the only thing a child cared to read was the product of a formula, then by all means he or she should be allowed to read it: it was better than nothing, and the child might be inspired to read something else as a result.

Another group of defenders took issue with the accusation of 'unreality' in school stories. Some emphasised the importance of escapist fiction as a means of consolation and compensation for lonely, dull or restricted lives. Since children's lives were frequently all of these things, reading provided a well-documented retreat from the problems and insecurities of growing up as well as a more positive means of wish-fulfilment and the acting out of fantasies.

Others questioned the notion of reality. 'What is real?' asked James Guthrie in 1958.

Philosophers, who are the people whose profession consists in asking themselves this question, tend to identify what is real with what is familiar to, and directly verifiable by, them. This, however, to my mind, makes the quite unwarrantable assumption that they are like us and that we both are like everybody else, past, present and future, all over the universe.[17]

Likewise, the critic's reality was not always the reader's, and greater confusion was caused by critics seeking to impose not only their own versions of reality upon the child but also their own interpretations of the *child's* reality.

That the critics and the defenders of popular fiction were at odds on *moral* grounds is nicely illustrated by two essays published in the *Junior Bookshelf* in 1943 in response to a competition asking readers for a written assessment of the Biggles books. Biggles was the fighter-pilot hero of a long and popular series of adventure stories for boys written by Captain W E Johns. They were clearly formula books and as such, unlikely to appeal to the editors of the *Junior Bookshelf*. The prize-winning entry, from Miss K E Bush of Southwark Public Library, found the novels factually unsound, their plots and characterisation weak, and the author's use of words slovenly.[18] But an essay submitted by a 14-year-old schoolboy offered a child's explanation of their appeal. The young reader first praised Biggles on moral grounds, pointing out that he was 'a true Britisher. He always fights for right against might.' He was a skilled pilot and 'a born leader of men, a man to look up to with admiration'. The boy found Captain Johns's subsidiary characters realistic and his plots engrossing; he could identify with the one and felt part of the other. To clinch matters, Biggles was a powerful role model: 'He is, in fact, the type of man I would like to be.'[19]

This young man's argument may surely be extended to the girls' school story – not necessarily in terms of the particular qualities admired here, which have the ring of patriarchy about them, but in terms of the reader's recognition of the heroine and his/her setting as possible realities as well as ideals. As with the Biggles books, the significance of the girls' school story lies not in the qualities for which it has been praised or damned: its realism, or its escapist potential, its literary merit or moral tone. And not in any stated values or explicit messages about class, race, sex roles, or any other political question. Rather it lies in an implied message and an unstated set of assumptions about what *might* be possible for girls and women. Just as Biggles provided 14-year-old boys with a hero to emulate, so schoolgirl stories gave girls their heroines, and in a patriarchal society, a rare vision of a women-only world.

AN INEXPLICABLE SUCCESS STORY?

The popularity of the school story has always defied its critics. Girls' school stories had a huge commercial success between the wars and for many years afterwards. Angela Brazil, their first great exponent, wrote 50 of them. Elinor Brent-Dyer wrote 59 *about one school*. Elsie Oxenham, at the peak of her popularity in 1936, had 52 titles in print. By the time Dorita Fairlie Bruce's *Dimsie Grows Up* (1924) appeared in its first Australian edition (1947), so the dust jacket tells us, sales of Dimsie books had reached half a million.

In the 1940s and early 1950s Enid Blyton entered the field of school story writing, adding 16 of them to her enormous output. Though excoriated by the critics, her books were appreciated by thousands of children, with the school stories ranking among her most popular series with her girl readers. In the 1950s Frank Eyre was writing hopefully that 'by 1950 the girls' boarding-school story seemed well on the road to extinction.'[20] Elinor Brent-Dyer, however, published 36 novels in the 1950s and had 65 titles in *British Books in Print* as late as 1961. She also had the distinction of having her own fan club, the Chalet Club, with close on 4000 members at the time of her death in 1969. In the 1950s large numbers of Abbey and Chalet School books were reprinted in hard cover, and by the end of the 1960s Collins Armada had begun

15

the lengthy process of bringing the latter out in paperback, a task which is only now reaching completion.

For a time in the 1960s and 1970s it seemed that the school story would in fact die the death its critics thought it deserved. A contributor to *Elinor Brent-Dyer's Chalet School* (1989) observed that after 1970, school stories became 'incredibly difficult to find – they even began to disappear from the libraries'. Only the paperback revolution in children's books kept the school story on the shelves of the retail book stores. As I remember vividly, reading school stories was very much a minority interest in this period. This meant, however, that there were many second-hand bargains to be had. All that changed in the 1980s. By 1980 Armada was selling 150,000 Chalet School paperbacks a year and the number had increased to almost 200,000 by the end of the decade. The 1980s saw a renewed demand for second-hand copies of the original hardback novels, with prices of £100 or more being charged by antiquarian dealers for first editions of some Chalet School books by 1991.[21]

So while it is true that some school story authors, popular in their day, are no longer read, the school story as an artefact did not die the death its critics thought it deserved. New generations are discovering afresh, through paperback adaptations, the schoolgirl classics not only of Elinor Brent-Dyer but of Angela Brazil, Enid Blyton and Antonia Forrest.

The resurgence of interest in girls' school stories suggests that the time is ripe for a new feminist interpretation. Cadogan and Craig's 'new look' at girls' fiction (*You're a Brick, Angela!* published in 1976) made no claim to be specifically feminist. While most of what it said about the genre was apt, and much of it amusing, for the feminist of the 1990s there are a number of problems with their analysis. First, though purporting to examine 'the intricate relation between a society and the kinds of expression it gives rise to', the authors frequently shift their focus from the social context to issues of stylistic merit, so that in the final result some novels are lauded and others condemned on grounds of 'quality' alone. 'Certain writers, like Angela Brazil and Dorita Fairlie Bruce, are unintentionally funny but nonetheless *good*; others, like L T Meade, are not.'[22]

Such a view permits sophisticated jokes at the books' expense but is unable to account convincingly for the enduring popularity of a long series of variable quality like the Chalet School books. Moreover, just as Cadogan and Craig distinguish between individual authors and books, so they also perceive series as being built around the personalities of individual characters, which is not always the case. This view fails them when it comes to explaining the success of the Abbey or Chalet School books where the original heroines grow up and leave the centre stage quite early on but the saga continues. They argue, for instance, that after Jo Bettany quits the Chalet School 'the books take on a factitious and sterile note from which they do not recover'.

> Their continuing popularity can be ascribed only to the fact that the glamour of the *idea* of the Chalet school had taken hold of children's imaginations to the extent that it was able to generate enthusiasm even for the boring intricacies of the old-girl network and the second-generation pupils' family relationships.[23]

This theory, however, is immediately contradicted by their singling out as the 'best' Chalet School books a group placed in the early years of Jo's marriage, when she is a mother with young children – well after she has left the school. We have, in fact, to look beyond individuals to the world of girls and women which these authors created. This in itself was a lasting attraction for readers.

Cadogan and Craig do note that school stories provide an 'exclusively female society' which allowed 'qualities which had been regarded as "masculine" . . . to occur in certain girls'. But they are critical of the way that 'The implications of this are rarely followed up: where a definite conclusion has to be drawn to a girl's activities, the sentimental equation

17

of marriages with "happy endings" has proved irresistible
– and . . . the idea that a girl's own ambitions should be
relinquished at this point is brought out.'[24] In making this
claim they are once again not entirely correct, since marriage
and motherhood do not debar Jo of the Chalet School, Joy
of the Abbey books, or Dimsie of her eponymous series from
pursuing their chosen vocations (writing, composing, and
herbalism, respectively). It could be argued that, in depicting
married women able to combine work and family, the books
presented an unrealistic picture of the possibilities for wives
and mothers of the period in which they were written from
the 1920s to the 1950s. The point is, however, that these
positive role models were put forward for girls to note, even
if they were difficult (though not impossible) to follow; in
any case, Cadogan and Craig were surely wrong to see
'ambitions' solely in terms of masculine-style careers.

My final criticism of Cadogan and Craig's analysis reveals
how much they were bound by the ideology of the era in
which they wrote. The early years of the current women's
movement were preoccupied with the struggle to obtain
equality for women with men, to be achieved through such
means as equal pay, the abolition of sex discrimination in the
workplace, and the free availability of contraception, abortion, and childcare facilities. In the educational sphere feminists launched an attack on 'sex-role stereotyping' in the classroom and children's reading material, considered to be
damaging to both sexes, in the hope and expectation that the
removal of sexist imagery and its replacement by sexually
interchangeable role models would create a climate of true
educational opportunity.[25] Cadogan and Craig criticised girls'
fiction covering the preceding century for representing
women 'essentially as passive, domesticated, brainless and
decorative'. They argued, however, not for a different, stronger brand of girls' fiction but for a unisex children's literature:

At the present time girls' fiction appears almost redundant
as a genre: the most interesting work which is being pro-

duced is capable of appreciation by anyone. Classification along rigid sexually-determined lines is, or *should be*, no longer valid.[26] [My italics]

Subsequent experience has shown that the elimination of separate provision for women (whether segregated schools and colleges, separate clubs and meeting-places for girls and women, or a sex-specific literature) has meant, in most cases, the reduction and sometimes elimination of provision for the female sex. Men tend to dominate and take over women's space. This is hardly surprising since we live in a patriarchy, a society organised in and for the interests of men, who possess more power than women. I argue that the decline of the girls' school story after the Second World War removed a potential source of strength for girls, and that its renewed popularity in the 1980s and 1990s points to a continuing need for a separate literature for girls and women which presents positive role models for their sex which are free from domination and control by men.

FEMINISM AND POPULAR CULTURE

The 1980s saw burgeoning feminist scholarship in the area of popular culture generally and women's literature in particular. Out of this has come a number of significant conclusions, among them, that popular fiction *is* worth studying, whatever literary critics say; that its message may not be entirely reactionary, but may include positive elements for women or elements which have been read positively by them. The messages have not been consistent across the twentieth century, but have varied according to historical circumstances. Even a specific era has contained contradictions and inconsistencies owing as much to contradictions in cultural attitudes to women at the time as to personal differences in authors' values and intentions. The effect of popular fiction on women's behaviour has not been proven, and perhaps cannot be proven – though this, of course, does not prevent speculation about it.

Establishing the credibility of research into popular literature was difficult for many feminist writers. Either the works studied were not considered worthy of critical attention – the reaction Nicola Beauman received when she told her former supervisor at Cambridge, a woman, that she was writing a book about women's novels of the interwar years (*A Very Great Profession*, 1983) – or the area was not sufficiently *politically* important in the view of fellow socialists and feminists, as Janice Winship found when she embarked on the study published as *Inside Women's Magazines* in 1987.

> Yet I continued to believe that it was as important to understand what women's magazines were about as it was, say, to understand how sex discrimination operated in the workplace. I felt that to simply dismiss women's magazines was also to dismiss the lives of millions of women who read and enjoyed them each week. More than that, *I* still enjoyed them, found them useful and escaped with them. And I knew I couldn't be the only feminist who was a 'closet' reader.[27]

Nicola Beauman's experience with women's novels was similar: 'For me, as well, a good novel must usually be one with a distinctively "feminine note", a novel which in some way or another illuminates female attitudes to experience, throws light on the texture of women's lives.' Quoting Anthony Burgess, who claimed to gain pleasure from reading only literature which had 'a strong male thrust' and 'a brutal intellectual content', Beauman remarked: 'Sadly, or happily, I only read novels with these characteristics under duress.' She found greater enjoyment in women's novels of the interwar years than in anything else she had read in the past 20 years, 'though they are clearly deficient in strong male thrust'.[28]

This personal engagement with the text is a distinguishing mark of modern feminist scholarship: both Beauman and

Winship wanted to study their particular branch of literature because they themselves read and enjoyed it. Their approach shows how far the women's movement had moved on since Cadogan and Craig were writing in the mid 1970s. No longer do feminist critics condemn images of femininity out of hand or criticise women's literature for portraying a sex thwarted from achieving in men's world on men's terms. Feminists in the late 1970s and 1980s abandoned their single-minded pursuit of equality with men, which meant aiming for masculine goals and attributes to the exclusion and suppression of feminine ones; they began to value many aspects of being a woman and to reclaim feminine ideals and qualities. As Janice Winship explained in 1987:

> Many of the guises of femininity in women's magazines contribute to the secondary status from which we still desire to free ourselves. At the same time it is the dress of femininity which is both source of the pleasure of being a woman – and not a man – and in part the raw material for a feminist vision of the future. For example, we don't so much wish to throw off 'motherhood' as demand that it be assigned a worthier place in society's scale of tasks and values . . . Thus for feminists one important issue women's magazines can raise is how *do* we take over their feminine ground and create new and untrammelled images of and for ourselves.[29]

This observation points the way to the second achievement of feminist scholarship in this area: the discovery that popular culture, with all its apparently reactionary values and traditional presentation of sex roles, can even so carry a positive message for women readers as I show in this book. Here work on popular romances of the Mills & Boon type has shown most development. This genre emerged roughly contemporaneously with the Women's Liberation Movement in the late 1960s; and perhaps this was no coincidence, as both can be seen as responses (albeit from very different political

21

standpoints) to women's increasing unease with their social position, described by Betty Friedan in *The Feminine Mystique* (1963) as 'The problem that has no name'. Within a decade, it had become big business on the grandest scale; by 1981 Mills & Boon sold 188 million novels annually worldwide, and the figures were increasing each year. Currently British women buy over five million Mills & Boon romances annually; some books sell over 100,000 copies; one in three British women reads them. Twelve new titles appear every month.[30]

Romance fiction engaged the attention of feminists at the outset of the Women's Liberation Movement as it seemed to embody most of what we were fighting against: the repetition of images of femininity and patriarchal power relations which, we feared, helped to keep women perpetually submissive to men and to divert their energies from rebellion by providing a temporary escape from the awfulness of real life. Largely because of their enormous popularity, romances were condemned as 'pornography for women', and the women who bought and read them with evident eagerness were pitied and deplored.[31]

Later studies, however, like that of American Janice Radway (*Reading the Romance*, 1984) took a more sophisticated approach. She argued that it was necessary to look at 'ethnographies of reading' as well as 'textual interpretation' to find the real meaning of literature.[32] By this she meant that we need to look at the ways the readers themselves read and use romance fiction as well as at the intended message of its producers.

This is particularly important to remember when scholars are examining a genre with which they are not personally familiar and do not themselves read for pleasure. Most feminist analysts of romances have never read the books by choice and want to investigate them purely to find out what role, if any, such literature plays in the construction and perpetuation of feminine ideals which help to keep women subordinate to men. They are outside the novels' intended audience and may read the text quite differently, with feminist consciousness, not to say cynicism. Radway concluded that:

> even the most progressive of recent romances continues to bind female desire to a heterosexuality constructed as the only natural sexual alliance, and thus continues to prescribe patriarchal marriage as the ultimate route to the realization of a mature female subjectivity.[33]

Romance can only flourish, however, in a society where heterosexuality fails to achieve that object: it exists 'as a protest against the fundamental inability of heterosexuality to satisfy the very desires with which it engendered women.' This failure, Radway argued, leads women to keep on reading in a perpetual search for the hero who will meet their needs. 'Romance reading, it appeared, addressed needs, desires, and wishes that a male partner could not.'[34]

Such was the feminist analysis. But non-feminist women readers, Radway found in interviews, saw the romance quite differently. The traditional message could not be denied, 'but it is essential to point out that . . . many of the writers and readers of romance interpret these stories as chronicles of female triumph.' The readers preferred to read about heroines who, in their view, had 'intelligence, a sense of humor, and independence', even though an outsider might judge them to be passive and helpless. Recently romance producers have claimed that the books are becoming more 'feminist', presenting more assertive heroines and nurturing heroes, or, as Radway puts it, 'incorporating a few of the least dangerous challenges to patriarchy into a literary form once thought to be a purely conservative reaffirmation or legitimation of it'.[35]

jay Dixon (1987) has argued that although Mills & Boon and the Women's Liberation Movement would seem to be at odds, they have one thing in common:

> M & B romances, too, put women first and see them as the true 'heroines' of the world. Women fight for what

23

they want, and win. They control their destiny and end up being both powerful and protected.[36]

She points out that it is important for feminists to realise that romances embody women's power fantasies and have a strong grip on the imaginations of thousands of women. This helps us to understand how more 'politically correct' literature, which turns its back on patriarchal certainties and points to unknown futures, seems so threatening and bleak to many women.

When English scholar Jean Radford wrote the introduction to *The Progress of Romance* (1986), she was able to state that the starting-point of most debates about popular culture was the question of whether it is 'merely a means of domination and control' or a form of resistance to the dominant culture.[37] This brings us to a further issue with which feminist scholarship has engaged in the last decade or so: the *effect* of popular culture on women. Granted that it may or may not carry a positive message, is there any evidence that popular fiction ever changed women's behaviour, for better or for worse in feminist terms?

Radway's work was important because it took us beyond the usual patronising if not contemptuous attitudes to women readers of romance fiction, and established that these women are discriminating and choose books with heroines who are, in their view, more independent and in control of their lives, and heroes who provide the caring and nurturing that real men for the most part do not. But she could not in the end answer the claim that romance-reading has a baleful effect on women. Typical comments by her interviewees indicated that it played an essentially compensatory role ('I'm able to escape the harsh world for a few hours a day'), while at the same time idealising heterosexual relations ('We can dream and pretend that it is our life').[38] Yet all the married women insisted that they were happy in their marriages, and there was certainly no evidence that reading romances led them to any kind of feminist consciousness, however that might be defined, or action against patriarchy (though some claimed it made them more assertive). The very act of reading disarmed the impulse for real change: 'Women's domestic role in patriarchal culture . . . is left virtually intact by her leisure-time withdrawal.' In any case, as Radway herself admitted, it is very difficult to trace the effects of romance reading on individual readers. Her guarded conclusion was nevertheless that romance-reading might well be, as feminists had always thought, 'an active agent in the maintenance of the ideological status quo because it ultimately reconciles women to patriarchal society and reintegrates them with its institutions.'[39]

All forms of popular fiction provide escape from a reality which may be less than ideal, but they also offer a vision of 'the possible or future or ideal' which may or may not be acted upon by the recipient.[40] There seems to be a fundamental difference between the reading of heterosexual romance and the reading of schoolgirl stories for the purpose of escapism. In reading romances, women escape into an idealised form of the patriarchal world, one in which patriarchal ideals and structures *work* for women, as they rarely do in real life. Although women do experience a sense of belonging to a community of women when they read women's fiction and magazines, they experience this separately and at a distance: the heroine stands alone and her goal is the *personal* achievement of heterosexual love and marriage. In reading school stories, on the other hand, girls and women escape temporarily into a world dominated by women – where patriarchal values, while rarely actually absent, may be softened by feminine influence, avoided as far as possible, or transformed at the hands of women into something positive for themselves. Certainly the books do not focus directly on men's power – a focus which, as Ann Rosalind Jones (1986) points out in the Radford volume, has important consequences for the romantic genre:

> For one thing, the narrative perspective in these novels still privileges the male gaze: the hero's perspective is always

the one from which the heroine's looks are described . . .
Another result of the centrality of the hero is that woman-
to-woman relationships are tangential or fraught; although
some novels represent strong families, including energetic
and capable mothers, the heroine is more likely to be given
a woman friend as a merely temporary confidante – or to
confront heartless or amoral rivals for the hero's love.[41]

Finally, if the reader is young, there is more possibility that
she will act upon the models offered to her by her reading;
the school story may therefore be more effective here since
its readership has generally (though not exclusively) been
young.

The contrast between girls' school stories and other juvenile fiction was remarked upon by Cammilla Nightingale in
one of the first feminist discussions of sex-role stereotyping
to mention the school story ('Sex Roles in Children's Literature', 1972):

I think that the great popularity of the school story must
lie in the fact that the girl heroine is allowed considerable
scope for adventure and rebellion against authority. There
are no men present, indeed, within the terms of reference
of the story, men hardly exist, except in [the] menial
capacity of gardeners and grooms. There is no need therefore to inhibit the girls to maintain a standard of femininity.[42]

The point was more fully developed by Gill Frith in the
first full feminist investigation of 'The time of your life: the
meaning of the school story' (1985). In her survey of schoolgirls she found that school stories were still popular among
8- to 12-year-olds in the mid–1980s, including some girls of
Asian descent, in her sample; and she accounted for this on
the ground that the books offer girls active, not passive, role
models. Of one 10-year-old she remarked: 'She was very
conscious that the school stories did not represent "real life",

but she enjoyed them because the girls *did* things, and the things they did were exciting.'

> The significant point here is that the school story presents a picture of what it is possible for a girl to be and to do which stands in absolute contradistinction to the configuration of 'femininity' which is to be found in other forms of popular fiction addressed specifically to women and girls.[43]

Where romance fiction showed girlfriends competing with one another in troubled pursuit of the one desired goal, a boyfriend, the school story emphasised working at friendships with other girls and in group endeavours with them. 'In the absence of boys, girls "break bounds", have adventures, transgress rules, catch spies . . .' Frith noted that the institutions within the school were run by the girls themselves, and the prefects had great power and influence and acted as ideals for the younger girls to emulate and adore.

> It is a fantasy accessible to any girl who dreams of vindication, independence, freedom from constraint; a fantasy which combines the dream of autonomy and control with the freedom to be irresponsible within 'safe' limits.[44]

But does this positive imagery have any lasting effect on its readers? Frith thought not. In Frith's view, the school story offers only temporary escape from the demands of a heterosexual, patriarchal world, for it is cast aside at puberty when the desire to achieve 'a more unambiguously "female" identity supervenes'.[45]

She may be right, for the pressures on women to adhere to society's heterosexual norms are strongest in adolescence. But few of us remain stuck at this stage of awareness; most of us grow up to question and replace this obsessive conformity with a more mature and balanced view of women's role, having learnt from experience. Particularly if we come under the influence of feminism, and even if we don't, ideas learned in childhood come back to help us make sense of our situation in society. Here, girls' school stories may be more powerful than we realise.

THEORIES OF WOMEN'S COMMUNITIES

Art historian Kathleen Adler has put forward an interesting theory about male and female artists in late nineteenth-century Paris. She argues that men's world (as their art reveals) was the city centre, where they could move about freely and go wherever they pleased. Women on the other hand had to be accompanied or chaperoned in town, and there were some places where no respectable lady went in any circumstances. Women's world was in the suburbs, and this was the world that women artists painted.[46] This is because, Adler contends, women *were* in control of their lives in the suburbs which, emptied of their male inhabitants in the daytime, became a world of women. Though constrained in the city, where they were forced to abide by men's rules, here they could create and operate their own rules in their own space.

By drawing a comparison between women's art and women's literature we may find some useful parallels. Women's fiction is often criticised for being domestic and trivial in its subject-matter. Girls' school stories are no exception to this rule. The boarding school for the English school-girl and mistress played a similar role as the suburbs for the Parisian bourgeoise: it provided a stage where women could act freely according to their own rules, unrestricted by the demands of the male-dominated world outside.

Of course both the Parisian suburbs and the girls' boarding schools operated within the patriarchal structure of the wider world. But inside the space set aside for them, women had considerable autonomy to negotiate their own lives. Provided they performed the services patriarchy expected of them, and conformed outwardly to patriarchal norms, men left them pretty much alone. Viewed at one further remove, the *art* produced by women on the subject of their suburban existence and the *novels* written by women about boarding-school life were potentially even freer than the reality, for they could be idealised to remove patriarchal influences as far as possible.

'Separate spheres' were as much the norm for the English middle-class as they were across the channel. Single-sex schools and, later, segregated university colleges were inevitable; mixed education would have been unthinkable for young ladies before the First World War. Once grown up, middle-class women were expected to marry and be mistresses of suburban households, enjoying a similar freedom on their own territory to those of their Parisian counterparts. Those who did not marry usually found a place within the domestic circle of a married relative.

For a select but increasing few, however, an acceptable alternative to the heterosexual family emerged in the late Victorian period. An increase in the proportion of women to men in the population, coupled with a decline in the marriage rate, left up to one in four women unmarried. This great band of 'superfluous' women helped Victorian feminists (many of whom came from its ranks) to push for and win educational, political, and employment opportunities for middle-class women who needed to be independent, since they could not be supported. This in turn paved the way for others to *choose* to work in the new female occupations.[47]

Nineteenth-century fiction often depicts the gathering together of women, at first in the home and later in the workplace, as Nina Auerbach explains in *Communities of Women* (1978). But until the current wave of feminism, this aspect of our cultural tradition was not appreciated by historians and critics trained in the masculine ideals of scholarship.[48]

Early feminists saw nineteenth-century women, in fact and fiction, as confined to their 'relative' roles of wife, mother, daughter.[49] Then in 1975, Carroll Smith-Rosenberg's ground-breaking article on 'The Female World of Love and Ritual' which appeared in the first issue of the American journal *Signs*, inaugurated a new branch of feminist scholarship, now flourishing: the study of women's relationships between and among themselves. 'What was once the stigma of a female community is now seen as a proud hidden profession.'[50]

Martha Vicinus, for example, has shown how some middle-class spinsters chose to live out their lives in communities of women, as teachers in girls' schools or women's colleges, nurses, deaconesses and sisters, and settlement workers.[51] For many (such as Florence Nightingale and the classicist Jane Harrison) this was a deliberate choice in preference to marriage, because it offered greater freedom.

While girls' school stories, like the schools themselves, were novel cultural products at the beginning of the twentieth century, both belonged to a longer and broader tradition which accepted and assumed communities of women. It was only when the twentieth century was well advanced that women's communities began to be seen as a threat to patriarchal power and thus to be belittled, derided, condemned and finally destroyed. So systematically was this carried out, however, that the very notion that a community of women might be something to value and celebrate, as contemporary feminists have shown, is still a matter of surprise to most of us.

2 The Writers' World

In *The Chalet School Goes To It*, 13-year-old Gwensi is a fan
of school stories. Her book case is crammed with them:
'Here's a whole shelf of Elsie Oxenham, and another of
Dorita Fairlie Bruce . . .'[1] Such was Elinor Brent-Dyer's
graceful tribute to her sister writers, who shared with her
the dominant position in the schoolgirl market at the time.
Throughout Brent-Dyer's novels we see repeated flattering
references to the works of Elsie Oxenham and Dorita Fairlie
Bruce, but she never acknowledges Brazil's or Blyton's; a
clear hierarchy of merit operated even among the prac-
titioners of this much-criticised art.

ELSIE JEANETTE OXENHAM

After Angela Brazil, Elsie Oxenham was probably the best-
known girls' school story writer of the interwar years. In
spite of the absence of a biography, the main details of her
life are tolerably clear. She was born in 1885 in Southport, the
eldest daughter of a businessman turned journalist, William
Arthur Dunkerley, and his Scottish wife, Margery Anderson
of Greenock. In his spare time Dunkerley wrote fiction and
poetry under the pen name 'John Oxenham'. So successful
were his books that he was able to give up hack journalism
and support his wife and six children entirely on the proceeds
from his writing, becoming quite famous for his devotional
works. The family lived in Bedford Park, Ealing, West
London.

The success of Elsie Oxenham's first novel, *Goblin Island*

(1907), which was reprinted almost immediately, led her to adopt her father's career as a writer. She also adopted his pen name, as did her sister Erica, another writer. She published more than 90 books for girls: school stories, light romances, and historical novels. Her recreations were listed in *Who's Who* (in which she appeared from 1927) as 'tramps on the Downs' and 'folk-dancing'. She moved to Worthing in Sussex in 1922 and died there in January 1960.

Oxenham's earliest novels are set in Scotland, where she had often holidayed as a child. The first of them, *Goblin Island* (1907), is about an unmarried woman writer who is acting as secretary to her father, another writer. It is written in the first person – unique in Oxenham's oeuvre – and may, like so many first novels, be partly autobiographical, in which case she may have lived in Scotland in her twenties. On the other hand, she may simply have chosen to set the novel there for the romantic landscape and quaint Scots dialect. Other early Oxenham novels have a Welsh setting.

In the absence of further explicit information about her life, and particularly about her friends and interests, I have relied on two readily available sources: the dedications in her books, and her will. Dedications are revealing about the people who are significant in a writer's life at the time the book is being produced, and often in relation to the events depicted in the story. For example, *A School Camp Fire* (1917) was dedicated 'To the girls who sit with me around the camp fire with love and all best wishes by [sic] their Guardian'. Camp Fire was a girls' organisation she was involved in at the time. In 1921 there is: 'To those members of the English Folk Dance Society from whom I have received so much helpful enjoyment this story is dedicated in grateful acknowledgment of all their kindness'; other titles dedicated to members of the Society followed, so we know that folk-dancing was an absorbing interest for her in the 1920s. Even family history may be chronicled in dedications. Several books before 1925 were dedicated to Oxenham's mother, but *Queen of the Abbey Girls* (1926) is to her memory: she died in 1925. These events are frequently reflected in the plots of the relevant books. The Abbey books of the 1920s are related to folk-dancing, and *Queen of the Abbey Girls* inaugurates a series of stories featuring bereavement.

More than 20 of Oxenham's books were dedicated to one or other, or both, of her parents, usually in loving acknowledgment of the inspiration, guidance and encouragement they gave her, together with a strong Christian faith. Others so favoured were her brothers, Roderic and Hugo; her sisters Marjorie (Maida), Theodora, and Erica Isobel; her sisters-in-law Daphne and Prim; her cousins Agnes and Mabel Dean; and, towards the end of her life, her great-nieces, Deborah and Sara.

They were a tight-knit family. In a biography of their father, Elsie's sister Erica wrote: 'as a family we were so extraordinarily unsociable – outside our own home . . . But within our own domain we had the jolliest and happiest childhood possible.'[2] That family was all-important to Elsie Oxenham was also borne out by the terms of her will. Made in November 1957 in a Worthing nursing home, it left everything to her surviving family. Her brother Roderic got the house (Inverkip, The Glen, Worthing), which she hoped he would keep in the family. Everything else was divided between Roderic and her two surviving sisters, Erica and Theodora, neither of whom had married. Erica, who was sole executrix, was still living at the Worthing address she had shared with Elsie before their father's death in 1941; we know this because Elsie Oxenham's last request was for her own books from her bedroom to be kept intact at Erica's house.

Just who Elsie Oxenham's close friends were, or whether indeed she had any, is difficult to ascertain. Her books frequently show a correspondence between certain characters in the story and its dedicatees, who clearly inspired them. For example, *The Abbey Girls Again* (1924) is dedicated 'To Madam, who teaches us and dances to us, and the Pixie, who gives us help and wise advice . . . with thanks for continued friendship'. 'Madam' and 'The Pixie' are characters in several Abbey books at this time and an earlier one, *The Abbey Girls Go Back to School* (1922), is also dedicated to them but under their real names: Helen Kennedy North and D C Daking. Both were officers in the English Folk Dance Society. It is hard to know how close they really were to Oxenham as she also dedicated a book to the Society's founder, Cecil Sharp (*The New Abbey Girls*, 1923), but clearly they were significant.

Three or four other friends are mentioned in dedications, especially after her father died, and her last book, *Two Queens at the Abbey* (1959), was 'for all the friends at Marlposts' (the nursing home where she was living) 'and to Janet Margaret Argent with love'. She probably knew Dorita Fairlie Bruce, to whom she dedicated *Secrets of the Abbey* in 1939 ('To Dorita Fairlie Bruce, with thanks for all the pleasure her Dimsie, Prim, and Nancy have given to me and so many others'). She certainly knew Elinor Brent-Dyer, who corresponded with her over the years; each dedicated a book to the other.

Elsie Oxenham's fame rests chiefly on her Abbey books, a series of novels about some girls who live near a ruined Abbey in Oxfordshire. There are 37 books in the series, of which the first – *The Abbey Girls* – appeared in 1920, and the last – *Two Queens at the Abbey* – in 1959. The original Abbey girls are Joan and Joy Shirley, red-haired cousins aged 15, who come to live in the Abbey; Joan's mother, a widow in reduced circumstances, has become the caretaker to the ruins. There is no money to pay for the girls' schooling, but Joan is given a scholarship to a school in nearby Wycombe, which she unselfishly passes on to Joy whose need is greater: Joy is a talented musician, though a difficult personality; Joan is the more pleasant character. Joy becomes May Queen of Wycombe school's Hamlet Club (to which we were introduced in an earlier novel, *The Girls of the Hamlet Club*, 1914). At the end of *The Abbey Girls* it emerges that Joy is heiress to the Hall, the big house in the grounds of which the Abbey stands, but her grandfather leaves the Abbey to Joan because of her great love for it. The girls and their mother, now wealthy, move into the Hall after his death. From now on they who have received so much will devote their lives to sharing their good fortune with others.

The theme of *noblesse oblige* runs through all the Abbey books and, indeed, through many of Oxenham's other books as well. Certainly the plot-line of a girl from a poor or ordinary background who becomes an heiress appealed sufficiently for her to repeat it over and over again; her earliest version of this story was in fact called *A Princess in Tatters* (1908). The part of the story that she always seemed to enjoy most was the dispensing of largesse by the heroine to the poor folk left behind – who were always grateful and never felt patronised. Her obsession with wealth and class badly dates the books but, more grievously, this impinges so strongly on the reader's mind that the other really striking feature of Oxenham's oeuvre tends to be overlooked. That is that she wrote about a world of women, to the almost complete exclusion of men. We expect this in girls' school stories, but the majority of the Abbey books are not school stories; they are light romances, which purport to deal with heterosexual romance but are really about women's relationships with their women friends. Certainly all the Abbey girls – Joan and Joy, and later Jen, Rosamund and Maidlin – marry and have families, but the men are peripheral and paper-thin and the children merely picturesque dolls until they, the girls at least, are old enough to form friendships of their own. Oxenham's women marry not because they want to spend more time with the men they love, and certainly not for economic support, since they all have private means; they marry because marriage allows them to spend more time with their women friends and it also produces the children who can all be friends in the next generation. The *Two Queens* of Oxenham's last published book are Joy's 15-year-old daughters, whose selection as May Queens of their school's Hamlet Club brings the series gracefully full circle.

Her interest in women's relationships led Oxenham to write books about different kinds of communities of women:

Girl Guides, folk dancers, Camp Fire, as well as many straightforward school stories. There were several Sussex schools, one in Yorkshire, and one in the Swiss Alps. This last is paired with a boys' school in the same valley, and the girls enjoy a healthy comradeship with the boys and later some unconvincing romances. The heroine of the Torment books, a solitary girl at a boys' school, also associates cheerfully with the opposite sex; but in both cases the girls are seen to prioritise their girl-only activities.

It is impossible divide Oxenham's output into neat series since the characters from one set of books stray into the others, and nearly all her heroines end up in Switzerland or at the Abbey at some point. This must have been fun for her readers, who could be sure of meeting someone they knew in every novel. She used a large number of publishers – 17 in all – and books in one 'series' might be shared among three or four publishing houses.

Oxenham's Swiss school pre-dated Elinor Brent-Dyer's Chalet School by four years and shows striking similarities: both are English schools which take pupils from all over Europe, and both are associated with a sanatorium for tuberculosis sufferers on the Alp above. We know from the dedications to *Expelled from School* (1919) and *The Twins of Castle Charming* (1920) that Oxenham travelled on the Continent with her parents after the First World War, but she must have taken all her English attitudes, beliefs and values with her; any international – indeed any Swiss – flavour is notably absent from these books. If her Scotland and Wales were altogether too quaint, any venture into continental Europe reads like a guidebook peopled with caricatures.

Indeed it is in her evocation of the *English* countryside and customs that Oxenham is at her best: the downs and coasts of her Sussex novels, the Chiltern beechwoods of the Abbey books, the bleak moors of the Rocklands series, the English country dances and May Queen crownings and afternoon teas around winter fires. Her world is cosy, comfortable, and nostalgic: a world of ruined abbeys, of leisured heiresses, of the rigid separation of men's and women's spheres; an ideal-ised version of a world that was fast disappearing, in reality, before Oxenham took up her pen to write about it.

DORITA FAIRLIE BRUCE

Dorita Fairlie Bruce was born in the same year as Elsie Oxenham – 1885 – but she was much older – 35 – when her first novel was published in 1920. She was a considerably less prolific writer than either Oxenham or Elinor Brent-Dyer, never publishing more than one or two books each year, but perhaps for that reason her work maintains a more consistent standard of interest and competence. Of her 39 published books, 28 were school stories.

Her real name was Dorothy Morris Fairlie Bruce, a name which suggests Scottish ancestry, and in fact she identified herself as a Scot. The majority of her novels are set in Scot-land, although she seems to have spent most of her life in London. She was educated at Clarence House, Roehampton, to the headmistress of which she dedicated her first book. The third was inscribed to the Old Girls of the same school, together with some verses which tell us something of her school life and the 'white-pillared portico', 'flower-fringed terrace' and 'the wide green playing-field'.[3]

Bruce may well have become a teacher herself, as one of her novels from the late 1930s is dedicated to the girls of a Twickenham school. Throughout the 1920s and 1930s she was keenly involved in an organisation called the Girls' Guil-dry, being Guardian of an Ealing company, then President of the North West London Centre.[4]

Like Elsie Oxenham and Elinor Brent-Dyer, Dorita Fairlie Bruce did not marry. Many of her books are dedicated to relatives: her mother, possibly a sister, cousins, a nephew, nieces, and later, great-nieces. Among the many friends hon-oured in this way were two fellow writers: Elsie Oxenham, and Margaret Stuart Lane, who was probably a close friend.

The latter (her real name was Margaret Ashworth) was a historical novelist whose children's books included stories about Brownies and Girl Guides.

Unlike Oxenham and Elinor Brent-Dyer, Bruce's work is not distinguished by one outstanding series. Rather it is divided into a half-a-dozen shorter series each of three to nine titles. Readers follow the progress of schoolgirl heroines into adulthood and eventual marriage. As with Oxenham, the different series often interrelate, with characters from one popping in and out of others; so that the eponymous heroine of the Dimsie books, for example, gets married in one of the Springdale books. Four of the series and part of a fifth are set in the same part of the west coast of Scotland. There is much friendly rivalry between St Bride's and Springdale, the two schools on the firth, while Colmskirk, scene of four later romances, and the school which features in the last three novels, are nearby. These overlapping characters and settings give a unity to Bruce's work which performs the same function as the longer series of Oxenham and Brent-Dyer.

Though Scotland was evidently Bruce's favourite territory, her first books were set in a school in Kent which seems to have been based on one she attended herself. *The Senior Prefect* (1920) was reissued as *Dimsie Goes to School* when the idea of a series about the senior prefect's young cousin, Dimsie, emerged. Sequels followed promptly: *Dimsie Moves Up* (1921), *Dimsie Moves Up Again* (1922), *Dimsie Among the Prefects* (1923). As well in 1923 appeared the first – and for a long time the only – book about the school on the island of Inchmore, *The Girls of St Bride's*, which was also the first with a Scottish setting. In *Dimsie Grows Up* (1924), Dimsie, having left school, moves to the family home in the same part of Scotland, where she quickly finds romance.

That Bruce regretted this precipitous leap into adulthood – and the consequent narrowing of plot necessitated by the closing off of most opportunities for adventure and independent action on the part of her heroine – is suggested by the appearance of *Dimsie, Head Girl* in 1925, which stepped back a year or two in time. In the same year Bruce made another attempt to establish a new school setting with *That Boarding School Girl*. Nancy, expelled from her Scottish boarding school – none other than St Bride's – makes a fresh start at Maudsley Grammar School, a day school in the south of England. *The New Girl and Nancy* and *Nancy to the Rescue* followed in 1926 and 1927, but the latter is sufficiently feeble to prompt the thought that this environment and set of characters did not absorb Bruce as much as Dimsie and her setting. So in *Dimsie Goes Back* (1927) we find ourselves accompanying Dimsie, engaged to be married, back to her old school to act as the headmistress's secretary for the interim.

With *The New House Captain* (1928) Bruce commenced the run of six books based on Springdale school, set on the mainland across the water from St Bride's and from Dimsie's home. The Springdale books appeared roughly at two-year intervals, interspersed in the alternating years with new volumes in the 'Nancy' series. The heroine of the first three Springdale books is Peggy Willoughby, Captain first of her house and then of the school; the last three are dominated by Peggy's sister, Anne, and her chum Primula Mary Beton. The last Springdale book appeared in 1939, but this was not the last we were to hear of either Anne or Prim.

Nancy at St Bride's (1933) fills a gap in Nancy's life-story, and links the St Bride's and the Nancy books, by taking us back to Nancy's calamitous term at the Scottish school from which she was expelled. Like most books written retrospectively, it is not altogether successful in recapturing the atmosphere of the earlier tales, and incidentally presents a number of inconsistencies with other books in the series covering a later period. In 1937 she wrote *Dimsie Intervenes*, a final retrospective glance at Dimsie's schooldays, in response to requests from readers 'all over the world' for another book about her most famous heroine.

The School on the Moor (1931) introduced Toby Barrett, a characteristic Bruce heroine. The plot concerns two ex-schoolmates of Dimsie, one a teacher at Toby's school and the other a famous cellist. We meet Toby again in *The School in the Woods* (1940). After this Bruce wrote no more school stories for 16 years.

Toby reappears, however, in one of the three novels set during the Second World War, which are not school stories but concern characters from the school series, now grown up. *Toby at Tibbs Cross* (1943) finds her assisting on the farm of Charity Sheringham, late of Maudsley Grammar. A satisfying relationship evolves between the two young women, until marriage presses its greater claims upon first one and then the other. *Nancy Calls the Tune* (1944) follows Nancy in her wartime occupation as church organist in a Scottish parish, where in the concluding pages she accepts the minister's proposal of marriage. The heroine of *Dimsie Carries On* (1942) is not really Dimsie herself, who is now married and mother of two children, but her assistant Anne Willoughby of Springdale, whom the final pages see happily settled with a (male) government spy.

With nearly all her schoolgirl heroines married off, Bruce closed the files on Dimsie, Nancy, Toby and Anne after the war and evolved an entirely new setting and characters in *The Serendipity Shop* (1947). Another light romance for young women, this was the first of four novels set in Colmskirk, a small town on the west coast of Scotland. Each novel featured different central characters, usually a girl in her late teens and one slightly older, but the same wider circle. Each ended with an engagement, Primula Mary Beton being resurrected for the last of the series *The Bartle Bequest* (1955). Bruce's final trio of books (1956, 1959 and 1961) returned to the school story genre, introducing Sally, a Canadian girl sent to a Scottish school with boarding houses in the town.

Although she published no more novels after 1961 – when she was 76 years old – Dorita Fairlie Bruce outlived both her exact contemporary Elsie Oxenham and the younger Elinor Brent-Dyer, dying, not in London as one authority states, but at her home named 'Triffeny', in Skelmorlie, Ayrshire, in September 1970.

ELINOR MARY BRENT-DYER

With Elinor M Brent-Dyer we are on safer biographical ground, thanks to Helen McClelland's fascinating study *Behind the Chalet School* (1981). The creator of the Chalet School was born Gladys Eleanor May Dyer in April 1894 in South Shields. Her home circumstances as a child were about as different as they could be from the large, happy, model families she described in her novels. Her father, who had risen from the ranks to become a commissioned officer in the Navy, abandoned his wife and two children when Brent-Dyer was aged 3; her only brother died in his 'teens. These were aspects of her past that she understandably preferred to forget, and, though readers in later years asked her repeatedly for details of her childhood, she never referred to her South Shields origins and the shameful secret of the broken home.

The comfortable leisure of the lady writer was not available to Brent-Dyer: she was obliged to go out to work, and began to earn her living at the age of 18 as an untrained teacher. During the First World War she studied at the City of Leeds Training College and then went on to teach in a variety of schools over the next 30 years. At the same time she wrote, to begin with poetry and plays put on by theatrical friends. Her career as an author took off with the publication in 1922 of *Gerry Goes to School*, the first of nearly a hundred books for children, including some historical and adventure stories, but chiefly girls' school stories. Her great achievement was the Chalet School series, inspired by a holiday in the Austrian Tyrol in 1924. This was to become the longest series of books for girls – there were 59 titles – and the second longest juvenile series ever written (after Captain Johns' 78 Biggles books).

In 1930 she took the unusual and courageous step, for that

time, of converting from the Church of England to Roman Catholicism; some years later she made the heroine of her Chalet School books do the same. With her mother and stepfather she moved to Hereford in 1933. There she obtained employment as a governess and entered fully into the life of the town, joining the Three Choirs Festival Choir and giving historical talks to local women's groups. But when her stepfather died in 1937 it became necessary for her to earn a better living to support herself and her mother. In 1938 she set up her own school for girls, called the Margaret Roper School after Sir Thomas More's daughter. The outbreak of the Second World War brought a fortunate influx of pupils sent away from the threat of air raids in the south, and the school – modelled to a large extent on its fictional counterpart, even down to the uniform and activities – prospered during those years. As headmistress, Brent-Dyer continued to write, turning out 14 titles in the 10 years of the school's existence.

The War also breathed new life into the Chalet School, which by the thirteenth volume had been in danger of coming to an end now its heroine Jo had grown up and, more significantly, because its Austrian home had been occupied by the Nazis. Unlike Elsie Oxenham, who ignored the arrival of war and continued to write 'in a timeless Never-Never Land',[5] Brent-Dyer used historical events to provide the plots for *The Chalet School in Exile* and half a dozen subsequent books. But unlike Dorita Fairlie Bruce, who, as we have seen, also set some of her books in wartime, Brent-Dyer did not reduce the conflict to one of patriotic Britons against the Hun. Art and life moved closer together during this period. She arranged for the Chalet School to be evacuated first to Guernsey (which she had visited in 1923) and then, as the Germans encroached into the Channel Islands, to Hereford, which she called Armiford in the books. Later the school moved to an island off the coast of Wales and finally to the Swiss Oberland, though Brent-Dyer herself remained in Hereford until a few years before her death. Her biographer is of the opinion that she never visited Switzerland, site of the Chalet School for the last 28 books, but gleaned all the necessary background information from tourist guides; this seems quite remarkable, since her settings are described in convincing detail.

The Margaret Roper School closed in 1948. McClelland suggests that Brent-Dyer was not a great success as a head-mistress, preferring to concentrate on her fictional school rather than the real one, and neglecting her lessons for her writing. She continued to share the big house with her mother until the latter's death in 1957, and with a number of elderly lady lodgers. In the years after she closed her school, and before her health began to fail in the late 1960s, Brent-Dyer's literary productivity escalated, for now she had unlimited time to write. In this period the Chalet School was earning a secure and self-perpetuating income for her. *Three Go to the Chalet School*, for example, published in 1949, sold almost 10,000 copies within a month or two of publication.[6] In the decade following, Brent-Dyer published 38 different titles, with anything up to six appearing in any one year.

These were not all Chalet School books. She had always, like Elsie Oxenham, produced a roughly equal number of titles which were not part of the main series. Some of these formed mini-series of their own, such as the La Rochelle books (seven in all, mostly set in Guernsey) and the Chudleigh Hold stories, intended for boys; others were one-offs or had only one sequel. Occasionally the characters from these books overlapped with those of the Chalet School; a notable illustration of this was that the second generation of La Rochelle girls all became pupils at the Chalet School. In her sixties, Brent-Dyer's output began to slow down and she confined herself, with only two exceptions, to Chalet School books. By the time of her last book, *Prefects of the Chalet School*, her heroine Jo was nearing 40 years of age, and although she had always played a prominent part in Chalet School doings, the series had for the past 40 books been primarily concerned with the second generation of Chalet girls: Jo's triplet daughters, the prefects of the title, and their associates.

In 1964 a friend, Phyllis Matthewman, persuaded Brent-Dyer to buy a house with her and her husband (who was Brent-Dyer's literary agent) in Redhill, Surrey. They occupied the ground-floor flat and she the upper one. She continued to write, though more slowly as two heart attacks had taken their toll. In September 1969 she died; *Prefects of the Chalet School* was published posthumously in the following year.

So high was her reputation as a children's author that not only the local *Surrey Mirror*, but also three national papers – *The Times*, the *Telegraph*, and the *Evening Standard* – accorded her an obituary. In her will she left £25 for Masses to be said for the repose of her soul, and the residue of her estate, including the copyright to all her books, to the Matthewmans.

All sources indicate that, apart from her mother, family was of minimal importance to Elinor Brent-Dyer. She was not close to her stepfather, and though she dedicated seven of her books to her mother (one together with 'Dad', and one in memory), the only other family member to receive a dedication was a cousin, Beatrice. Two 'aunts' who were mentioned on different occasions were not true relatives. In the event of the Matthewmans predeceasing her she had arranged for a couple called Rutherford to be executors and residual beneficiaries of her will, and these may have been relations since Mrs Dyer's maiden name was Rutherford.

By all accounts, though, she had a large circle of friends, practically all of them women. A great many of them are named in dedications. Some have been identified by her biographer, like Miss Rose Farr and Miss Mary Middleton of Hereford; others remain untraced, like the 'Lilian' who accompanied Brent-Dyer on that momentous trip to the Tyrol in 1924, and the 'Madge Russell' who gave her name to a central character in the Chalet School series. McClelland interviewed a number of people who had known Brent-Dyer and concluded that 'Elinor often tended to blow very hot in the early days of a friendship but to cool off very suddenly later on'. She pointed out that although the Chalet School heroines kept their girlhood friends into their thirties and forties, while making new ones all the time – 'and this is obviously something of which Elinor approves whole-heartedly' – nevertheless 'a number of the friends Elinor herself made along the way dropped out of sight and out of mind altogether'.[7] Not all of them, however. Phyllis Matthewman had been a school contemporary who came back into Brent-Dyer's life in Hereford, when both were successful writers of juvenile fiction. She became the friend most often honoured in dedications, especially in later years; and, as we have seen, she and her husband inherited almost all of Brent-Dyer's considerable estate on her death.

ENID BLYTON

I had not originally intended to include Enid Blyton in this book. Unlike the other three authors she is not known primarily for her school stories, and her far more prolific output and fame have won her very much greater critical attention, much of it adverse. Yet, when I discussed my interest in school stories with other women, I found, time and time again, that it was Blyton's Malory Towers and St Clare's books which were most frequently recalled from childhood reading. Some women, indeed, were reading them again in current paperback reprints, or even for the first time, in the 1990s.

There is much, in fact, that the four women have in common. Enid Blyton was a contemporary of the others, born in 1897 and dying in 1968. Like Elinor Brent-Dyer and Dorita Fairlie Bruce, Blyton chose teaching as her first career. She was trained in the Froebel kindergarten teaching methods, and was, by all accounts, a skilled and inspired teacher for the few short years she practised this profession.

But literary success and marriage at the age of 27 freed her to write full time, and this she did for the rest of her life. Her income from writing enabled her and her family to live sufficiently comfortably to be able to afford cooks, nannies, big houses and cars and boarding school for the children. She lived a lifestyle which eluded the other three authors.

Unlike the other authors, Enid Blyton married – twice – and gave birth to two daughters. As the younger daughter has testified, however, motherhood was not her strong point, and it could be argued that, like Brent-Dyer, she was more interested in the imaginary children of her pen than the real ones in her care.

Blyton's first work, a book of poems for children, was published in 1922, and her first full-length novel in 1937. Between 1940 and 1951 she produced 16 school stories. There are three series – the *Naughtiest Girl* books (three, published by Newnes 1940–45), the *St Clare's* books (six, published by Methuen 1941–45) and the *Malory Towers* books (six, published by Methuen 1946–51) – plus one novel originally published under the pen name of Mary Pollock, *Mischief at St Rollo's* (Werner Laurie, 1947). Alongside the 21 Famous Five books, the 14 Secret Seven books and the hundreds of Adventure, Secret, and Mystery books and stories for younger children, the school stories make up only a small part of Blyton's output, but in the view of Sheila Ray, they 'not only constitute some of her best work, they also represent a final peak of achievement for the genre.'[8]

The Naughtiest Girl books are intended for younger readers and feature an interesting co-educational boarding school where the children are responsible for discipline through monitors chosen by themselves and a school council. St Clare's and Malory Towers are more conventional girls' boarding schools, whose heroines move up through the ranks from green first former to prefect in successive volumes. Blyton is clearly happier dealing with the younger pupils and makes no attempt to make her twins (of St Clare's) or Darrell (of Malory Towers) show the type of emotional growth and reaching into adulthood that Oxenham, Bruce and Brent-Dyer do with their heroines. It is estimated that Enid Blyton produced about 600 books in all, and she herself reckoned she had written every kind of children's book and for every age group. This is not true, since she generally wrote for a younger audience than the other three mentioned authors, and she never attempted anything in the line of their adolescent romances, either in an historical or in a contemporary vein.

Even more than Elinor Brent-Dyer, Enid Blyton went to extraordinary lengths to conceal certain aspects of her life story from her family and fans. Fortunately for us, her autobiography has been supplemented since her death by a biography and the memoirs of her younger daughter, which have helped to set the record straight. Like Brent-Dyer, Enid Blyton was the product of a broken home, her father (a clerk) having left his wife and children to live with another woman when Enid was aged 12. Like Brent-Dyer, she told nobody, either then or later; as her biographer Barbara Stoney observes, 'Keeping up appearances was a very real factor in 1910 suburban Beckenham.'[9]

Unlike Brent-Dyer, she had been close to her father – she was the eldest of three children and the only girl – and she continued to see him after his defection, but she did not get on with her mother, and took the first available opportunity to leave home at the age of 19 herself, never to return. Neither of her two husbands nor her two daughters were ever allowed to meet her mother, who died in 1950 never having been visited by the daughter she had not seen for nearly 30 years.

The other big silence concerned Enid Blyton's own adultery, divorce and second marriage. In 1952 she published *The Story of My Life*, a misleadingly titled set of chatty vignettes about her childhood and work which we now know to be decidedly economical with the truth. Chapter 19 introduces 'My Little Family'. 'There are four of us in the family – my husband, whose name is Kenneth Darrell Waters, and my two girls, Gillian and Imogen.'[10] No one reading this account would guess that her husband was not the father of the girls, or that both she and her husband had had to divorce their existing spouses in order to marry each other. Once divorced, Blyton never allowed the girls' father to see his children again.

A myth is perpetuated in these pages:

> As you can imagine, we are a happy little family. I could not possibly write a single good book for children if I were not happy with my family, or if I didn't put them first and foremost.[11]

Her younger daughter Imogen Smallwood recalls family life quite differently. She remembers the day when she first realised that the autocrat of the household was, in fact, her mother. She had read about mothers in story books and knew 'that a mother bore a special relationship to her child'. But in her case, she said, the theory did not fit the facts. 'There was no special relationship. There was scarcely a relationship at all.'[12] Since Enid Blyton tended to spend all day writing, producing 6000 to 10,000 words by 5 p.m., perhaps this neglect of her children was not surprising. She was, in fact, able to write literally dozens of books each year (in 1951 the total was a staggering 37, all typed by herself on a typewriter sitting on her knees), and these entertained millions of other people's children.[13]

Blyton liked to say that she read her stories to her children as she wrote them. Imogen Smallwood, however, recalls her reading to them only once. Blyton claimed that many of the incidents in her school stories were based on her girls' experiences at boarding school. This was not so, states Smallwood; the earliest ones were published well before either girl went to boarding school.[14] (Blyton herself had attended a day school.)

Unlike Elinor Brent-Dyer, Enid Blyton did not have a large circle of women friends. As a teenage girl, rebelling against her mother's narrow domesticity, she was encouraged by the aunt of her best friend, a spinster 20 years her senior. Through this woman, Mabel Attenborough, Enid met the Hunts, whose daughter had taken a Froebel teacher training course at Ipswich, and persuaded Enid to do the same rather than take up a planned place at the Guildhall School of Music. But Mabel and Ida Hunt disappeared from her life when she became a writer, and from then on, apart from social acquaintances taken up and left behind as she moved from Chelsea to Beckenham, Bourne End and Beaconsfield, her only close woman friend seems to have been Dorothy Richards, who came to be a nurse to baby Imogen in 1935. They fell out, however, when, as Dorothy perceived it, Enid behaved selfishly to some of Dorothy's relatives who came to stay after being bombed out of their home during the Second World War.

By this time, Blyton had begun her relationship with the man she was later to marry as her second husband, Kenneth Darrell Waters, a surgeon. Imogen Smallwood observes: 'It was as if her work gave her time for one close relationship only.' She also comments that: 'from my childhood to her death in 1968, I never knew my mother to have another woman friend, outside her own household staff.'[15] Though she resumed seeing Dorothy Richards after a 10-year gap, Blyton centred her emotional life on her husband until his death a year before her own. Perhaps it is significant that her books carry none of the fulsome dedications to friends common to the other three authors discussed here.

In the late 1950s Enid Blyton began to suffer from pre-senile dementia, which caused her to lose her memory progressively and to confuse past and present, and fantasy with reality. 'So much of her life she had kept hidden from those around her, and what little she had revealed had been embroidered into stories she now half-believed herself,' wrote her biographer.[16] Her literary output dwindled, with only four titles appearing in the last year of her life though even this is an enormous output compared to almost any other writer except Barbara Cartland – and even she is out of the running here. She died in a nursing-home in November 1968. Her memorial service in St James's Piccadilly, in January 1969, was attended by representatives of her many publishers and the children's clubs she had founded.

Enid Blyton remains the best-known, the most successful and popular children's author of all time. At the time of her death she was the fourth most translated author in the world – after Lenin, Marx and Jules Verne – whose stories, even those set in boarding schools, gripped the imagination of children in many different cultures notwithstanding their quintessential Englishness.[17] Like Elsie Oxenham, she divided her favours among many publishers – in Blyton's case, 53 – the main ones being Newnes (for which her first husband worked), Hodder & Stoughton, Collins and Methuen. Like Elinor Brent-Dyer, she had fan clubs (the Famous Five Club enrolled 40,000 members in the first eight months of its existence in 1954) and her own magazine.[18] She is still the most widely read children's author, especially among girls of the 11–14 age group.[19] Almost all her books are still available in paperback and cheap editions today, nearly 25 years after her death. It is the school stories (particularly the Malory Towers series) which are among the most popular.

THE WRITERS AND THEIR WORK

Are there any general conclusions that can be drawn from these four potted biographies? First, it seems that the typical successful writer of girls' school stories was female, middle-class, and unmarried. Leaving Enid Blyton for a moment – for she was unique in many ways – we cannot be surprised that the others lacked husband and family; the incidence of spinsterhood among middle-class women was sufficiently high even before the First World War to cause concern among those who advocated traditional roles for women, and the

War itself so reduced the pool of available men as to make marriage for women of Bruce and Oxenham's age (early thirties around that time) extremely unlikely. We have no evidence as to whether either wished she had married, or chose not to do so. As for Elinor Brent-Dyer, who was younger – only 20 at the outbreak of war – her biographer cites evidence that she sometimes regretted her single state. As a spinster without large private means, she was obliged to earn her living all her life, and this was probably also true for Elsie Oxenham and Dorita Fairlie Bruce.

As professional writers they were following one of the two traditionally acceptable careers for 'ladies' – teaching being the other – and one which, moreover, was (rather more than teaching) a source of pride rather than embarrassment or resignation. So much is obvious from the fact that Oxenham includes no fewer than three unmarried women writers in her Abbey cast (Mary, the 'Writing Person', and Rachel), while Brent-Dyer's Chalet School heroine Jo is a successful author in spite of marriage and eleven children. All of them write girls' school stories. In contrast, Oxenham's teachers are perfunctorily described, though Bruce and Brent-Dyer are rather more sympathetic – probably because they themselves had taught.

Being unmarried threw these three women upon resources other than husband and children for providing an emotional focus and a home. In Oxenham's case, this brought her closer to her parents and siblings, while Brent-Dyer (though she lived with her mother) seems to have drawn more on women friends for support. Too little is known about Dorita Fairlie Bruce to be able to speculate about her position.

Their interest in writing for girls could be – and doubtless was – seen as a substitute for motherhood, just like teaching. It could be argued that all three decided to specialise in school stories partly because these were certain money-spinners at the time; in other words, that their choice of genre was dictated more by shrewd business sense than frustrated maternal instinct. They were, after all, dependent on their own exertions to survive. But all three women seem to have had an interest in and commitment to girls which was independent of their writing.

Brent-Dyer's biographer puts forward the idea that her books served as a means of wish-fulfilment for someone who had experienced her share of disappointments in life; that she created an imaginary world she would have liked to live in herself, peopled by characters she would have liked to have been. Clearly there is some truth in this observation, but we must guard against over-simplification; just because all Brent-Dyer's heroines marry happily, have hordes of attractive children, live in lovely homes, and so on, does not necessarily mean that she would actually have wanted to change places with them. She might just as easily have been writing to a formula acceptable to her publishers and the Sunday School prize market. Certainly when she tried to run her own school on the model of the Chalet School, she found the real experience less rewarding than the fiction.

There is however plenty of evidence that Brent-Dyer tried to construct an image of herself which in her view was more acceptable than the reality. She changed her name, not once but several times, and not simply for writing purposes. She fudged her date of birth and gave people to understand that her mother had been widowed, not deserted. So it is probably not accidental that her heroines have large, happy families – in an era when this was not only not the norm, but tended to be frowned upon – when she herself came from a small and broken home. It is particularly interesting that Jo's eldest daughter, a heroine, and a central character in the later Chalet School books, is called Len, short for Helena – the name by which Brent-Dyer herself was known to her friends.

If there is any truth in the wish-fulfilment theory, then Oxenham's pretensions were even more preposterous than Brent-Dyer's. She, too, changed her name, cashing in on her father's fame. Her characters, usually from quite ordinary (genteel) backgrounds, repeatedly marry into the titled classes; in the end nearly all the Abbey girls have become

Lady Something. What we see in Oxenham's books is a deliberate perpetuation of a pre-First-World-War world, not just in its outmoded notions of class, private wealth and *noblesse oblige*, but also in its separate spheres for men and women. This allows her to go on writing about a women's world in which men simply appear as romantic objects and then disappear as husbands, long after both sexes had actually begun to mix more freely together. Most school story writers ignored the Depression and social movements of the interwar years, and Oxenham went on writing through the Second World War as if it had never happened.

Bruce's values are equally old-fashioned – her treatment of the Second World War is jingoistic in the extreme – but one is less conscious of the escapist element in her books. Her heroines are, however, highly idealised, and the men less than convincing. It seems fair to say that if the popularity of these authors' works lay primarily in their depiction of a women's world, then this was equally a source of pleasure to their creators; that they deliberately chose a genre that enabled them to enter into a world where girls and women controlled their own lives, in contrast to the reality of many women's experience in Britain from the 1920s onwards.

What of Enid Blyton? She stands apart from the others in, first, being married; second, not focusing her output or even a large part of it on school stories; and third, preferring to write for a younger age group than the others, and never taking her characters past school age. She was in truth a very different sort of writer, one who merely tried her hand at school stories as she did at practically every type of children's literature.

On the other hand, Blyton's life does bear many similarities to the others'. Financial success freed her from most of the burdens of housework and motherhood, and she was able to devote herself fairly single-mindedly to her craft. Like Brent-Dyer, she endeavoured to construct an image of herself which was preferable, in her eyes, to the truth, concealing both her parents' failed marriage and her own, and representing her domestic situation as the sort of happy family she gave to her storybook heroines. And among the idealised worlds she offered her readers were the two series set in girls' schools (the third is co-educational), which share many of the characteristics of those which came from the imaginations of Oxenham, Bruce and Brent-Dyer. 'For surely,' wrote her biographer,

> her secret lay not only in her extraordinary creative and imaginative gifts, her great vivacity and charm, her amazing capacity for hard work and shrewd business acumen – but also in her very ability to look with childlike wonder on to a world of constant enchantment and surprise, putting aside those things which were unpleasant and keeping only her dreams of life as she would like it to be.[20]

For her girl readers, growing up in the real world, the appeal of these shared dreams is understandable.

3 The Schoolgirl Code

At Miss Macey's school in Wycombe, juniors can take part in the Hamlet Club activities (rambling, folk dancing, and the May Queen ceremony) or they can play cricket; they are not permitted to do both. Jen, with several brothers, is an excellent cricketer, but she prefers to belong to the Hamlet Club where she is Maid-of-Honour to the reigning Queen, Joan. Disaster strikes the junior cricket team when its best bowler leaves the school. If Jen took her place, the school would have a chance of winning its fixtures; without her, they are doomed to lose them all. But to help them out, Jen must give up the pleasure of being with her adored Joan and taking part in the May Day procession. Under pressure from the Games Captain, she turns in despair to Joan, who helps her to make the right decision.

What Joan says to Jen echoes the sentiments, the very language, of school stories across the generations:

> If you're brave enough and give up everything for the sake of the school . . . you'll get those two very big things – the fun of the games and the satisfaction of having played up and been really sporting.[1]

To someone unfamiliar with the English idiom, the words 'played up' and 'sporting' might seem to refer to Jen's prowess on the cricket pitch. English readers, however, know that something quite different is being suggested. It is Jen's potential behaviour which is being praised, if she gives up the activity she likes best in order to help the school out. What we have here (and in practically every girls' school story) is an illustration of the schoolgirl code in action in the context of its birth: the games field.

What was this schoolgirl code, and where did it come from? Its roots clearly lie in the vocabulary of sport. The priority given to games was in part a legacy of the male model, and the code of conduct came with it. The schoolgirl code was a modification of the schoolboy code, just as the girls' boarding school, where it flourished, was modelled on the boys' boarding school, and girls' school stories emulated and adapted boys' school stories.

THE STORY GOES TO SCHOOL

School stories were a Victorian creation, a product of the middle class that emerged in Britain after the Industrial Revolution in the nineteenth century. The long haul up the social ladder was accomplished by means of education. New public schools such as Marlborough and Rugby, set up for middle-class boys, were later copied by the pioneers of girls' education at Cheltenham (founded in 1854), St Leonard's (1877), Roedean (1885), and Wycombe Abbey (1896). Lacking an alternative model for a genuinely equal schooling, feminists disagreed over whether the structure and curriculum of the new schools should be 'identical with that of men' or 'as good as possible, but in some way or other specifically feminine'. Emily Davies, founder of Girton College, argued the former.

> Every effort to improve the education of women which assumes that they may, without reprehensible ambition, study the same subjects as their brothers and be measured by the same standards, does something towards lifting them out of the state of listless despair into which so many fall.[2]

Others, like Dorothea Beale at Cheltenham, initially took a

different approach; but Davies' was the one which prevailed. Middle-class girls' schools thus acquired the characteristics of the new middle-class boys' schools – an academic education, examinations, uniforms, houses, prefects, compulsory games and a moral code based on honour, loyalty, and playing the game – with the odd concession to feminine accomplishments. Molly Hughes remarked, for example, on the rule at Miss Buss' Camden School, that every girl should be able to make a button-hole.[3] These ideas were taken over in turn by the girls' High Schools and passed on, after the Education Acts of 1870 and 1880, to board-school children by ex-students who went into teaching, and, after 1902, to secondary school girls. Although the schoolgirl culture and the books which described it were the privilege of a small proportion of the population, compulsory education created a large new reading public, steeped in middle-class ideals and aspirations, which was to become the main market for the schoolgirl story.

As a literary form, the girls' school story owed as much to the emerging tradition of boys' school stories as it did to any real school tradition. This was also a Victorian creation. Stories about schooldays were not new, even at the beginning of the nineteenth century. But it was the growth and reform of the public school system in the mid-nineteenth century that inspired the modern school story. Thomas Hughes' *Tom Brown's School Days* (1857), based on his own experiences at Rugby, is generally held to be the corner-stone of the genre. This book sparked off two literary traditions: the public school novel for the juvenile market which, refined progressively by the pens of Dean Farrar, Talbot Baines Reed and others, paved the way to the fictitious havens of the schoolgirl story; and the public school novel for the adult market which, in contrast, tended to be founded in fact and critical of the institution it described.

The *Boys' Own Paper*, the first issue of which in 1879 included a story by Talbot Baines Reed, proved an important force in shaping the boys' school story. Its appeal lay in its depiction of heroes who were real enough for middle-class readers to identify with. It also preserved a strong under-current of idealism in the consistent emphasis on a composite quality known as 'manliness'. Manliness encompassed notions of honour and service as well as certain assumptions about class, race, and sex. The stories, set in public schools, concerned well-to-do boys; the lower orders and non-whites were treated in a kind but patronising manner. The problem of sex was ignored: in these pages, girls did not exist.

The *Boys' Own Paper* was quickly imitated by a succession of boys' weekly papers featuring stories by noted school story writers such as Bracebridge Hemyng, Gunby Hadath and P G Wodehouse, as well as various Fleet Street hacks. The most famous exponent of the genre, and one of the most remarkable writers of all time, was Charles Hamilton who, under a series of pen names, between 1907 and 1961 produced no fewer than 5000 stories and dozens of full-length novels (over sixty million words in all) about one hundred different schools. As Frank Richards he created St Jim's and Greyfriars, the adventures of whose immortal pupils Tom Merry, Harry Wharton and Billy Bunter were still being chronicled at the time of his death in 1961. [4]

The *Boys' Own Paper* had its opposite number, the *Girls' Own Paper*, which likewise had its competitors: the *Girls' Friend*, *Peg's Paper*, *Girls' Weekly*, *Girls' Favourite*, *School Friend*, *Schoolgirl* and *Schoolgirls' Own*. Charles Hamilton wrote for these under the pseudonym Hilda Richards; indeed, as Cadogan and Craig point out, 'the whole girls' enterprise was conceived, created and sustained by men'. [5] The weekly papers form yet another branch of school fiction, designed as they were for girls from poorer homes and largely pro-duced and written by men.

The girls' school story, like the girls' public school, emerged about 50 years after its masculine counterpart. L T Meade (Mrs Elizabeth Thomasina Smith), who died in 1914, was the most prolific writer for girls in the late-Victorian period. Among her 250 books, published at the rate of half-a-dozen a year, were several pioneering school stories including *A World of Girls* (1886); she also ran a girls' magazine called *Atalanta*.

The founder of the genre as we know it today is, by common consent, Angela Brazil.[6] Though born in 1869, she did not begin to write until she was 30; her first successful school story, *The Fortunes of Philippa*, appeared in 1906. Forty more followed before her death in 1947, establishing her as Queen of the girls' school story. Even today, hers is the name that most people associate with girls' school stories; she is the only exponent (apart from Enid Blyton) included in Janet Todd's *Dictionary of British Women Writers* (1989), and the only one discussed in any detail by Isobel Quigly in *The Heirs of Tom Brown* (1984). (Not that Quigly appears to think very highly of Brazil and her sister-writers; in a book of 276 pages about school stories she devotes only one perfunctory chapter of ten pages to girls.)

THE IMPORTANCE OF SPORT[7]

One of the most significant characteristics which girls' boarding schools derived from their male counterparts was the emphasis on team games. Organised sport was a Victorian creation, introduced into boys' schools to help the boys to use their leisure time not only in a healthy and disciplined manner but in a way which promoted useful social values such as leadership, the team spirit and competitiveness. Its introduction into girls' schools was not simply because what boys had, girls had to have too. Victorian feminists had long campaigned against the way in which girls were denied healthy exercise in the interests of femininity and because it was held to impair their reproductive abilities. While boys enjoyed the rough and tumble of games and outdoor pursuits, girls had sat indoors or made do with ladylike walks in constricting garments. Feminists recognised that this predisposed girls to weakness and ill-health and hampered their achievement in other fields. Thus games were encouraged by the women reformers from the start for physical reasons.

As feminists struggled against the restrictions and disabilities which limited women in education, employment, law and politics, sport became one more male-dominated area to campaign for. It also had symbolic value: sport represented freedom in a very real sense, the freedom to abandon feminine decorum and run about in (relatively) light clothing in the open air, with other girls, for personal enjoyment rather than in the service of some abstract ideal or concrete person.

In attempting to persuade reluctant parents that games would be good for their daughters, the reformers also drew on the moral advantages beloved of the Victorian educators of boys. Team games, they argued, encouraged discipline, loyalty, and determination: qualities as relevant to girls as to boys. In the 1920s an official history of the first girls' public school, St Leonard's (founded in 1877), attempted to explain the tremendous significance that schoolgirls attached to their games:

> No mere physical enjoyment can explain the intensity of excitement in shield matches. The truth is that each house, through its team, is conscious of being put to a public test. Not only quickness and skill, but staying power, combination, resource, the courage to play a losing game, and the generosity to be a good winner, all these qualities, *the very qualities once supposed to be untypical of girls*, are on their trial as house meets house [my italics].[8]

In boys' schools, sport played an important role in training the leaders of the future in their respective roles, whether as wise leaders or unquestioning followers, working together for a common goal. The suppression of individual desire was an important part of team-work – individual decisions might be made, but in the interests of the team – going hand in hand with the general stunting of emotion in the interests of reason, moral strength and 'manliness'. These qualities were seen as necessary to train the future rulers of industry and empire. In the context of the girls' school, sport took on a radical significance, since it gave women access to what were seen as 'masculine' values. Leadership, for example, had never been seen as a feminine role; women were generally viewed as undisciplined, whimsical, unable to make reasoned judgments or to co-operate with each other. Whether these assumptions were true or not – and contemporary accounts suggest that the conventional education of girls tended to make them self-fulfilling prophecies[9] – sport provided an opportunity for girls to prove them wrong. It also gave practical expression to a code of values which, seemingly traditional and patriarchal, meant something quite different for girls. If the goal was, as Emily Davies had argued, that girls should 'be measured by the same standards as their brothers', then the standards referred to were not only academic but also moral. That is, honour, 'sportsmanship', loyalty and discipline – the ingredients of the schoolgirl code.

GAMES IN THE SCHOOL STORY

Beginning with the enthusiastic pages of Angela Brazil, who always regretted not having had enough games at her own school, they became a *sine qua non* of girls' school stories. The works of our four authors were no exception. Cricket was taken seriously at most of Elsie Oxenham's schools, with tennis as the preferred sport of the older girls. They seem not to have been keen on winter games, but then folk dancing and Camp Fire absorbed a good part of their energies.

Dorita Fairlie Bruce was also most devoted to cricket, as the title of one of her 'Nancy' books (*The Best Bat in the School*, 1931) indicates. But hockey, netball, tennis and rounders feature importantly in all her stories, and inter-school matches provide oportunities for heroines from one series to cross into the pages of another.

The Chalet School, though set up in Austria, is determinedly English in its choice of games, with cricket and tennis being played in the summer and hockey in the winter. Continental pupils take to the games with enthusiasm, which leads to an initial misunderstanding when a rival English school takes up occupation on the other side of the lake. Its girls naturally assume that the Chalet School with its mixture of nationalities will be 'dud at sport'.

> 'Foreigners never *can* play games for nuts. If they do anything, it'll be battledore and shuttlecock, you'll see. As for cricket, I don't suppose they would dare to do anything with a ball that wasn't *soft!*'[10]

They are soon proved wrong.

Capitalising on their lakeside location, the early Chalet schoolgirls are privileged to enjoy skating in winter; and in the summer, although the spring-fed waters are too cold for swimming, they take up rowing. It is ironic that, although the school is firmly situated in the Alps, it never seems to have occurred to Brent-Dyer that the girls might *ski!* It would appear that in the 1920s and 1930s skiing was still too novel a sport as far as the average English person was concerned – though not for the Austrians themselves or for wealthier tourists – for the idea to cross her mind. When the Chalet School moves to Switzerland in the 1950s, however, almost the first thing the girls do is learn to ski.

In between Austria and Switzerland, the school is located in the Channel Islands, England, and Wales, and there the typical British team games are pursued with the usual inter-house and inter-school fixtures. Water sports come to prominence once again when the school spends two years on an island. But the move to Switzerland takes away most of the outside competition, and games become more social. There is still swimming on Lake Thun in summer; tennis, cricket, lacrosse, netball and hockey enjoy shorter seasons, and the wintry months are given over to skiing (cross-country, not competitive) and tobogganing. And as in most school stories, the games prefect at the Chalet School is second only in authority to the head girl herself.

For Enid Blyton, sporting ability is a virtue equal in importance to academic excellence. Her heroines excel on the playing field and in the swimming pool, and her gravest criticisms, and often ridicule, are reserved for the girls who don't enjoy games, like Gwendoline, the butt of the six Malory Towers books, who is driven to lament:

> Why aren't there any nice *feminine* girls here – the ones who like to talk and read quietly, and not always go pounding about the lacrosse field or splash in that horrible pool.[11]

When Alison of St Clare's asks why games are compulsory at school, her form-mate Janet replies in terms of the school-girl code:

> We have to learn to work together as a team – each one for his [sic] side, helping the others, not each one for himself. That sort of thing is especially good for *you*, Alison – you'd sit in a corner and look at yourself in the mirror all day long if you could . . .[12]

This was very much the philosophy of the nineteenth-century headmistresses who saw games as a corrective to feminine frivolity and self-obsession. It is not, however, without significance in the increasingly anti-feminist atmosphere of the postwar period when some leading educationists were returning to the old idea that women's place was in the home and were, accordingly, advocating increased emphasis on appearance, personal relationships, and domestic skills to fit girls for their 'real' work.[13] Clearly Blyton did not subscribe to this view.

Games are a literary device of school stories as well as a reflection of their role in real schools. Accounts of matches fill any number of pages and provide twists to plot lines in nearly all the novels. It is important for us to read them not as literary padding or as vehicles for the mindless reiteration of conventional values, but with an awareness of what they might have meant to the schoolgirls of earlier generations. What seems conventional – even reactionary – now, was radical then in contrast to the Victorian girl's almost complete lack of physical freedom and her attenuated sense of self-worth. The achievements of sporting heroines showed that girls could be as 'good' as boys both in their performance on the games field and also in their personal qualities. Support for the team also encouraged feelings of identification with a community of women.

A reaction against the emphasis on sport for girls occurred in the early years of this century when educators such as Sara Burstall, headmistress of Manchester High School, argued that the sporting trend had gone too far.[14] This attitude is reflected in the first novel (1920) of Dorita Fairlie Bruce, where the headmistress decides to reduce games practice time for the girls and instead introduce domestic science.

THE SCHOOLGIRL CODE IN FICTION

If sport had different meanings for schoolgirls from those it had for schoolboys, can we say the same for the schoolboy/girl code which the girls also took over as part of the masculine curriculum? I think it is simplistic to say that girls accepted the ideals of honour, loyalty and the team spirit unthinkingly, just because they wanted to adopt every aspect of boys' education. The early headmistresses were obliged to be very careful to reassure parents that school would not 'unsex' their girls. Feminine skills and decorum were never lost sight of, and girls were educated to take their places in the home as well as in higher education and jobs. Thus, loyalty and the team spirit had to fit into a scheme of teaching which represented a compromise between femininity and feminism, between women's roles as they were conventionally perceived and those which campaigners hoped to open up. The girls' school stories reflect this uneasy compromise; they show how completely these values, hitherto seen as masculine, were absorbed into the schoolgirl culture, but also how the feminine world refined and manoeuvred round them.

Because the schoolboy code evolved in the Victorian era, it is often seen as inseparable from the worst aspects of British imperialism. We who have read countless literary analogies between playing the games on the sports' field of Eton and playing it in the colonies or in the trenches find it difficult to view the idea in a neutral light. Discipline and loyalty are firmly tied to fascism in many minds; honour seems a meaningless concept in the context of modern politics. Yet I would argue that although the values of the schoolboy code have been used in the service of ideals we might not support today, they are not in themselves necessarily bad; certainly they were not perceived as such by girls' schools and school story writers in the early part of this century.

Reading *Tom Brown's School Days* (1857) is an education in how unexceptionable the values of the mid-Victorian schoolboy code mostly were. Apart from the endorsement of violence, an important distinction, there is little that the modern reader can object to in its ideals. Tom Brown's father sends him to school not to make a scholar of him but so he will 'turn out a brave, helpful, truth-telling Englishman'. And although he is a Tory, Squire Brown holds egalitarian views about rank; he declares that 'it didn't matter a straw to him whether his son associated with lords' sons or ploughmen's sons provided they were brave and honest.' (Of course, Tom was not likely to come across ploughmen's sons at Rugby.) We can hardly be surprised at the Squire's attitude to women – Tom is instructed not to 'listen to or say anything you wouldn't have your mother and sister hear' – but while patronising, this was surely not very oppressive.[15]

Such chivalrous sexism had no place in the girls' schools, though there was probably a fair amount of agreement about which subjects were suitable for children's ears generally. (In the school in L T Meade's novel, *A World of Girls*, 1886, Charlotte Brontë's *Jane Eyre* is banned!)[16] But the rejection of class distinctions *was* taken up; indeed, the girls' school stories make rather a feature of it. In *Dimsie Goes To School* (1921), Dorita Fairlie Bruce depicts 10-year-old Dimsie arriving at school for the first time, expecting her schoolmates to ask her what her father does. 'Rosamund stared. "Why should we? Your father isn't coming to Jane's, is he?" '[17]

Elinor Brent-Dyer takes a similar stance in *The Feud in the Fifth Remove* (1949) where, we are told

> the atmosphere of the Abbey High School was utterly unsnobbish. The girls stood on their own merits – not what their fathers might chance to be, and, as Miss Heriot, the Head Mistress, said on one occasion, 'the only thing that mattered was whether a girl was honest, honourable, and courteous.'[18]

If Brent-Dyer tells us once, she tells us in a dozen books that 'Our Lady was the Wife of a carpenter.'[19] Elsie Oxenham takes on class in *The Girls of the Hamlet Club* (1914), while Enid Blyton is less earnest but perhaps more honest in her understanding of the attraction that wealthy, well-to-do girls have for their less privileged schoolmates. Yet she too exposes snobbery in a series of stock situations which are nevertheless cleverly crafted. In *Claudine at St Clare's* (1944), two new girls vie with each other to boast about their wealth. Says the Hon Angela Favorleigh, 'I bet you haven't more than one bathroom in your own home. We've got seven.'

'We've got nine, if you count the two in the servants' quarters,' returns Pauline Bingham-Jones instantly.

'The other girls join in mischievously. 'Let me count *my* bathrooms,' says Bobby. 'Three for myself – four for Mother – five for Daddy – two for visitors – er, how many's that?'

'I can't remember whether we've got a bathroom at home or not,' adds Hilary . . . [20]

It has to be admitted that there are very clear bounds to

this social egalitarianism in all school stories. Heroines are universally middle-class and white; even 'poor' characters turn out to be 'ladies', [21] and every book contains throwaway lines which reveal the limits of the author's awareness, or even concern, for class divisions. [22] Elinor Brent-Dyer ties herself up in knots when she tries to explain just exactly why Joan, in *A Problem for the Chalet School* (1956), is *not* a lady; [23] Dorita Fairlie Bruce constantly associates 'cheapness' and 'vulgarity' with the working class. Other critics have exposed the class bias of most of these stories, and I see no reason to disagree with their analyses. With respect to the other aspects of the schoolboy/girl code, however, just as different schools emphasised honour, loyalty and discipline in different degrees, so too did the school story writers.

Dorita Fairlie Bruce was politically the most conservative of our four in terms of her unswerving allegiance to Empire, militarism, royalty and the ruling class. Not unnaturally, then, she is inclined to use the values of the schoolgirl code to uphold these ideals: ideals more commonly supported in her time, of course, than today. Elsie Oxenham was also a conservative, but her schoolgirls are less influenced by the schoolgirl code than by nineteenth-century notions of feminine morality; if they are honourable, it is because gentlewomen *are*. Elinor Brent-Dyer and Enid Blyton take a more light-hearted approach. As the values of the schoolgirl code came to be taken for granted, as fixed and immutable as the curriculum itself, girls' stories came to focus on their heroines' attempts to negotiate around them to achieve a just result without actually bringing the ideals themselves into question.

In the libertarian climate of the 1960s and 1970s there was a wholesale attack on the values of the schoolboy/girl code, and its component parts were for the most part summarily rejected. Subsequent experience has shown us, however, that good things may unthinkingly be lost with the bad in this kind of clean sweep, and that women may choose to retain and reclaim for their own use features which men have rejected. The team spirit, for example, may be reinterpreted as feminine co-operation; women may derive strength from seeing it in terms of sisterhood, and in so doing may present themselves as a stronger force against patriarchal oppression.

For Dorita Fairlie Bruce, as for so many writers of juvenile fiction, the pre-eminent value of schoolgirl existence was that nebulous quality 'honour'. It is best explained by reference to what was considered *dishonourable* conduct. Breaking rules was not necessarily dishonourable – the difference between honourable and dishonourable rule-breaking is explored in *Captain at Springdale* (1932) – but failing to own up for one's misdeeds was, as was letting other people take the blame for them, and 'sneaking'. 'I think you'll find that sneaking isn't appreciated at Springdale. It just happens to be one of those things which aren't done at any decent school,' Primula tells one of the new girls in *The New House at Springdale* (1934).[24] The plots of several Bruce tales hinge on the heroine's code of honour, which frequently gets her into scrapes which could have been avoided had she not stuck rigidly to it. Refusal to speak out, because to do so would implicate another girl, makes for compounded confusion, and this is only resolved when someone – generally a junior – decides to tell all. This is not a breach of the code because, confusingly, 'There are times when sneaking is the only right and proper thing to do.'[25]

Loyalty is an aspect of honour. In Bruce's novels, loyalty to the school sometimes takes contradictory forms of expression. It is used by the Senior Prefect as a weapon to break a strike by the girls of the Jane Willard Foundation, when the new headmistress, as described above, has reduced the time allowed for games.

I warn you, girls, this isn't playing the game. . . . How can you think it best for Jane's to stir up this rebellion against the teachers? Miss Darrel used to say that the school was just like the nation in miniature, and I think it was awfully true. We have to be loyal to our head and the people over us, just as the nation has to be loyal to the King.[26]

In contrast, loyalty to an individual may actually be subversive to the state. In one situation it involves breaking the law. In *Sally's Summer Term* (1961), Sally refuses to give evidence against the man who criminally damaged the local fir plantation, because his daughter

> is my pal . . . And if all this came out and got into the papers, when everyone knows she's his daughter, I – I believe she would die of shame! I simply couldn't! Not to save all the trees in Scotland![27]

But this is nothing to Toby Barrett's decision in *The School on the Moor* (1931) to shelter an escaped convict of whom she knows nothing except that 'in that momentary ebb of the fog the man's eyes had met hers – wild, driven, terrified, yet somehow straight and trustworthy'. When he asks her, not unnaturally, why she helped him, she replies simply that, 'I sort of feel you wouldn't do anything mean, or – or beastly – or any of the kind of things for which people are sent to prison.' She has an additional reason, which clinches the matter: 'Besides, you're rather like some one I know – a mistress at our school.'[28]

Of course, he *is* Miss Musgrave's brother, and of course he is innocent of the crime for which he was convicted, so we end up feeling that Toby was perfectly right to pervert the course of justice. But as a lesson for girls – that they should trust a lightning glimpse of a face and an instant character assessment when faced with a fleeing criminal, or take it upon themselves to interfere with the agents of the law – it is hardly consistent with Bruce's usual respect for authority, and might be positively dangerous if followed. Replete with false assumptions which were, however, typically held by people of Bruce's class and era, the sentiments expressed here are revealing of the uneasiness with which the values of the schoolboy code sat on women brought up with very different notions of individual moral responsibility and the infallibility of women's moral judgments.

For Elsie Oxenham, too, such things as eavesdropping, breaking promises, sneaking, betraying confidences, letting others take the blame for your misdeeds, and disobeying when a mistress has put you 'on honour' are all, generally speaking, dishonourable actions, and all make their appearance in the plots of her school stories. In an early book, *The Abbey Girls* (1920), she shows sympathy for a new girl who does not instantly grasp all that the schoolgirl code entails. 'They think any girl who is fourteen and cannot understand their ways must be an absolute idiot.'[29] After that she is forced to take it on board.

Writing about international classrooms, Oxenham followed the jingoistic traditions of boys' school stories in presenting honour as a peculiarly English virtue. The new pupil Sally, at St Mary's in Switzerland, finds French Louisette 'catty', but 'Nell's jolly and really English, which means all that's sporting, of course!'[30]

Honour is also associated in Oxenham's mind with the male sex. Gard's older brother keeps her up to the mark: 'You do have to mind what you're about when you're living with boys. He'd be awfully upset if I did anything he thought was rotten.'[31] For Oxenham it is a middle-class attribute – working-class people are shown not to understand its significance – but not *all* middle-class people have it. Dick and Della are well-to-do and English but lack the vital quality. Under the influence of the Abbey chums, Della awakes to a 'new sense of honesty, born of the knowledge that these girls with whom she was living had different standards from hers . . .'[32]

Honour includes the ability to be *sporting*; or to do the right thing in a particular dilemma. Gard rescues her old enemy Rita after an accident on the Downs, but the car which stops to help them can only convey one girl to the pageant on time. Gard gives way because Rita's part is more important. Rita, who was in the wrong all along, immediately gives up the rivalry, full of admiration for Gard: 'She didn't think of herself at all. She's a brick; and absolutely sporting.'[33]

The language of the games field sprinkles these exhortations, hardly surprising since the code had been borrowed from the boys' public school. But girls' school stories prove that honour and sportsmanship need not only be elements of 'manliness'. Oxenham adapts the code to form the basis of the morality of the Abbey books' Hamlet Club with their more feminine problems. The day girls at her Wycombe school, who live in the hamlets round about, are excluded from the regular school societies because they cannot afford the subscriptions. Along comes Cicely, a day girl with plenty of money, who refuses to band with the exclusive clubs and joins up with the outcasts to form the Hamlet Club whose motto is, of course, 'To be or not to be'. This means 'whether we are or are not to be out of everything in the school,' as Miriam explains.

> But to some of us, it means the question all have to decide sooner or later, whether they'll just have a good time and please themselves and get all they can and care for nothing else, or whether they'll put more important things first, and – are about other people, and try to do great things in the world.[34]

This broad interpretation allows Oxenham to carry the Hamlet vision into the adult lives of her Abbey girls (they go on being 'girls' well into their thirties). When Joy and Jen decide to take on Mary and save her from the unhealthy dream world she has become immersed in, they recognise that 'It's up to us to hand on to her and see that she never goes back. . . . It's a big job for us, but we can't shirk it.'[35] In a later book, Mary herself – fully recovered and now a wise adviser in her own right – tells Jen and Ann: 'When we funk a difficulty or shirk a plain duty or are slack and lazy, we're failing to do our part in a plan that may spoil things for other people.'[36] For Oxenham, this plan is God's design for humanity; in books written at this time, she drew a good deal on religious justification for comfort. We have come a long way from the playing field, but our rules are still adhered to.

Loyalty to the school is also a favourite theme of Elsie Oxenham's. Cicely unites her schoolfellows by insisting that Hamlet Club members be on good terms with everyone and contribute to all school activities. 'She puts the school first.'[37]

The loyalty that prevails even over law is present in Oxenham's books as in Bruce's, though in a less dramatic form. Jinty trips and shouts on purpose when stalking would-be thieves so that they will not be caught. 'I wanted them to get away. Because of Roger [a dog]'s mistress, you know [a gypsy lavender seller, whose son was one of the thieves]. It would have been so horrid for her.'

Typically, the owner of the goods which were almost stolen does not mind:

> You saved me the trouble and annoyance of police-court proceedings, and yet saved my treasures as effectually as if you had caught the thieves. We will hope the fight will deter them from doing the same thing elsewhere.[38]

Elinor Brent-Dyer's early books represent no radical departure from the usual notions about honour. Even foreign schools like her Collège des Musiciens in 'Mirania' have English standards:

> The tone of the College was very high, and the Principal held a tremendous standard of honour. He detested anything in the nature of meanness, and the girls, on the whole, developed a sense of 'playing the game' which would have done credit to any English public school.[39]

In *Heather Leaves School* (1929), Brent-Dyer engaged with the contemporary debate over the role of sports in girls' schools. Heather's parents take her away from her school because:

> Ripley has a great name among schools, but it seems to me that they are in danger of making a little tin god of sport, and forgetting everything else. After all I, for one, don't want my daughter to grow up into a kind of boy-girl!

Heather, however, has fully imbibed the moral value of sport. When a companion opines that playing games is a waste of time, she declares: 'What rot! Why, it's games that help to make you sporting and unselfish! When you play, you've got to play for your side – not for yourself! And you learn not to howl when you get a knock or anything like that!'[40]

There is also an acknowledgement that, in the pursuit of high standards of conduct, girls are following in the footsteps of boys. Eustacia, for example, tells tales. Miss Wilson tries to explain to her the enormity of her offence:

> Cannot you understand, Eustacia? In a boys' school you would have been thrashed well by one of the fellows, and everyone would say it served you right. I do not imagine that the girls here will proceed to such lengths, but I am afraid you are making things hard for yourself. . . . School-girls, you will find, are as strict as their brothers in matters of honour – and rightly so.[41]

In later books, Brent-Dyer moves beyond the clichés to the exposition of a much more helpful set of principles. A war-time novel introduces a difficult new girl, Lavender, whose aunt/guardian has always tried to shield her from war news. Miss Wilson tries to reason with Miss Leigh.

> After all, it will be, in great measure, the boys and girls who are now in their early teens who will have to rebuild

life, once the war is over. How can they do it adequately if they don't understand what it is they have to consider in laying the foundations for what *must* be, to quote Hitler's words, a new order? And, apart from that, it doesn't do to wrap children up in too much cotton-wool. It may have answered in our mothers' day, when a girl was, in the main, expected to stay at home until she married, and went to a home of her own. But these children will have to go out and face the world; and unless we who are responsible for their present training give them some backbone, many of them will crumple up and fall before what they must meet.[42]

This quotation is interesting for its mention of Hitler's 'new order'. Anyone who has followed the Chalet School series will know, however, that Miss Wilson is no supporter of Hitler; she was among the Chalet School personnel forced to flee Nazi-occupied Austria, an incident which permanently crippled her and turned her hair white. Miss Wilson has every reason to hate Hitler; she only invokes his name to reinforce her idea that women must play a more significant role in the postwar era.

For Enid Blyton, honour is essentially an English virtue. 'But Suzanne was French,' she says in one novel. 'She hadn't quite the same ideas of responsibility as the British girls had.'[43] In *Claudine at St Clare's* (1944) the eponymous heroine (based on a real girl at Blyton's own school, as she tells us in *The Story of My Life*),[44] when new to the school, copies another girl's work, and is astonished to be accused of cheating. 'You all see me do it,' she protests. 'Cheating is a secret thing.'

The form head girl tries to explain that cheating is dishonourable, whether done openly or on the sly. 'Besides, it's so silly of you to copy from Mirabel. She gets so many answers wrong. Miss Ellis will find out and then you'll get into a row.'

'You think then it would be better to copy from Hilary?' returns Claudine, missing the point completely.[45]

On another occasion she is caught sampling strawberries after the girls have been put 'on their honour' not to touch them. 'This honour of yours, it is a funny thing,' she observes philosophically.

> It stops you from doing what you want to do. I have no honour to worry me. I will never have this honour of yours. I do not like it.[46]

But of course she is won over in the end, after a series of misunderstandings and scrapes, and is able to agree with the headmistress that the one thing she will take back with her to France is 'the English sense of honour'.[47]

DISCIPLINE

Discipline was another essential virtue inculcated by the schoolboy/girl code, but also imposed to a greater or lesser extent by the school authorities. Discipline in girls' schools varied, as it must have done in real life, from the rigid structures of Dorita Fairlie Bruce's books to some fairly relaxed institutions in Elsie Oxenham's; with Elinor Brent-Dyer and Enid Blyton in between. The head girl and prefects of Bruce, Brent-Dyer and Blyton wield considerable power and are responsible for enforcing most school regulations. In Oxenham's stories, the older girls rule more by personal influence. But through all the books, order is maintained as much by a general adherence to the school code as by any written constitution.

Bruce's educational philosophy is conservative. Her schools are organised on traditional hierarchical lines with fixed and punitive regulations. This is true even of her last school, St Michael's, in which (though it is a day school, and the books were written in the late 1950s) the pupils' lives seem to be as completely controlled as they were in her boarding schools of the 1920s and 1930s. What is more, the girls *prefer* it that way. In both *The New House at Springdale* (1934) and *Sally's Summer Term* (1961) there is criticism of schools where the girls have too much freedom. Of Braidwood School, a St Michael's girl remarks: 'They don't take anyone under fifteen, and they don't seem to have any rules to speak of; they're allowed out and around in a way that would make our Head's hair stand on end.' To which her friend replies, 'I'd rather have a straight-laced Head than one who is lax, like Braidwood's. It's more comfortable, somehow. After all, school is school.'[48] It *is* more comfortable, of course, having your moral decisions made for you, instead of having to make your own; but not much of a training for autonomous adulthood.

One of Bruce's favourite breaches of discipline, for plot purposes, is gambling at cards. Her very first novel involves a scandal about Dimsie's mother and some card-sharpers, and *Dimsie Goes Back* (1924) features a syndicate of schoolgirls who play behind closed doors (thoroughly dishonourable), causing one poor girl to lose not only all her pocket-money for the term but her Christmas tips pledged in advance. Another stock situation is breaking bounds, such as to go to a dance in town or for a midnight picnic. The one breach of discipline not found in Bruce's work is the schoolgirl prank, of the kind beloved of Elinor Brent-Dyer, Elsie Oxenham and, especially, Enid Blyton, whose descriptions of 'tricks' played on unsuspecting staff members are still unexpectedly, irresistibly funny. Bruce's heroines are serious young people. As a child, Dimsie asks if the girls put hairbrushes in new girls' beds:

> 'What for?' inquired Rosamund, who was not fond of reading [a dig at contemporary school stories]; 'it sounds a silly sort of thing to do.' 'Nor jugs of water on the top of the door?' pursued Dimsie . . . 'You *are* a queer kid,' said Rosamund in a superior voice . . . [49]

By contrast, discipline is pretty lax in Elsie Oxenham's schools. She is not a strict observer of rules and none of her heroines is a serious student. Jandy speaks for most of them when she declares that she wants 'to have all the fun of being at school, but not to trouble about the work! . . . I'd rather just enjoy myself . . .'[50] Breaking bounds to meet the boys of the neighbouring school does trouble the form captains at St Mary's – not because there is any intrinsic harm in mixing with boys, but because of the disobedience involved. But in the somewhat anarchic atmosphere of the Abbey School, girls easily get permission from the headmistress to scamper off to explore secret tunnels or dig up Abbey treasures.

At the Chalet School, prefects have a lot of power. A favourite device of Elinor Brent-Dyer is to contrast their role with that enjoyed by their counterparts in other schools. When St Scholastika's amalgamates with the Chalet School, Miss Browne's girls are quickly made aware of the difference. The Chalet School prefects have *real* power, and because they are trusted to enforce their discipline with actual sanctions they are treated with due respect.

Agents of social control though they clearly are, wielding only delegated power, the prefects are nevertheless strong role models for the younger girls, as they must have been for readers. By and large they are shown to rule by the force of their personal influence, not by imposing punishments. And while the idea of enlisting older girls to manage younger girls has a repugnant feel to those who view teachers and pupils as either natural enemies or natural allies, prefectship was an excellent training ground for girls who were going to have to move into the hierarchically organised professional or political world. It provided younger girls with female models to admire and emulate, at a time when there was a dearth of these, both at school and in the wider world. It proved that the female sex could handle management quite as well as the male, and paved the way for women to prove the same thing in the much more difficult patriarchal society outside.

In an ideal world, girls might well choose to act collectively on an egalitarian basis. In fact, to some extent the prefect system of the girls' schools did approach this ideal, since prefects often acted collectively and in co-operation with other girls. In Enid Blyton's Naughtiest Girl series, a democratically chosen school council drawn from all ranks of the school is responsible for discipline, and decisions are made by a vote of the entire school. On the other hand, many girls welcomed a hierarchical system as recognising the difference in age and experience between the young women of the top forms and the little girls of the bottom. And the natural inclination of younger girls to look up to their elders was often a pleasant experience for both, and preferable to focusing one's emotional energies on to boys.

Enid Blyton examines the subject of discipline in *In the Fifth at Malory Towers* (1950). Maureen has come to the school from Mazeley Manor, where girls are allowed to do pretty much as they choose. She finds the rules at Malory Towers difficult to accept but eventually concludes, 'Perhaps – yes, perhaps it *was* better to *have* to do things that were good for you, whether you liked them or not, till you were old enough and responsible enough to choose.'[51]

It is not clear on what grounds Maureen makes this judgment and, in fact, Blyton's attitude to discipline seems in most respects quite relaxed. Her girls indulge disproportionately in 'tricks' which disrupt lessons and in midnight feasts which the headmistress does not worry much about. After one such incident, Miss Theobald scolds the girls involved but adds, 'your escapade is not in the same rank as, for instance, meanness, lying, or disloyalty' – a refreshingly sensible view to take.[52] In Blyton's view, a good boarding school 'makes you stand on your own feet, rubs off your corners, teaches you common-sense, makes you accept responsibility'.[53] These effects, a universal argument for community life, are illustrated by the development of her characters through the series from undisciplined juniors to mature seniors, ready to take their place in the adult world.

A POSITIVE MESSAGE FOR GIRLS

As the offspring of two educational institutions, the school and children's literature, school stories are by nature didactic. But just as educational ideologies change over time, so the messages of the school story have come under attack from later generations. Not everyone has been happy about their messages. By the second half of the twentieth century, literary critics had become as vocal in their condemnation of the values promoted in school stories as they had been about the lack of literary quality. Their attack on this aspect of the school story was two-pronged, based on both ridicule of the inflexible, outmoded schoolboy/girl code which regulated the characters' conduct and despair at the absence of any consideration of 'realistic' contemporary issues such as class and race. The critique was part of a reaction against the social mores of an age which had come to be seen as jingoistic, sexually puritanical and class-bound.

There can be no doubt that the popular support enjoyed by school stories in the years between the wars was at least partly due to the value system they were believed to espouse and propagate. Many of these books began life as 'Sunday School Rewards' and were marketed as such. The 1920s and 1930s was an era of both social unrest and conservative reaction. Then, as now, a return to the old ideals of discipline, family life, hard work and deference to authority was seen as the answer to economic and social insecurity. These were all values promoted by the school story. School stories therefore enjoyed conservative support because they represented, or at least did not challenge, conventional values.

It would be wrong, however, to overlook the existence in the schoolgirl code of a positive message for girl readers of the interwar years. Their commercial success was not, I am sure, solely due to the Establishment; I suggest these books may have been bought by many whose outlook was progressive, not to say feminist. The right to education had been one of the great battles fought by the Victorian women's movement, and the victory was still fresh in the minds of its beneficiaries. As Sara Burstall wrote in 1933:

> For generations men have felt loyalty and gratitude to their schools: emotion which has found its way into song not only at Eton and Harrow and Clifton. Stirring and beautiful as these songs are, they do not express more than is felt by women who, under the new era, have gained from their schools opportunity, knowledge, discipline, fellowship, and who look back in loyalty and affection to those who taught them.[54]

School stories were literary proof that (middle-class) girls' education was at last being taken seriously and that (middle-class) girls should have access to a masculine curriculum, including games, and a masculine value–system, perceived in a patriarchal society as the best available. This in itself was a source of pride for schoolgirls. A still greater source of strength and pleasure was, no doubt, the fact of studying, playing, and learning to live together in a community of girls and women, free from the constant patronage, harassment and competition of the male sex.

Along with school songs, uniforms, prefects and games, girls' schools took on as part of the educational package a moral code which was genuinely believed to be the best available: the code which made boys into men, into soldiers and leaders and Empire builders; the code which made England 'great'. This code was now being used to transform girls into honorary boys: that is, individuals with high standards and a capacity for individual judgment and action, usually denied to women in the heterosexual world outside schools, where men made decisions and women obeyed.

Paradoxically, the traditional view of women as the moral guardians of society made it easier for them to adopt the ideals of the schoolboy code. Women were expected to have an *active* moral sense in what was perceived as a fundamentally passive nature. This was in spite of the fact that women had to exercise this morality from a position of relative powerlessness – economic, social, legal and political – made worse, often enough, by ignorance and inexperience. Putting women in a higher moral position gave men licence to err – innately less moral, they were therefore less culpable – and placed on women the responsibility for all that was wrong in the world. If a man sinned, the woman was to blame for leading him on or for failing to curb him. If children were delinquent, the mother was to blame for not bringing them up properly. To carry most of the moral burden of society, women had to be trained. All the more reason, then, why schoolgirls should feel so at home with honour, loyalty, and discipline. Morality was intrinsic to womanhood, a lesson girls learn very early on.

The same tension between working to reduce women's responsibility for parenting and nurturing, and celebrating these roles, exists in the women's movement today. It is a tension that schoolgirl readers of the interwar period would have recognised, and school story writers compromised by accepting and indeed emphasising women's moral responsibility, while giving it a masculine 'equal rights' basis in the adapted schoolboy code.

Objections which arise are: first, the code is inadequate for dealing with many of the important moral issues faced by schoolgirls; second, that principles originally intended for guidance came to be reinforced so rigidly and unthinkingly as to preclude reasoned consideration of the moral issues and autonomous decision-making and action. Clearly this is illustrated in some school stories. Nancy and her friends completely missed Barbara's real problem in *The New Girl and Nancy* (1926). The novel focusses on her permed hair, which she wishes to wear loose at school, causing a great stir: 'It certainly won't pass. What made you do it in such a weird way?' The girl's reluctance to subdue her hairstyle is regarded as a breach of discipline with important moral implications. 'That kid will have to find her level before she's much older. She's got a good deal too much side on at present.'

Meanwhile, her real problems are ignored. Thirteen-year-old Barbara has lived since her mother's death with the latter's relations. Her father, lately re-married, has now decided he wants his daughter to live with him. He goes to court to get custody, and wins. Barbara not unnaturally does not want to leave her present home; but the validity of her feelings is never really addressed in the novel, nor the morality of either her father's getting custody of a teenage girl or her uprooting at such a time. All that seems to matter is that Barbara has permed hair and that this, with its implications of non-conformity (and worse, *cheapness*) cannot be tolerated in a good school.

Honour, loyalty and discipline are not much use if you limit the application of these values to people like yourself; they cannot train you to put yourself into other people's place and help them on their own terms. (There have been plenty of honourable, loyal and disciplined fascists in history.) Bruce in particular leant heavily on discipline to peddle her own homilies against modern ideas in schooling and fashions for girls. There *are* arguments against lax school organisation or make-up and permed hair on schoolgirls, but we will not find them in the pages of Bruce's novels. Instead of presenting a reasoned case, Bruce opted for authority that was in no way democratic, and for enforced conformity.

Even discipline, however, can be understood in the context of the 1920s and 1930s as a source of strength for girls. Being seen to maintain the same standards as boys put girls on an equal footing with them in the eyes of the external world. Discipline was also a necessary adjunct to emancipation, for parents of the time would have been unwilling to allow their daughters to attend modern schools if they had not been assured of the high moral tone of the institution and a scrupulous superintendence of the girls. Moreover, the stringent regulations and duties were not always resented by pupils. As Bruce correctly shows, adherence to an arcane set of customs bound the girls together into a community, like membership of an exclusive club of which they alone understood the rules. Readers of stories about imaginary schools would have enjoyed entering vicariously into this fellowship, particularly if they themselves had been denied the real (and often very much less pleasant) experience of boarding-school life.

Strict discipline also offered opportunities for rebellion both independently and in alliance with comrades, which provided not only relief from the boredom of school life but also a staple device for innumerable school story plots. These acts of defiance prompted both demonstrations of power by prefects and acts of moral rectitude on the part of younger heroines. Only a structure built on clear rules of conduct and values gave scope for these roles to be played out by girls, and to be admired and perhaps imitated by the readers of girls' school stories.

If in real boarding schools there was probably very little opportunity for this sort of rebellion by the hapless pupils confined therein, nevertheless the fictional school settings fed the imaginations of an incomparably greater number of readers who had never experienced the reality.

4 Heroines

THE EVERLASTING SCHOOLGIRL: ELINOR BRENT-DYER'S JO

What is remarkable about the heroine of Elinor Brent-Dyer's Chalet School books, Jo Bettany, is that she gets married in the fourteenth book in the series, yet remains a more or less central character throughout the 45 succeeding volumes. In spite of marriage and motherhood, 'which by rights should debar her from playing the lead in a school-story',[1] the adult Jo is presented (as the author herself asserts in more than a few novels) as 'the spirit of what the school is meant to be'.[2]

Jo starts life very much in the mould of Louisa May Alcott's Jo March, a girl who finds it hard to conform to feminine conventions and who is reluctant to leave girlhood behind for the uncertain delights of womanhood. 'You'll have to grow up some day, Joey,' the 16-year-old Jo is advised by Jack Maynard – who has a vested interest, since he intends to marry her.

'Not a day before I have to!' Jo retorts. 'I'll be like Jo March in *Little Women*, and "wear my hair in two tails till I'm twenty!"'[3]

Yet, despite her name, Jo Bettany is not portrayed as a tomboy, and in the 1920s her rebelliousness against a less repressive regime than that faced by Jo March takes the simpler form of girlish mischief and naughtiness, for which there is ample scope in a boarding school. As a child she is delicate, prone to illness and accidents (again good plot material for school stories). In the best tradition of heroines, she is striking but not pretty ('Joey made up in distinction what she lacked in beauty'),[4] with short, black hair and black eyes. Her talents are musical – she has a lovely singing voice – and literary; like so many writers' heroines she grows up to be a writer herself. She is not particularly academic, and there is no thought, this being the 1930s, of her going on to university or college when she leaves school.

What then is special about Jo Bettany? Brent-Dyer's biographer, Helen McClelland, observes: 'As a schoolgirl, Jo is portrayed with quite a realistic mixture of good qualities and faults. . . . It all adds up to a convincing and attractive presentation which, in the early books, is always seasoned with a touch of humour.'[5] Prettiness, goodness and brilliance have little appeal for readers, and Jo exhibits none of these. Rather, she is sensitive and creative, and her intense feelings are something which girls growing up might well identify with: 'A nature like hers is sometimes more of a curse than a blessing. She has wonderful moments of happiness, I know. But her sufferings more than pay for them.'[6]

She is also a natural leader. At the age of 16 she is told by the senior mistress that she has tremendous power in the school, simply by force of her personality. 'You have the most responsible gift of all, and I want you to realise it, and try to live up to it,' Miss Annesley says. 'Wherever you go, you are likely to find friends, and people will be anxious to win your liking. What you do and say will have a great influence on them.'[7] When the time comes, she very reluctantly assumes the mantle of head girl, but in her four terms of office comes to appreciate the influence this position gives her.

Yet she continues to rebel against growing up. This is explained in two ways, both of which must have struck chords in her readers. First, she wants to hold on to the carefree irresponsibility of youth, the safe fun and companionship of her girl friends. 'I've had such a jolly time at school, and I can't bear to think that it's nearly over!' Second, she cannot envisage a satisfying adult life ahead of her.

Grizel and Juliet are teaching; but there isn't anything of that kind for me to do. I shall just stay at home, and help with the children [her nieces and nephews], and practice my singing, and so on. It does *not* appeal to me after the full life we lead here – it seems so – so *little*, somehow. It's doing little bits of things that aren't important.

Her friend Marie expresses the hope that Jo will marry. 'It is why God created women.'

But Jo 'simply can't imagine myself darning someone else's socks, and pouring out his coffee.'[8] Neither, no doubt, could many of the girls who read these words.

The fact that it did come to this – that in later books we do meet Jo darning someone else's socks and pouring out his coffee – changes Brent-Dyer's message to her readers. There is no doubt, however, that the early books accurately represented a real fear of young womanhood.

As a grown-up, Jo is not so successfully portrayed, perhaps inevitably becoming:

less a character than a collection of stereotypes, designed to evoke admiration; a woman of unusual insight and boundless compassion; an incredibly successful writer and at the same time a wife and mother of inexhaustible patience (she needed to be with eleven children . . .); a friend of wonderfully sympathetic understanding and steadfast loyalty . . . ; a mature adult, though still at heart a schoolgirl with a would-be delicious dottiness and sense of fun. It is all quite simply too good to be true.[9]

And sometimes even ridiculous. For instance, Matron (unmarried, unemotional, crisp and efficient) considers Jo the light of her life, 'Matey's heart's dearest', long after the girl has left school and married. But this relationship can only subsist as long as husband and children are ignored: 'Inside, Joey, you're just the same tiresome, naughty girl you ever were.'[10] If Jo as the perfect wife and mother is impossible to believe in, Jo as the mischievous schoolgirl still holds her appeal.

That Jo Bettany was also Brent-Dyer's 'heart's dearest' is not, in itself, sufficient to keep her readers' loyalty and admiration for her heroine throughout the 59 Chalet School books. Idealised characters are rarely the most attractive to readers. What holds us is the series format. Having met and loved Jo as girl, we are her friends for life. As with real friends we tolerate all sorts of flaws and deviations for the sake of our shared past; we are invariably pleased to meet them again, to catch up on old times and find out what they're up to now. As Helen McClelland puts it:

> Elinor's principal achievement would seem to lie in having created at the beginning of the series, where it mattered most, a set of characters who gradually assumed an almost independent existence in her eyes and those of her readers. Then, by employing various devices, she was able to keep at least the most important of these characters on stage throughout the series. Later their multitudinous children were to follow in their footsteps at the school, often learning from the same teachers as had their parents. And what amounts to a personal relationship between readers and characters was slowly established.[11]

FAIRY-TALE HEIRESSES: ELSIE J OXENHAM'S HEROINES

Nicholas Tucker has observed that 'when adults write for children, they may also be writing for that part of themselves unfulfilled by the adult culture in which they live.'[12] For Elinor Brent-Dyer this was undoubtedly the ability to combine social acceptability through marriage and motherhood with the retention of schoolday connections and companions, both of which her heroine Jo achieved – though Brent-Dyer herself achieved neither. For Elsie Oxenham it was the same, with the addition of one further ingredient: the acquisition of wealth and a higher social status. If Brent–Dyer's heroines stay comfortably middle class and relatively 'ordinary', Oxenham's aspire to greater things; as in fairy tales, most of them become heiresses and marry noblemen.

The story of the Abbey girls is but one example of a theme so often repeated in her books it comes to seem like an obsession: that of the young woman of restricted means who is suddenly elevated to great wealth or a title or both. Joy Shirley inherits Abinger Hall and marries a baronet. Maidlin di Ravarati inherits a fortune. Jen Robins marries a baronet. Rosamund Kane goes one better and marries an earl. And so on. The standardised plot makes it difficult to distinguish the different heroines in their similar circumstances.

Darling Doranne (1945 – not an Abbey book) provides a representative example. Doranne, a small-time musician, lives in a bedsit in a working girls' hostel in London. She gives up her home and job to go as companion to her elderly aunt in Sussex. This is quite a sacrifice, as she is a gregarious young woman who enjoys her work and London life, but she wants to do her best for the old lady, of whom she is very fond. Her life in Sussex is quiet, consisting mostly of caring for her aunt and the cat, gardening, taking her aunt out for drives, and shopping.

She knows that she is her aunt's heir but imagines that only the cottage and perhaps a small income will come to her. She wonders whether, after her aunt's death, she will remain in the country 'and ask folks from Town to come and stay with me' or whether to return to London. Whatever she chooses, she feels that if there is enough to live on she 'can't take a job that some other girl would be glad to have . . . it wouldn't be fair'; though her friend Gwen sensibly points out that she must do something or be bored out of her mind.[13]

The aunt duly dies, and it turns out that Doranne has inherited a mansion and a fortune. Her response is typical of the many Oxenham heroines faced with her dilemma:

I've been living in one room in a hostel, on £150 a year, and playing my fiddle for dance classes to make a little extra money! How can I turn suddenly into a millionairess?[14]

The problem of what to do with the money and the house absorbs the rest of the book, apart from the obligatory romance – precipitated by the obligatory near-fatal accident – in the closing chapters. Doranne's solution is sweeping in its breath. Not simply convalescent homes for poor East End children and 'tired London girls', nor just a musical foundation: Doranne decides to build a whole new village. And these will not be 'charity places', but homes for:

> people like you and me, who are longing to feel they have a home but can see no chance of ever finding one; people with tiny incomes who don't need to live in Town.[15]

It is clear that Oxenham is drawing a careful distinction between Doranne's project, which is for 'people like you and me', that is, middle-class people, and local authority or housing association provision which she would view as 'charity places'.

For many would-be readers of Oxenham's books the pervasive snobbishness presents an insuperable barrier to enjoyment. As an Oxenham fan myself, I have to confess to some impatience upon encountering the umpteenth heroine whose sole dilemma is what to do with her money-bags, or whether to marry the nearest available baronet. Yet recognising wealth and class as devices to endow her heroines with power and influence may go a long way towards reconciling readers to their use – even as we sense the weight of feminine powerlessness the author must have been labouring under to have had to rely, in the twentieth century, on such external factors.

Fortunately, some of her characters are memorable in a positive way. The Abbey girls, for example, are carefully distinguished. Jen is perhaps Oxenham's ideal: tall, fair, blue-eyed, a jolly 'straight' English schoolgirl with at the same time, a thoughtful beauty-loving side to her nature. There is little that is really special or memorable about Jen, except her capacity for friendship; and her credibility is almost destroyed by her subsequent fecundity – she has nine children.

Joan and Joy, the original Abbey girls, are set in temperamental opposition to each other: cousins, physically so alike as to be taken for twins, Joan is the thoughtful one, Joy the thoughtless. If Joy inherits Abinger Hall because she turns out to be Sir Antony's sole grandchild, Joan is left the abbey because he recognised her love and care for it. Oxenham must have tired of Joan's goodness so she married her off at the end of the third book in the series; she is revived, however, in seven retrospective volumes about Jen's schooldays where Joan is seen through the younger girl's adoring eyes. 'She's head over heels in love with you,' remarks Joy, not unkindly.[16] This makes for quite a successful portrayal of love between two young women, with Joan as the sensible, sensitive, protective older partner.

Rosamund and Maidlin, the 'new' Abbey girls, are similarly juxtaposed: the one outgoing, practical, apparently uncomplicated, the other introverted, artistic, and difficult. But Rosamund reveals unsuspected depths, and Maidlin triumphs over her psychological problems to become a brilliant concert singer. Rosamund is intentionally the more attractive character, as the more straightforward. Our interest in Maidlin's development lies primarily in her relationships with Rosamund, her best friend, and Joy, her adoptive mother, which give Oxenham scope to explore the varied manifestations of love between women.

It is the Joy of these mid-series novels (*The New Abbey Girls*, *The Abbey Girls Again*, *The Abbey Girls in Town*) who is the most engaging heroine because she is the most realistically drawn. Oxenham charts her transformation from the self-centred tomboy of her 'teen years into a woman painfully awakened to adult responsibilities. This change is precipitated by a motor-cycle accident in which she nearly kills Jen, by the marriage and departure of Joan on whom she has always relied, and by the coming into her life of the two schoolgirls, Rosamund and Maidlin, of whom she assumes care and control. Maidlin in particular, another heiress from a deprived background, needs careful bringing up. Then there is the problem of Joy's fortune and how it can best be used for the benefit of less privileged people.

In spite of the country trips for 'cripples', the holiday home for London working 'girls', the music school, etc., Joy never becomes totally good. Her wealth, her beauty, and her friends conspire to shield her from real self-knowledge, and she continues to display the old selfishness and thoughtlessness at intervals throughout her adult life.

A favourite device of Oxenham's is to introduce each new Abbey book from the point of view of a new character who is brought face to face with the Abbey girls and then drawn into their world. The focus subsequently shifts to the old Abbey heroines, but the technique has allowed us to view them initially from afar, through the eyes of an outsider. There is nearly always a tableau, rendered in highly visual terms, and much is made of the glorious setting that is their home (stained glass, polished oak, ancient beech trees and abbey ruins in the background).

The great gray [sic] Hall, with its gardens and lawns – the gentle welcome of Joy's aunt, a frail little lady who made an ideal hostess for the old house – the beautiful bedroom set apart for them, with windows wide open and looking over the woods – and tea in the big entrance-hall under the portraits of Joy's ancestors – had all blended into a wonderful kind of fairy-tale for Mary and Biddy.[17]

We are let into the minds of the newcomers so that we can experience the effect the Abbey girls have on them. Here is Mary again:

These girls, happy, wealthy, full of joy in life, and music, and laughter, and friendship, were a new type to her; in her narrow life she had never come in touch with anything quite so young and radiant . . . They fascinated her; she watched each one of them without a trace of envy, unconsciously absorbing the atmosphere of happy life which radiated from them all . . . [18]

Mary Devine is a rare heroine for Elsie Oxenham in that she is the recipient, not the giver, of largesse; taken up by Joy and Jen, she becomes their lifelong companion and friend. When they first meet she is a poor secretary, supporting a young sister: genteel, unmarried, and ten years older than either of them. She never marries, never comes into a fortune, but lives out her days at the Hall writing successful girls' school stories and providing both paid and unpaid services for the Abbey girls. Though her influence declines in the later books (on account of her advancing years, it is implied), in the middle series she is one of the most interesting of Oxenham's characters because she is less of a fairy-tale character and more of a real person than the others.

In the beginning her shabby, cosy flat in London, her restricted life and simple pleasures are lovingly described by Oxenham who, one suspects, was more at home with this lifestyle than that of her wealthy heiresses. Her appreciation of the thrilling new world of folk culture and sisterhood is realistically portrayed, reflecting Oxenham's own association with the English Folk Dance Society, and her emergence from an emotional life of futile romantic dreams into the joy of real friendships with Joy, Jen, and the entire Abbey circle is very satisfying, as is the discovery that her creative urge can be put to productive use in writing. I suggest that though these mid-series Abbey books present the Oxenham theory of *noblesse oblige* at its most seductive (or irritating, depending on your point of view), the overwhelming impression one is left with is not of the wealthy patronising the poor but of love and caring by women for women.

I cannot leave Oxenham's heroines without a word on the

subject of hair. Elsie Oxenham makes a feature of it: red hair, like that of the Abbey girls', is a particular attraction, but black and yellow are also favoured. Her heroines spend a lot of time brushing their long, thick tresses. An oft-used trick is to describe tomboyish girls with plaits, or their hair 'up', who then let it out to gasps of admiration from onlookers at its quantity. When Jen, for example, un-does her plaits 'a shining yellow veil shrouded Jen from their gaze'.[19] In *The Tuck-Shop Girl*, part of another series, Jinty says to Barbara: 'I want to watch you do your hair. I do like yellow hair. I want to see yours when it's out of its plaits.'[20] There is a sense of transformation – from boyishness to femininity – which is surely significant. For while Elsie Oxenham liked to endow her heroines with some of the attributes of men – action, independence and power – she also wanted to remind us that they were women, and took a sensual delight in making the point. Of all girls' writers, no one has written more passionately about the delights of womanhood.

THE PERFECT SCHOOLGIRL: DIMSIE, NANCY, TOBY AND THE REST

Women writers have often been accused of being in love with the heroes of their novels. Such a suggestion has been made about Dorothy L. Sayers, the assumption being that the way Lord Peter Wimsey was depicted suffered because of his creator's lack of objectivity.[21] True or not, the proposition that the authors of schoolgirl stories idealise their heroines because they are in love with them makes for an interesting reversal of the heterosexual norm. Dorita Fairlie Bruce, for instance, has been accused of excessive partisanship in the portrayal of her most famous heroine, Dimsie Maitland. In the words of Mary Cadogan and Patricia Craig, Dimsie symbolised for Bruce 'the perfect English schoolgirl', but 'at the cost of her credibility as a character'.[22]

A brief description of her salient features will denote some idea of what that means. Dimsie is neither especially pretty nor especially talented. She is only average at games. She must be bright, for she obtains a place at medical school, though family losses prevent her from completing the course. Her most obvious quality, however, is her moral sense; her principles lead her to jump in wherever she thinks the situation calls for her intervention.

The strength of Bruce's feeling for her heroine is apparent in the author's tendency to tell us how wonderful Dimsie is, rather than let her actions speak for themselves. Dimsie is the headmistress's favourite pupil, and as a little girl she manages to endear herself even to the unpleasant Nita Tomlinson, the mean, vengeful anti-heroine of the early Dimsie books and the villain in *Dimsie Moves Up* (1921) who says, after saving Dimsie from drowning, 'since I had to save somebody, Dimsie Maitland, strangely enough, I'd rather it was you.'[23]

Later, as a prefect, Dimsie is loved and feared by the younger girls:

at sight of her the heated argument ceased abruptly. There was something about the youngest prefect at Jane's, popular though she undoubtedly was, that instilled a certain awe into unruly juniors. Not even Erica Innes herself [the head girl], nor even Pam, the mighty sports captain, was held in greater respect by the small fry.[24]

Her influence persists into adulthood, where it frequently takes the form of a religious crusade. She takes on morbid Kenneth Orde, turned unbeliever in the aftermath of the First World War and personal misfortune. Her actual words are not particularly convincing but the ensuing paragraph drives home the point that it is what Dimsie *is* rather than what she says or does that gives her morality its power.

She spoke rather wistfully, her gaze going past him to the loch shimmering below them in the morning light, and as he looked up at her quiet reverent face, the sarcastic retort died on his lips, and instinctively he raised his cap to the Unknown God who was enshrined in the girl's deep eyes.[25]

Bruce's other heroines are usually cast in a similar mould. We first meet Nancy Caird in *That Boarding School Girl* (1925) as a new girl at the Maudsley Grammar, having been asked to leave her last school, St Bride's, after a term of persistent rule-breaking. It is not easy to recognise the conscientious, law-abiding Nancy that Maudsley knows with the carefree irresponsibility of her past reputation, and indeed Bruce never convincingly does so: the carefree irresponsible is simply not a type in her repertory. The Nancy of *Nancy at St Bride's* (1933), the book which describes that past but was written much later, is in fact a shadowy creature of unclear motivation. The later Nancy, however, is true to type: high-principled – 'I should have had the sense to realize that, if the whole school went crooked, you would still go straight,' says Charity Sheringham, one of the prefects, in *The New Girl and Nancy* (1926)[26] – with a tendency to rush to the assistance of weaker mortals (*Nancy to the Rescue*, 1927), and to convert those of little faith (*Nancy Calls the Tune*, 1944).

As a young adult Nancy is 'strong and wholesome and good to look at, with no "make-up" – we are never allowed to forget Bruce's views on cosmetics.[27] The slick phrases have a sanctimonious air, and recur from book to book and from heroine to heroine. Dimsie's cousin Daphne, for example, is 'slim and grey-eyed, straight alike in body and mind, untiring at tennis or cricket'.[28] Chris McLean of St Bride's is 'tall and yellow-haired and looked the personification of a healthy mind in a healthy body;'[29] while of the heroine of the early Springdale books, Bruce wrote: 'Without being exactly pretty, Peggy Willoughby had a wholesome, jolly look about her that attracted most people with whom she came in contact, and made her popular among her school-fellows.'[30]

Dimsie and Nancy are but two of 'the engaging but out-

spoken juniors in whom Dorita Fairlie Bruce was to special-
ize', as Cadogan and Craig observe.[31] Toby Barrett is an
older version of the same. She is set up as unconventional
because she did not go to school until she was 17, having
kept house for an absent-minded artist father who let her
'run wild in that careless fashion'. Her aim in life is to be
like other girls, but her friend Jane Trevor tells her not to
bother: 'It's more amusing to have you different from the
rest of us.'[32] Clearly Bruce wants her heroines to keep their
innocence into adulthood; perhaps the use of make-up, which
she so deplored, symbolised the debased sophistication into
which she felt the young womanhood of the interwar years
was in danger of falling.

The subsidiary characters who can in fact be seen as heroines in Bruce's novels are mostly lightly sketched in the usual
school story manner. But among those who stand out as
more fully developed are two of the head girls in the Dimsie
series. They are worth considering in some detail as Bruce
has allowed us to see them, perhaps, in better perspective
than her heroines, since she is herself far less attached to
them.

Dimsie is not in fact the heroine of the first novel which
bears her name. Rather, it is her cousin Daphne, the 'senior
prefect' of the original title. Daphne is a good deal more
rounded a character than the stereotyped pen portrait quoted
above would suggest; she is permitted weaknesses, moments
of doubt, jealousy and irresponsibility. In contrast to her
stands her chum, Sylvia Drummond, the head girl. Sylvia is
a goddess. One of the juniors describes her as 'rather like a
mistress, you know. Not even the other seniors can cheek
Sylvia Drummond.'[33] The headmistress herself appears to
regard Sylvia as an equal; in one scene Miss Yorke 'glanced
across at Sylvia with a smile, which showed the mutual
understanding between them'.[34]

This image of mature dignity impresses itself on the young
reader. Sylvia, we are told, maintains order by the sheer force
of her personality. Though normally she addresses people in

'the simple direct fashion which made her popular with her school-fellows,' she is mistress of a 'cool sarcasm' – an adult skill usually attributed only to teachers – voiced in a 'nonchalant drawl' which she reserves for unpleasant characters like Nita Tomlinson.[35] She is naturally well-bred, well-off (a 'tall, slim girl, dressed simply but expensively in the height of the fashion'), and clever into the bargain, and she carries herself 'with an unconscious air of distinction, which seemed, somehow, to make prettier girls look ordinary by comparison'.[36] After she leaves school she establishes herself as 'one of the finest novelists of the day'[37] (not 'lady novelists', note; and unlike Brent-Dyer's Jo and Oxenham's Mary, Sylvia does *not* write girls' school stories).

In being encouraged to view her from the perspective of a younger girl, with awe and respect, readers are presented with a very effective role model to admire, if not to emulate. While Dimsie is shown as an idealised version of an ordinary schoolgirl, Sylvia is deliberately portrayed as beyond ordinariness, a person of almost unattainable gifts and distinction. It is possible that, in making her a writer, Bruce created an *alter ego*, endowing her with some of her own aspirations and fantasies. Most significantly, while she provides romance and husbands for all her other main characters, she leaves Sylvia unmarried. This is the only alternative model for girl readers and, it has to be said, one that sustains its appeal rather more than the wives and mothers do.

Ursula Grey is a very different person – in artistic terms more successful because she is presented as imperfect. Not morally so – 'She is such a good, conscientious creature', declares Miss Phipps – but in terms of strength of character: 'the way in which those juniors bully her is abominable – simply abominable!' Well might Miss Yorke look astonished at this. 'If the head-girl allows herself to be bullied by a parcel of impudent juniors, then she is scarcely fit to be head-girl.'[38]

In discussions before the election for head girl, Ursula is initially passed over. 'I suppose because she has no force of character', as one girl observes. Another says: 'She carries no weight in the school. Just compare her in your mind with Sylvia Drummond or Daphne Maitland.' The qualities required of head girls are considered, and Ursula is found wanting.

> She lacks self-confidence, which you need in dealing with our juniors – I believe it's because she doesn't do anything well. If Ursula suddenly broke out in any one direction, stood first in the form instead of third, or won the medal for drill, or developed a swift service at tennis – oh, I don't care what it is! but if she could only make her mark, she'd have a position in the school, and we'd soon discover that she had got heaps of character behind all her diffidence.[39]

Two people have sufficient faith in Ursula to put her to the test: the headmistress, Miss Yorke, and Dimsie Maitland of the middle school. Between them they ensure that Ursula is elected. It is Dimsie who discovers Ursula's hidden talent and enables it to flourish: Ursula, it turns out, is musical. As an orphan whose guardians see her simply as an adjunct to their own gifted girls, Ursula has been allowed to play the piano, but only to accompany Betty's singing. Dimsie arranges for her to take cello lessons with Miss Phipps, and within a short time she is making rapid progress both musically and in self-confidence. By the end of the book Ursula is not only an excellent head girl, spoken of in the same breath as Sylvia Drummond and Daphne Maitland, but has found her vocation in life.

By the time we meet her again in *The School on the Moor* (1931) Ursula is on the way to becoming 'one of the foremost lady 'cellists in England'.[40] Unfortunately, she is one of the heroines whom Bruce singles out for romance. In deciding to give up her career as a concert artist to marry a former schoolmate's brother, Ursula abandons the pursuit of self-fulfilment which made her development at school so interesting and convincing. By contrast Dimsie, having been thwarted in her medical studies, continues to practise as a herbalist after her marriage to a GP, and to lead a full and rewarding life as wife, mother, and professional in her own right.

THE PERFECT STEREOTYPE: ENID BLYTON'S CHARACTERS

Enid Blyton's school stories, like everything she wrote, took a familiar formula and reduced it to its barest bones. This is not a criticism, for she accomplished this with consummate skill, and in such a way that her books appealed to a much wider audience than those of any other author in the genre. But it does mean that there is less variety and less of particular interest in the portrayal of her characters, and consequently less to say about them. The formula requires that each character be given one or two traits by which s/he can be recognised: thus, among the girls of St Clare's, Bobby is boyish, Alison vain, Carlotta wild (she is a foreigner), Angela snobbish, Janet naughty, Gladys mousy, and so on.

One of the reasons given for her enormous success with young readers is the range of characters Blyton provides, so wide that everyone, potentially, can find someone to identify with. In fact, readers tend to identify with the heroine of the story, who in this case must combine the most attractive qualities of the stereotypical English schoolgirl. So she has to be fond of fun and tricks, but capable of responsibility; both popular and a leader, but compassionate towards those less fortunate than herself; honest and honourable; keen on games; loyal to her school. All Blyton's schoolgirl heroines fulfil these criteria.

Blyton has been criticised because the personalities of many of her characters remain fixed throughout each book and even whole series. For example George, the tomboy member of the Famous Five, scarcely develops (indeed, does not even age) through a dozen and a half novels.[41] (This does not stop her from being probably Blyton's most memorable and beloved child creation among girl readers as the character that every tomboy identified with.) This criticism may certainly be applied to the O'Sullivan twins, the central characters in the St Clare's series. One wonders whether their dullness was intended as a foil to the more highly-coloured personalities of Claudine and the others around them, or whether such a collection of static traits must inevitably lack appeal.

However, this criticism does not fit either Elizabeth, the 'Naughtiest Girl', or Darrell Rivers of Malory Towers. The three stories about Elizabeth at her unusual progressive, co-educational boarding school are concerned with her development from a rebellious little girl who hates school into a responsible member of the school community (*The Naughtiest Girl is a Monitor*), and with her growing friendship with Joan, a girl from an emotionally deprived background. Sheila Ray explains that:

> In her school stories Enid Blyton intended to show mental and moral growth as well as physical growth, and certainly her treatment of characters seems likely to give even her least mature readers some idea of why people behave and develop in the way they do.[42]

Ray also makes the point that Blyton refused to rely on the debased, wildly improbable plot lines that were current in girls' popular fiction at the time. Nothing happens in her stories that might not happen in any ordinary school. 'The action in her school stories is constructed around the personalities of the characters: the girls are what their families, their upbringings, their circumstances and their special gifts have made them . . . Much of the interest and appeal of the stories lie in the very simple but comprehensible psychology of these characters.'[43]

Ray sees Darrell Rivers as Blyton's 'most successful and convincing heroine'.[44] She is an ordinary, nice, middle-class girl, with no memorable peculiarities – except a bad temper, which sometimes leads her to hit other girls – whom it is impossible not to like. The six Malory Towers books chart her progress through the forms, from naughty first-former to responsible head girl. It has to be said that as her heroines reach the late 'teens, Blyton tends to shift her focus to a new set of characters in the junior forms; she never seems entirely comfortable in the portrayal of older children and Elizabeth, indeed, never reaches that stage. This unease is reflected in the fact that none of her girls ever grows to adulthood in the books, unlike the heroines of Brent-Dyer, Oxenham and Bruce.

THE SIGNIFICANCE OF SCHOOL STORY HEROINES

The traditional starting point for literary criticism is the hero or heroine who, in children's literature, has also been conceived in terms of role model. To concentrate on one atypical individual may seem inappropriate for an essentially social genre like the school story, especially the school story for girls which has generally emphasized relationships along with individual growth. But given that whole series like the Dimsie books were built around the personality of one girl, and that readers' attachment to one major character like Jo of the Chalet School or Darrell of Malory Towers is frequently put forward as a reason for the books' enduring popularity, it seems sensible to study the schoolgirl heroine on her own before examining other aspects of the school story. In particular, we want to see whether the schoolgirl heroine provided the suitably conventional model for her readers that her critics have assumed or whether, in fact, the paradigm contains radical elements which have tended to subvert the apparently conformist morality.

What is conventional about the schoolgirl heroines discussed here is that they are brought up to be good wives and mothers. Most of the heroines do, in fact, get married and have children. But our heroines are clearly educated to do more than this, and even as wives and mothers they do not always follow the prescribed lifestyle. In the interwar and immediate postwar years marriage and a career were generally held to be incompatible for women, yet both Brent-Dyer's Jo and Bruce's Dimsie continue to work after their marriage. Even Oxenham's Joy does a bit of composing on the side, and Maidlin returns to the concert platform between babies.

Though the nuclear family of father, mother and children remains the unquestioned norm, as adults the Abbey girls at least inhabit a virtually all-female world. Lip-service may be paid to the idea that men should come first with women, but once a husband has been obtained, our heroines' lives revolve around their children, and their women friends and their children. Even though Brent-Dyer's and Bruce's female characters put their husbands first in principle, in practice they go on relating primarily to other women. Courtship results in a tiny blip on the normal pattern of events. The message is made all the more clear by the presentation of men as one-dimensional, limited characters ('Men are like that,' Jo remarks of one inept father[45]), and largely absent (exploring in Africa, conducting orchestras in America, or dead). Women friends by contrast are present, caring, and fun to be with.

Jen, for example, is clearly reluctant to accompany her husband on a trip around the world to speed his recovery from a serious accident. She does this – but breaks off the journey early to return home to her children and women friends. Joy's second husband has to come and live in *her* house, because that is where she wants her children to grow up – and incidentally, next door to Jen. Dimsie's adult life is spent in Scotland where, although they were at school together in the south of England, her old friends Jean, Erica and Pam all end up, living near her.

These deviations from the patriarchal norm are but logical extensions of the woman-centred, man-free existence of their shared schooldays. In the world of the girls' school as depicted here, female ambition and leadership are recognised and encouraged, and relationships between and among women are prioritised. Girls' loyalties are directed indivisibly towards other girls and their love is confined to females. Thus Jen openly loves Joan; Maidlin adores Joy. Boys are utterly irrelevant. Occasionally allowed as friends, they have no greater intrinsic importance – in contrast to the world outside the school.

Tomboyishness – perceived to be a serious problem in the post-Freudian decades, which viewed this trait as at best transitory and at worst perverse – is acceptable in a community which encompasses a wide range of human attributes instead of a very limited number allocated by the wider society to the female sex. In fact, tomboys appear throughout the novels of Brent-Dyer, Oxenham and Blyton; one of Oxenham's books is called *Tomboys at the Abbey*. The proliferation of boyish nicknames borne by crop-headed girls is testimony to the popularity and acceptability of this type of girl. Both Brent-Dyer and Oxenham have important characters called Jack; Brent-Dyer in addition has a Tom and a Ted, and Blyton has Bobby and Bill. For some characters, tomboyishness is seen as a phase: Oxenham's Jen, Joy and Jack (the *Tomboys at the Abbey*) all eventually marry and settle down. But even where the trait persists into adulthood, there is no criticism: Brent-Dyer's perhaps aptly named Tom Gay is presented simply as a different but equally worthwhile kind of woman, pursuing her carpentry and social work in the East End. Spinsterhood is all right, too. The central heroines all have to marry but for women such as Brent-Dyer's Mary-Lou and Bruce's Sylvia, fulfilment with the right vocation is the true reward – Sylvia, indeed, is permitted fame.

After the First World War, the post-feminist restoration of the Victorian ideal – that a girl's real destiny lay in marriage and motherhood – was reinforced by the heterosexual pressures of women's magazines and the cinema, all insisting that girls' main object in life was to make themselves attractive to men. Attractiveness was held to lie in feminine beauty and adherence to fashion, but also in service, self-denial, and putting others first – particularly men. Again, though lip-service is paid to these feminine attributes in all school stories, the message is undermined by the significance attached to the development of 'character' in the heroines. Our heroines may be caring and thoughtful about others but they are rarely self-sacrificing to the extent required by the feminine ideal. They are self-confident even during their courtship days and continue to display qualities of leadership and responsibility well into adulthood. Enid Blyton's Darrell Rivers is a fine example of a girl who would find it difficult to transform herself into the type of woman her mother and all Blyton's mothers are portrayed as: the kindly, full-time housewife, devoid of interests beyond husband, home and children.

In these novels, too, girls' physical beauty exists for themselves and their women friends. If looks and personality certainly help some to win husbands, these qualities are never wholly assigned to those men. Women retain control of their own bodies and lives in a way which to a considerable extent contradicts the social assumptions of the interwar and post-war years.

As schoolgirls these heroines have a moral sense which includes the male ideals of honour and sportsmanship, and they make moral decisions which affect their own and others' lives. Some girls are not good at all; some have weaknesses, and are loved in spite of them, and some grow over time – and their moral development is regarded as important. The fact that women had a literature relating to their self-development is testimony to the discord between the social ideal, which minimised women's individual worth, and the girls' school story, which emphasised it.

Girls' school stories contradict the idea that only men are historically significant, that only men can change the world. Oxenham's heroines are always taking on social ills and trying to improve conditions for selected groups, often women. Bruce's heroines are moral crusaders. It is true that they campaign in a limited and uncritical fashion, which does nothing to challenge the patriarchal capitalist society which they inhabit nor their own privileged position within it. But at least they are not just doing nothing while enjoying their privileges. In going about reform in the personal, piecemeal manner traditionally employed by women they have attracted male and left-wing criticism which tends only to recognise revolution on a large scale. But because they see no real attack on the class system these critics have over-looked the possibility that these stories, whether or not intended to do so by their creators, may have made subvers-ive inroads into patriarchy.

Such manifestations of female power are at odds with the prevailing social ideology, but are a logical continuation of the school ethos. They are also at odds with social reality. Many school story heroines, as we have seen, resist growing up, fearing the narrowness of adult life for women. But they always eventually navigate the stormy passage successfully, to reach a haven of fulfilment in marriage and motherhood. In real life, however, Brent-Dyer, Oxenham and Bruce never reached this haven, and for Blyton it was far from ideal. Many readers of girls' school stories would have reached the goal only to discover that to achieve real fulfilment in mar-riage and motherhood was a difficult, if not impossible, task in a patriarchal society. Most would have experienced what sociologists such as Jessie Bernard have termed the painful disjunction of married women's lives, where their indepen-dent action, income, status and lifestyle are abruptly ended upon becoming wives and mothers, and their personalities compulsorily submerged in the family.[46] But then most of these readers would not have had the servants, the paragons of husbands, the perfect children, and the financial means which made a satisfying and comfortable wedded life possi-ble, let alone the rewarding employment and bands of women friends which all the authors thoughtfully provided for their heroines.

These adjuncts are provided for a reason. Our authors

could not bring themselves to suggest, falsely, that in marriage and motherhood alone, without other work, friends, help in the house or sufficient funds, women could recreate the fulfilment of their girlhood years. They knew from their own experience and from what they saw about them that this fulfilment could not realistically be achieved. So by providing additional help in the form of friends, servants, money and employment, school stories minimised the jarring discontinuity which characterised the lives of most married women of their time. But they also offered an implicit critique of the romantic and patriarchal ideal: that women should confine themselves to marriage and motherhood and not wish for any greater sphere of action. Their heroines, our writers contended, should have everything: husbands and children, work and leisure, wealth and power, friends and servants. The storybook schoolgirl's full and satisfying life of the school should not end with marriage. It should continue into womanhood, as it did for all these school story heroines.

5 Bosom Friends

Friendship is a central theme in girls' school stories. Sometimes it forms the basis of the plot: friendships are formed, break up, resolve themselves one way or another. Dorita Fairlie Bruce specialised in this type of story, more dependent on character than plot: *The New House Captain* (1928) is a classic example. Diana and Peggy fall out because Di expected to be made house captain and Peggy got the job instead. Di's attitude spoils the terms for both of them until she realises that their friendship is more important than her pride and that her jealousy showed her to be unsuited to the job.[1]

More commonly, friendship is presented as part of the context in which the characters' tales are played out, a fixed point in the background requiring no explanation or justification. Loyalty to one's friends and love and concern for them are unquestioned values in the novels. Perhaps surprisingly, though, close friendships are not confined to schoolgirls. In these stories, adult friendships are often portrayed as fundamental and are valued not only among single women (who have no husbands or children to absorb their emotional energies) but also among wives and mothers. Indeed, it is clear that, to Elsie Oxenham at least, these friendships between married women were more important than their relationships with their husbands.

FRIENDS ARE FOR SHARING

All four writers have much to say about friendship. For Elinor Brent-Dyer the main message in connection with the subject was that friendship should not be exclusive. From the very first book in the Chalet series she attacked the jealous possessiveness that certain girls showed towards a chosen companion. Jo is enthusing over the arrival of some new girls at the school. This causes Simone, who desperately claims her as her *amie intime*, to wail: 'Oh, Joey, don't have any more friends!'

> You've got Grizel, and Gisela and Bette love you, and I've only got you! And now you want those two new girls that you don't know at all! Oh, Joey, don't be so selfish!

Jo is indignant. 'Selfish!' she repeats.

> It's you who are selfish! I've told you over and over again that I'm going to have all the friends I want, and it doesn't make one scrap of difference to my being pally with you! I don't mind *your* having other friends – I don't see why you don't![2]

Years later, 10-year-old Mary-Lou learns the same lesson from her wise Gran in her first term at school:

> Learn to share your friends with other people. If they're friends worth having, and if *you* are a friend worth having, they and you will be all the closer for it. It's the people who demand everything and won't share who are to be doubted.[3]

It is rare for Brent-Dyer to feature heroines who have only one special friend. There are Nesta and Sally in *Nesta Steps Out* (1954): 'The other girls called them David and Jonathan.'[4] Peggy Bettany and Daphne Russell are also among those who 'hunt in couples', though Brent-Dyer assures us hastily that: 'There was nothing silly or sentimental about their friendship.'[5] But trios, quartets and larger groupings are much more common. Among the distinguished triumvirates of Chalet history are Daisy, Beth and Gwensi, and Gay, Gillian and Jacynth, all from the English books.[6] Jo herself is one of a foursome who remain friends into adulthood, while Mary-Lou heads a gang which at one point numbers 14 Middles.

Clearly Brent-Dyer felt there was safety in numbers, for many of the one-to-one relationships in her novels are troubled. In the later Chalet books Jo encourages her triplet daughters not to be content simply with their own company. But when Margot, the youngest and most 'difficult', takes up with Emerence, the naughtiest girl in the school, Jo is not very happy, especially since Emerence is three years older than Margot.

> Emerence was all that Margot could talk about. 'She's got it hot and strong – at the moment, anyhow. . . . I'm glad for them to make their own friends. But oh, how I wish Margot hadn't fallen for Emerence!'[7]

In the case of Elizabeth Arnett and Betty Wynne-Davies, in their day the naughtiest girls in the school, the partnership in crime ends when Elizabeth grows out of her childish insubordination during the trying war years and Betty does not. 'She had bitterly resented the change in her friend, and instead of trying to talk with her had . . . set herself more stubbornly "again the government" than ever before.' Betty's conduct goes from bad to worse; she bullies some of the juniors and, when one of them stands up to her, avenges herself on the child by betraying a family secret to a German spy who is able to use the information against the British government. Found out, Betty is expelled from the school as a traitor. All the girls refuse to say goodbye to her except Elizabeth, who is full of remorse: 'I should have stuck to you.' Brent-Dyer, however, is not the sort of writer to use friendship as a means of transforming a character already warped by her past, as Betty's is shown to have been. Elizabeth goes on to be head girl of the Chalet School; Betty disappears unmourned.[8]

FRIENDSHIPS ARE MADE IN HEAVEN

In contrast to Elinor Brent-Dyer, Dorita Fairlie Bruce prefers pairs of friends to larger groups. For her, friendships, like marriages, are made in heaven; the right combinations will sort themselves out and the wrong ones will never be made to work. For someone who sets herself against 'soppiness', Bruce is capable of writing scenes where friends discover their affinity for each other which are as powerful as adult romances. In *Dimsie Moves Up Again* (1922), for example, we meet Ursula Grey, an apparently uninteresting girl from an emotionally deprived background. She is well enough liked by her form mates but has no particular friend or circle. One night Ursula and her room-mate Lesley are awake late worrying about three Middle school girls who have gone missing. Lesley slips into Ursula's bed to talk, and Ursula confides how one of the missing girls – Dimsie – had been a good friend to her: 'I should have been awfully lonely, without her.'

Lesley is amazed. 'Lonely? How can you possibly be lonely here at Jane's, with all of us?'

Ursula explains. 'Ever heard of being alone in a crowd, Lesley? Because that expresses it more or less.'

Lesley thinks over Ursula's school life and realises how she has always been a loner. 'I fancy we've all thought you rather preferred mooning about by yourself.'

'I should have been more sociable,' Ursula admits. '. . . I'm a self-conscious idiot, but I've always been afraid of not being wanted.'

Suddenly Lesley's strong impulsive arms were wound

tightly round her, and Lesley's voice, with a break in it, exclaimed:

'Don't be such a dear idiot! Of course you're wanted – especially by me. If I'd had any idea that you felt like this, Ursie, I should have undeceived you long ago. As it is, I feel I've been a pig for years – but a purely involuntary pig – you do believe that, don't you? Anyhow, let's be pals after this.'[9]

It is true that Bruce's heroine Dimsie has no one special friend, belonging to a group of six contemporaries with many other friends both older and younger. But if she is as opposed to exclusivity as Brent-Dyer's heroines, most other Bruce characters are to be found in twosomes whose relationships strain and grow, or break, like any heterosexual romance.

Perfect equality in a pair, even a pair of schoolgirls, is hard to find. Realistically, Bruce often portrays one girl as the stronger party, but provides opportunities for the other to develop – as Daphne finds when she returns to school to find that Sylvia has sprained her knee and won't be back till half-term. 'I know just how you are feeling,' says the headmistress sympathetically:

but I believe it will be good for you to stand alone for a bit and shoulder your own burdens. You'll make a better friend for Sylvia when she returns if she finds that she can do a little of the leaning in your partnership instead of being forced to do all the supporting.[10]

Sometimes, as in love affairs, one person cares and the other doesn't. In *Captain at Springdale* (1932), new girl Norma is very taken with Gwynneth, who is cool towards her, while Polly, who would really like to be chums with Norma, is left out in the cold. Norma has a secret, and Gwynneth's view is that there's no point in being friends with a girl who doesn't trust you enough to tell you everything about herself.

Rebuffed and tearful, Norma is found by Polly, who takes her 'into her kind young arms'.

> Don't fret any more than you can help, Norma, old girl! and if – if you feel a bit lonely, there's always me. I know I'm not Gwynneth, but I like you rather a lot, and I really don't mind whether you tell me things, or whether you don't.

Bruce's message is that Polly, not Gwynneth, shows the real trust by not prying: 'I can carry on being friends with you just the same, if you care to have me.'[11]

Because of her less critical attitude to exclusivity, Bruce treats jealousy rather differently from Brent-Dyer. Take *The Girls of St Bride's* (1923), for example, where Winifred (an unusual instance of a disabled heroine: she uses a wheelchair) seeks Morag's attention:

> There and then was born in the cripple's [sic] unreasonable mind a jealous determination to oust Cynthia from her place in her friend's affections. Morag, she resolved, was to have one chum, and one only – Winifred Arrowsmith by name.[12]

Bruce links Winifred's character defects to her physical disability in a crude attempt to show how social and environmental factors affect personality. 'I wonder if she can have made mischief between Morag and Cynthia,' the head-mistress muses, in a way in which makes the modern reader cringe. 'One never knows what twist those poor warped natures may take, especially if they are inclined to be jealous.'[13] But by and large Winifred is presented as a positive character, who overcomes her jealousy and eventually forms a cosy triangle with both Cynthia and Morag. In a later book, as school secretary, she is able to advise Helga (who wants to be friends with Chris but has been thwarted by Chris' possessive chum Sybil) after her own experience. 'You will probably have them both in the end, if you have patience', and she turns out to be right.[14]

Some friendships, however, are not to be. In the Nancy series, Barbara resents the fact that although Desdemona likes her, she prefers Nancy. She tries to win her back:

> Barbara began by following a primitive feminine method; she made vigorous advances towards Elma Cuthbert, much to that young person's astonishment, and always when Desda was somewhere in the neighbourhood.

The plan to make Desda jealous fails miserably, for Desda's reaction is to say approvingly, 'I'm awfully glad you're chumming up with Elma, Babs.'[15] These 'primitive feminine methods', it is shown, will never work; anyone who tries them is clearly unworthy of the friendship.

SEPARATE SPHERES

There is no question but that Elsie Oxenham prized women's friendship above all else. Her depiction of it is Victorian; she did, after all, grow up at the end of Victoria's reign, and clearly never outgrew her formative impressions. For Oxenham, friendship is premised on the notion of separate spheres, the idea that men and women perform different roles in society and therefore, from schooldays on, occupy different worlds. As adults they fall in love, marry and make families, but continue to associate chiefly with members of their own sex. Men's role is public, so they are largely absent from these essentially domestic stories – though because many of Oxenham's men are gentlemen of leisure they may be present at unexpected times – and women occupy the private sphere, so may foregather, with or without children, to carry out their feminine pursuits in feminine company. These for Oxenham do not, of course, include housework or compulsory childcare; servants and nurses attend to such tasks. This

113

means there is plenty of time for music, dancing, and putting energy into friends.

The single-sex school is but a preparation for this life, so friendships are a matter of course. In the early Abbey books, Jen's 'chum' is Jack (Jacqueline), but Jen's relationship with the older Abbey girls is deeper and ultimately more enduring. This may be because, unusually, neither Joan nor Joy has a close friend of her own age – perhaps because as cousins they always had each other. Jen and Jack refer to each other as 'wife' and 'husband', and even the headmistress goes along with this innocent fiction when, aged 13, they are evacuated with their school to Abinger Hall and Jen asks if they can share a room. The head assents: 'Run along and be married, or be chums, however you like to put it! But don't lead one another into mischief!'[16]

Even as young women Jen and Jack refer to each other as a married couple and remain close, though geographically separated, till their respective real marriages. When Jen visits Jack in London, they sometimes share a bed: 'I'd tuck in with my husband. You know she always wants me to!'[17] (References to shared beds were perfectly acceptable in school stories in 1924, though such were omitted from the abridged editions of the 1950s and 1960s.)

Likewise, Rena and Nancy in the Rocklands books: 'Nancy's my chum, my Squaw! We're twin souls, and we mustn't be parted for too long, or we pine away and get ill!'[18] Here the role-play is taken further:

I go first to find the way and help her over walls and up cliffs, and to protect her from cows . . . She trots behind, carrying the sandwiches and the buns; and when we camp for lunch she makes the tea. And when we wash-up, she does it; I'm only supposed to be able to dry things.[19]

Rena is clearly joking here, sending up the institution of marriage, but Lisabel, a new friend, cannot understand: if Rena and Nancy are so like a married couple, how can Nancy bear the fact that Rena has so many other friends? Lisabel herself – another character damaged by an emotionally deprived background – craves exclusivity: a friend who belongs to her alone. Nancy explains. 'Everybody likes Rena!'

> Its the same wherever she is; she always has a crowd round her, and lots of fun goes on where she is. I've been to school with her for three years, and I'm used to it. But that doesn't interfere with our being chums. If she wanted anybody for anything important, she'd come to me . . . She laughs and plays with them, but – well, she *talks* to me![20]

This sounds even more like marriage. But as they grow up Lisabel and Rena are thrown together – both take up gardening as a career – while Nancy gets married. 'Liza's glad; she was always jealous of Nancy,' Rena confides.[21] Later Rena and Lisabel themselves marry brothers, a convenient way to continue the association throughout their adult years.

In her school stories Oxenham treats many of the friendship themes that we find in the work of other writers. Like Brent-Dyer, she is against possessiveness: as American Marsaili tells the young heroine of the 'Torment' books:

> Money isn't the only thing you lose the good of if you try to keep it to yourself, and gain by using. I believe friendship's another. If you share your friends with other people, you risk losing them, of course; but if they're friends worth having you may make them more yours than ever.[22]

Jealousy is the central theme in several Oxenham stories. Astrid, one of the head girls in the St Mary's books, is 'crazy' about her friend Gulielma, and 'eaten up with jealousy' if she 'looks at anyone else'.[23] Several books turn on the difficulties that this poses.

In *The School Without a Name* (1924) Oxenham emulates

Bruce in making a new junior the agent of reconciliation between warring factions, pupils of two old schools which have been deadly rivals and which have now amalgamated to form the new school. When Rita insists that Beryl should not be friendly with anyone from the other camp, Beryl explodes:

I'm not going to be friends with anybody who says if I'm her friend I can't be someone else's! . . . I'll be friends with anybody I like. If I'm one of your crowd, that doesn't mean you can choose all my other friends.[24]

Like Bruce, Oxenham believes that friends should be loyal to each other, even when they do not understand their behaviour. In *The Crisis in Camp Keema* (1928), Maribel decides for the sake of her school to give up Camp Fire to join the Guides. Her chum Phyllis refuses to follow suit; she can't understand how Maribel can give up the pursuit she loves best, and she 'can't be friends with anyone I don't understand'.

'But isn't that just the time one wants to be friends?' Maribel asks. 'I mean, when we're friends although we don't understand, it shows our friendship's real and worth something.' In this case the friendship does not survive, but Maribel finds a new friend who is sympathetic to her decision, and Phyllis comes off worst because of her lack of trust.[25]

Like Bruce Oxenham is conscious of the problem of dependence in some girls' friendships. Both Rosalind and Jansy are seen to be leaning too much on dominant Littlejan; she has to go away from the Abbey for three years (and return married) so that their own strengths can emerge.[26]

The importance of girlfriends is spelled out in *The School Torment* (1920), where Dorothy is worried that her young sister has never had a close friend: 'knowing the importance of a girl-chum at this time of her life . . . Dorothy felt her life would be incomplete and lacking in enjoyment until she

116

found the girl who could be her friend.' But Tormy was to go to a boys' school.

> No boy could be, at this stage, what another girl could be; she would no doubt make many friends among the boys, but they would be merely chums and comrades. There was no fear of anything else with Tormy. Dorothy could imagine the scorn with which her sister would greet any attempts at what she would describe as 'silliness', if not 'utter bosh' . . . the close intimacy of friendship and perfect understanding, of confidences and secrets, could only be with another girl.[27]

Leaving aside the vague and coy treatment of adolescent sexuality, we have here a view of same-sex friendship as an important stage preceding sexual awakening. It is frequently described – and not only by Elsie Oxenham – in terms similar to those used for heterosexual love. Tormy remarks, for example, that Antonia and Marsaili have 'fallen in love with one another at first sight'.[28] The use of such language may be due to the paucity of words in the English language dealing with love; it may also be because the writers of girls' school stories recognised that girls experienced these emotions with the same intensity as adults experienced their love affairs. What is interesting is that, in contrast to children's literature of 50 years hence, it is the intense same-sex relationships which are approved and the heterosexual ones which are condemned as 'silliness' and 'utter bosh'.

LIKE AND UNLIKE

Enid Blyton's friends are in couples. Sometimes the two partners are alike in character and interests – like naughty Alicia and Betty or horse-mad Bill and Clarissa of the Malory Towers books – and sometimes each complements the other: like mousy, reliable Gladys and loud, bossy Mirabel in the

St Clare's series. Dependability is the quality Blyton most esteems in a friend:

> Sally Hope, the steady, loyal, kindly, sensible Sally. Darrell's best friend. Sally might not be top of the form, but she would always listen to anyone in difficulty. Sally would not do brilliantly in exams, as Alicia would – but she would always help a younger girl at games or lessons. [29]

Both Sally and Darrell have leadership qualities but their characters are otherwise quite different. Darrell is impulsive and creative; Sally keeps her cool. 'Sally hadn't much imagination – she was sensible and sturdy and solid.' [30] Needless to state, it is Darrell, not Sally, who is the heroine of the Malory Towers books.

Sally can be jealous but Darrell is completely free of this fault. In her first term Sally denies the existence of her baby sister because she cannot bear to share her mother. When this interesting psychological defence collapses, partly thanks to Darrell's rough intervention, Sally turns into the ordinary, not to say colourless, character Blyton requires as a foil to her heroine. Later Sally has spasms of jealousy because Darrell seems to be more friendly with Alicia than with her. But neither jealousy nor any other manifestation of friendship is explored in any depth in the pages of a Blyton novel. Representative of the level of commentary on friendship is the following example, Mirabel's pleased response on learning that Gladys has attained a place in the lacrosse team: 'That was the best of friends – they shared your troubles with you, and they doubled your joys.' [31]

FRIENDSHIP AND INFLUENCE

All four authors present friendship as an institution in its own right with its own laws, which may be natural or socially constructed – according to the author's viewpoint. But it may also be seen in a functional light. Friendships between older and younger girls, or mistresses and students, might provide important role models for the junior party. Friendships between pairs of girls might be a preparation for the give and take of marriage. And friendships among groups serve to prepare young women for living in the community.

A special kind of friendship is that between a younger girl and an older one, or a pupil and mistress. All four authors are in agreement that where the older party provides a positive role model for the younger, the relationship has the potential to be an important and healthy one for both of them. Indeed the English boarding school system provided for 'influence' to be passed down the hierarchy from mistress to older student to younger one; prefects, house captains, patrol leaders and the like were chosen for their 'leadership' qualities, and younger girls were expected to admire and look up to their seniors. Fagging, a perverted version of this hierarchy based on enforced servitude and privilege rather than voluntary devotion and duty, was never common in girls' schools, which relied more on personal qualities.

Blyton's books do not tend to emphasise relationships between older and younger girls. Seniors who have sisters in the lower forms, like Darrell in the Malory Towers books, do have a certain amount of contact with them, but otherwise the relationships are fairly formal, such as that between sports captain and junior team members. Even the unusual arrangement in *Last Term at Malory Towers* (1951), where brilliant sportswoman Amanda of the sixth form undertakes to train promising but unsporting June of the second form, is based on mutual respect rather than affection – rather the reverse, in fact, as they proceed to fall out completely. But in a dramatic turn of events, the arrogant Amanda, having chosen to swim out to sea rather than confine herself to the school's pool, is caught in a current and dashed against the rocks, only to be saved from drowning by the arrival of June herself in a boat. Amanda is so badly injured she may never play games again.

When June asks to see the invalid, Matron issues a lecture:

> I know all about your clash with Amanda, and I don't care who's right and who's wrong. That girl will want a bit of help and sympathy, so don't you go and see her if you can't be generous enough to give her a bit. You saved her life – that's a great thing. Now you can do a *little* thing, and make it up with her.[32].

'I'm going to,' June assures Matron; and she does. Amanda starts to feel better when June promises her that she will go on training. 'June – I shan't mind things quite so much – being out of everything, I mean – if you *will* get into the second teams. I shan't feel I'm completely wasted then.'

Freed of her single-minded determination to get into the Olympic Games, Amanda becomes a humbler, more generous sportswoman. When June does get a place in the second teams, Amanda feels 'a prick of pride – but a different kind of pride from the kind she had felt before. This time it was a pride in someone else, not in herself.'[33]

Last Term at Malory Towers is, in critic Sheila Ray's view, Enid Blyton's most mature work, her sole attempt to depict girls on the brink of adulthood. As always with Blyton, the emotional response is understated, clothed in cliches and matter-of-factness in her very English way; but Ray is right, I think, to argue that this is a successful portrayal of an emerging friendship between an older and a younger girl.

> The bargain struck by Amanda and June completely lacks the sentimentality to be found in many girls' school stories, and they embark on a most convincing love-hate relationship, intolerant of each other in many respects but both determined to achieve their joint objective and in the process developing into much more admirable characters.[34]

These two different characters are seen to have been transformed through their relationship and the testing events that befall them into responsible members of the school community.

ROLE MODELS

Elsie Oxenham sums up the role model philosophy in *The Reformation of Jinty* (1933), whose heroine is 13 years old:

> Theo and Barbara were Jinty's idols, and no one could have been better for her untrained little mind. Every impulse she had was good, but there was hardly one which was not sorely in need of guidance. Barbara and Theo were patient, however; Barbara because she understood, and Theo because she could not let down a younger girl who relied on her.[35]

Barbara's success in 'understanding' the juniors in her bedroom and her Guide patrol leads the headmistress to make her head girl: the relationship that existed between the younger girls and the older is to be extended to the whole school.

> These qualities of devotion to the senior, of loyal hearty work for a common aim, of keenness and earnestness, and even in certain cases of sacrifice, . . . seem to augur well for our school work next term. If Barbara can infuse the same spirit into the school in general we shall do well . . . [36]

Mistresses may play this role, too. Suffering from a friend's betrayal, sixth-former Dorothy wonders if Miss Dickinson may be able to help. 'If I could only tell Dicky! I've always loved her; she understands, and she's such a dear.' Miss Dickinson responds by suggesting a walk over the Downs to talk it over; Dorothy can forget she's a 'school person' and think of her as a concerned relative. Later, back in the school context, the mistress has a moment's anxiety that the familiarity may have weakened her authority; should not a mistress be distant and formal with her students? But the parallel which is drawn between this relationship and that of Dorothy with a younger girl, Dot, affirms the appropriateness of dropping the barriers in such situations. In both instances an effort of understanding binds the pair together. 'You'll find Dot easier to manage next term because of this,' Miss Dickinson tells the prefect. 'She'll give you real love and loyalty now.' The chain of discipline is shown to be exercised through personal influence rather than reliance on rank.[37]

Elinor Brent-Dyer presents the same view. The responsibility of older girls towards younger is a frequent theme in her books, and special friendships like that of Jack Lambert and her dormitory prefect Len Maynard are encouraged, provided there is no sentimentality attached.[38] The Chalet School also prides itself on the close relations enjoyed by the older girls and the mistresses. Though this professed intimacy is highly exaggerated by modern standards, Kathie Ferrars is surprised and confused by it when she joins the school as a mistress straight from Oxford;[39] while Miss Bubb, temporary headmistress when Miss Annersley is injured in a bus crash, finds it impossible to accept. To Miss Bubb:

> a mistress must be someone quite apart from the pupils, and the friendship that existed between many of the older girls and the Staff struck her as undignified for the Staff and bad for the girls, as giving them too high an opinion of their own importance.[40]

The real specialist in the older/younger friendship is Dorita Fairlie Bruce. One such is that between Primula Mary Beton of the Upper Third at Springdale and prefect Diana Stewart; likewise Christine and Cynthia in *The Girls of St Bride's* (1923), and Hilary and Dimsie in *Dimsie Among the Prefects* (1923). The friendship is generally the younger girl's idea, to which the older assents with amusement; there are clear elements of affectionate protection and patronage on the one hand and admiration, if not adoration, on the other. Di, for example, takes Prim out from time to time: 'So what do you say to buying cookies and cakes at Macwhirter's and having our tea up in the old quarry . . . ?'

> 'I'd simply love it!' declared Primula, who would probably have said the same if Diana had suggested a picnic in a coal-pit.[41]

The rewards are shown to flow both ways. Bruce writes with understanding of both the younger girl's excitement and the older's motherly satisfaction in their roles. Dimsie, for instance, finds that when she becomes a prefect she is brought into closer contact with the juniors. In church one Sunday:

> something of that mother-sense, always strong in Dimsie, woke in her anew as she met Nan's shy friendly smile, and felt Hilary press up against her with a babyish movement which seemed strange from any one so sturdily independent. Dimsie drew the child's hand through her arm, and decided that this was the nicest part of being a prefect – the influence it gave one with the 'kids', and the power of making them happy, even if it meant a slight sacrifice on one's own part.[42]

But with Bruce, the *influence* also works both ways. It is Primula who makes Diana see how senseless is her jealous estrangement from her friend Peggy,[43] while both Dimsie and Nancy, as juniors, are shown to shame seniors whose laxness or dishonourable conduct is brought into sharp relief by the younger girls' straight and honest dealing with their trust and faith in the older.[44]

The relationship between Toby Barrett and Miss Musgrave – the 'Lesley' of the Dimsie books, now a mistress at *The*

School on the Moor (1931) – is similar to the junior–senior paradigm, but with about five years added to the age of each. Toby is 17 but, having come late to school, retains the original, disarming manner of a much younger girl. A drama involving an escaped convict – Miss Musgrave's brother, wrongfully imprisoned – bring the two together:

> As long as I live I shall never forget what you have done [declares Miss Musgrave]. At school, of course, nothing can be different. I am still one of the staff, and you in the sixth – but out of school-hours, and in the holidays, I hope we shall always be friends.[45]

A clear distinction is drawn between this healthy type of friendship and the practice among some weak mistresses of 'making favourites'. Prim and Anne, for example, are horrified to learn that the new housemistress at Wistaria is guilty of this crime; typically, her 'chief pash among the seniors' is the aptly named 'Silly' (Selina) Duncan.[46]

FRIENDSHIP AS PREPARATION FOR ADULTHOOD

If novelists saw schoolgirl friendships as a training ground for marriage, they certainly never said so. Nowhere have I found in the pages of these stories any version of the psychological truism perpetrated in my own youth in the 1950s and 1960s that girls' affections 'naturally' shifted in the 'teen years away from their own sex and towards males. Not one heroine is encouraged to give up her female circle upon marriage to devote herself to her husband's associates. All remain close to their schoolfriends in adulthood.

The Abbey girls' men, for example, are perfectly aware that though they may nominally come first in their wives' affections, in reality the women friends are more important. Maidlin even contemplates giving up her intended marriage if Joy should die, in order to devote herself to bringing up Joy's orphan children.[47] (Why she couldn't marry as well as bring them up is not made clear; what *is* clear is that loyalty to her friend takes precedence over her commitment to her fiancé.)

In fact, in these books schoolgirl friendships are presented unequivocably as a preparation not for marriage but for adult friendships between women. We see these among the Abbey characters as wives and mothers, and also among professional women who do not marry. The boarding school was an obvious place for adult friendships to flourish. As Martha Vicinus has shown in *Independent Women* (1984), single-sex communities such as colleges, hospitals and schools provided women with what were perceived as substitute families, with all the opportunities for the formation of emotional ties, emotional stress and fulfilment that families offer.[48]

That certain mistresses should become specially intimate with particular colleagues was accepted as natural and inevitable, at least in the early days of the evolution of the modern girls' school. School stories reflected this. Dorita Fairlie Bruce mentions in one novel that Miss Rogers is over at another house visiting Miss Thomson: 'They're rather matey, those two.'[49] Just as some schoolfriends are shown as devoted couples, so we find some adult friends on this model.

ADULT FRIENDSHIPS

Of all our authors, Elinor Brent-Dyer was uniquely skilled in depicting schoolmistresses. A teacher herself, she had an insider's insight into their ways and feelings, and never hesitated in her stories to show us the mistresses from their own point of view as well as through the eyes of their pupils – something rarely attempted by Elsie Oxenham or Dorita Fairlie Bruce, for example. In most of her Chalet books there is a chapter or two where the reader is invited to relax with the staff off-duty in their common room, or to join them in private deliberations over school affairs, or even to take their part in an interaction with a girl or girls. Across a series of nearly 60 books we get to know some of the long-serving staff such as Miss Wilson and Miss Annersley pretty well. We know what they look like, their histories, temperaments, idiosyncracies. We know where their emotional ties lie and how these change over the years.

There is good reason to believe that the presentation of adults in girls' school stories is more important than that of girls because it offers truly alternative role models for readers. Girls cannot usually choose whether or not to go to boarding school and live like their storybook heroines, but they may have some choice about their future careers and lifestyles. By depicting adult women outside marriage in an attractive light, school story writers may provide an alternative vision for girl readers. Girls may learn that not only is it possible to find fulfilment in careers but that spinsterhood does not necessarily leave a woman in an emotional vacuum; she may find not only companionship in the women around her, but also love.

It is true that Miss Wilson (in *Gay from China*, 1944) feels it necessary to compare her situation with that of Jo, a wife and mother, almost as if the former is a mere substitute for the latter. But a later friendship between two Chalet School mistresses is presented with no such apology. The relationship of Nancy Wilmot, maths mistress at the school from the thirtieth title, and Kathie Ferrars, her assistant from the thirty-seventh, runs as a constant theme through all the remaining books in the series. It is accepted, even taken for granted by both staff and students. Miss Wilmot and Miss Ferrars are a fixture, a certainty, in these pages; it is inconceivable that either of them should ever marry or leave the school. In this sense their relationship represents an interesting development on Miss Wilson's story; Miss Wilmot and Miss Ferrars belong to a younger generation (Miss Wilson actually taught Miss Wilmot when she was a pupil at the school) and, surprisingly, for the books in which their story unfolds were published in the 1950s and 1960s, theirs is the more explicit partnership.

Because it features always in the background of the plot, one could easily miss the significance of this relationship; yet I would argue that its steady development and constant presence through successive books impart a message which, though subliminal, makes its point as effectively as if it formed the main focus – perhaps more so. For that reason I think it worth spending some time here examining the relationship as it emerges and grows within the last 22 books in the Chalet School series.

Nancy Wilmot is one of a select group of teachers who are Old Girls of the school, though in her case it was for a very brief period when the school she attended across the lake in the Austrian Tyrol closed down and was taken over by the Chalet School. She was then in her final year, a prefect, described as plump, good-natured and lazy. She detested maths and described herself as 'the world's worst dud at languages'.[50] The war finds her in the WRENS[51] but she subsequently graduates in, remarkably, maths, and even more remarkably, eventually returns to the Chalet School (where the ability to teach in three languages is a prerequisite) as its maths mistress in its first term in the Swiss Oberand. She is now described as 'plump' and 'pretty'; all traces of laziness seem to have gone, though she remains relaxed and cheerful.[52]

Kathie Ferrars arrives at the school two years later as *The New Mistress at the Chalet School* (1957). Fresh out of Oxford, she is about ten years younger than Nancy Wilmot, and is described as small, attractive though not pretty, with bobbed, brown hair. Her first friend at the school is the history mistress, Biddy O'Ryan; but Biddy is shortly to marry and leave. ('Oh!' It was all Kathie said, but she felt a sudden disappointment.')[53] The friendship with Nancy Wilmot develops more slowly. When the prefects entertain the staff that first term, 'Kathie found herself making a threesome with Biddy O'Ryan and Nancy Wilmot.' Biddy and Nancy also start her off skiing before breakfast so that she should not appear a complete novice in front of the girls.[54]

By her second term at the school Kathie Ferrars has clearly been set up as Elinor Brent-Dyer's model teacher. She is already:

> a great favourite with the girls. . . . They liked her crisp way of dealing with them and, while they admired her and enjoyed the friendliness she showed them out of school hours, they remained in sufficient awe of her to take no liberties with her. . . . She was willing to listen to the girls' side of a question and they had always found her strictly just.[55]

The Chalet School specialises in mid-term expeditions to places of interest and Kathie is scheduled to take her own form, Intermediate V, to Solothurn. At the last minute Nancy joins her: her extra coaching has been cancelled because the pupil concerned has toothache, 'so I decided to make the most of it and come with you.'

> 'Oh, good!' Kathie Ferrars and Nancy Wilmot were very good friends, and it would certainly be more fun for the younger mistress to have one of her colleagues with her.[56]

Two books later the relationship is fully established: Kathie is described as Nancy's 'great friend and coadjutor'. This term Vb is off to Zermatt with Mademoiselle and Miss Ferrars for half-term. Nancy, whose plans to visit Biddy O'Ryan (now married and the mother of twins) have fallen through, asks if she can join them. Very properly she makes her request of Mademoiselle, who is the senior of the two; but she happens to be sitting next to Kathie.[57]

Brent-Dyer often uses conversations between members of staff as a device to further the plot through their comments on the girls. With increasing frequency in the Chalet School books these interchanges occur between Nancy Wilmot and Kathie Ferrars. Nancy remains placid and relaxed: she 'had the reputation of being one of the most easy-going mistresses imaginable, as a rule, though she could always pull in the reins when she felt like it.'[58] When Kathie is ground down by the responsibility of producing the Christmas play, Nancy is sympathetic and supportive:

'Hey, Ferrars, my love! Don't you want any Kaffee und Kuchen?'
　'Nancy! How long have you been here staring at me?'
　'Oh, about two minutes. Come on and stop looking as if you had the cares of the world on your back!'

But she engages seriously with the problem, which concerns two of the girls who refuse to act properly in one scene. 'What's gone wrong with them?'

'I haven't a clue! I rather think,' Kathy [from now on she spells her name this way] said, stopping at the head of the stairs to lean against the banisters and look up at her big friend, 'that there's some sort of private feud going on there . . .'

They discuss it, and Nancy advises her to 'give the whole thing a rest till next week and hope for the best.'

And Nancy slung an arm round her friend's shoulders and ran her along the corridor to the Staff sitting-room where Kaffee und Kuchen was in full swing. She brought two cups of Mdlle's [sic] unsurpassable coffee and the plate of cakes over to the corner where Kathy Ferrars had subsided and then stuck into the conversation . . . [59]

Book by book, further details of the friendship come to light. The bedrooms of Kathy Ferrars and Nancy Wilmot, we are told, are at the same end of the staff corridor; in a later book we learn that the rooms adjoin.[60] At every staff gathering, formal or informal, Kathy is to be found sitting beside Nancy 'as usual'.[61] Always described as 'great friends', they are always together outside school hours, attending lectures in Basel on Friday evenings, leading the salvage operations when the school dinner is ruined by vandals, rescuing two girls and the school cat from the snow-covered roof.[62] By the fifty-first book in the series they have bought a car together and go off together in it.[63] Any ramble or half-term excursion worth recording is led by them jointly: 'Oh, good! We've got Willy and Ferry for staff . . .'[64]

Something interesting is happening to their appearance, at least to Nancy's. From girlhood 'plump' and 'pretty', she is now 'big' and 'sturdy' and, it seems, increasingly masculine in demeanour. Suddenly she is six feet tall, with 'long arms' and 'powerful shoulders' – useful for rescuing girls and cats off roofs – and a dab hand with the lasso – useful for saving another girl's life by hauling her up a cliff.[65] We learn that she grew up with five brothers who 'insisted I mustn't grow up a sissy'.[66]

This is in stark contrast to Kathy. 'The long and the short of it!' Margot Maynard giggles to her sister Con.

> Miss Wilmot was both tall and broad while Miss Ferrars was on a miniature scale. But there was more to it than that. Nancy Wilmot was fair with blue eyes and honey-coloured hair under her big hat. Kathy Ferrars was brown-eyed, brown-haired and brown skinned. Nancy was a placid, happy-go-lucky creature, though she could be as icily dignified as anyone when she chose. Kathy was quicker in movement, thought and temper.[67]

By the time this book appeared Brent-Dyer was not writing as skilfully as she had done in her prime, and her books made greater use of stock situations and characters. It may be that Miss Wilmot, who once had nothing of the masculine about her, became confused in Brent-Dyer's mind with other big characters like Tom Gay and Dickie Christy who are seen as having a masculine style to go with their masculine nicknames. Perhaps in linking her with Kathy Ferrars, Brent-Dyer felt the need to develop her into a butch counterpart to the smaller, younger woman. But this was surely not a conscious decision: Nancy keeps her feminine name and her prettiness. Meanwhile the relationship with Kathy develops and deepens.

In the fifty-third book there is a '*monumental*' row over a caricature of 'Ferry' on the blackboard, and 'Willy' is 'mad'.

> 'Oh, well, she had a cold coming,' Judy said tolerantly. 'A 'flu cold, too. I expect she was feeling upset anyhow and that caricature of Ferry was the last straw. She and Willy are great friends, you know.[68]

In the fifty-fifth book, Miss Annersley goes off on a tour with other headmistresses of schools around the world. Miss Wilmot is appointed to act in her place for the term. At the beginning Nancy's cool, relaxed manner deserts her and, unlike the headmistresses in practically every other school story, she is shown to be 'as nervous as she could be and was devoutly wishing that she had never agreed to take on this job'. 'I must have been out of my mind when I agreed to it,' she complains to her 'bosom friend' Miss Ferrars. Kathy is deeply sympathetic: 'Poor old girl!'[69] Later she gains confidence, and whenever she has to deal with school problems, her friend is there to talk things over with her.

Soon after this, however, Kathy is rushed to hospital to have her appendix out and Nancy loses her support for the rest of the term. The incident where Kathy is struck down with a severe attack of appendicitis in front of her class is perhaps the most intimate testimony we have of the friendship, and for that reason worth recounting in detail. Nancy, happening to be 'striding down the corridor at that moment', hears a commotion in the classroom and enters to find her friend writhing and crying out with pain.

The Head was beside her at once. Waving the frightened

girls back imperatively, she bent over her friend, asking, 'Oh, my dear, what's wrong?'

She sends some of the girls to get help and dismisses the rest, but one, Victoria, stays in case she should need another messenger.

> Miss Ferrars was in severe pain and once her defences had slipped they had gone altogether. She was moaning at intervals and the Head's face when Victoria glanced at her was a revelation to that young woman.
>
> 'I – I'll just wait outside the door, Miss Wilmot,' she said. 'I can hear if you call.' She slipped away, leaving the door slightly ajar and Nancy Wilmot, along with her friend, thought no more about her.
>
> 'Kathy – Kathy darling!' she said. 'It's all right. Matey will be here in a sec, and the doctor, too.' She took one of Kathy Ferrars's slim hands in hers and was quite as frightened as the girls, the hands felt so weak. The next moment she gave a squawk, for a fresh pain shot through Kathy and her grip tightened until the signet ring Miss Wilmot always wore was cutting into her flesh.[70]

This is surely an unusual scene to find in any school story, let alone one written in the mid–1960s. It is unusual partly because it represents a very clear statement of love between two women. Although, as we have seen, Brent-Dyer often focuses on the staff, it is rare for their private dramas to be pushed to the fore like this, and rarer still for her to show any girls as privy to them.

Fortunately, Kathy recovers from her operation, and after her eventual return to the school the relationship resumes its comfortable continuity. In the fifty–seventh book Nancy and Kathy go off to Zug and Zurich with Upper IV for the last half–term in the series.[71] They have now been together for six years, and all the signs are that they will stay together, a settled pair in a community of women for the rest of their working lives.

It is not my intention to question whether Brent-Dyer meant to portray Nancy Wilmot and Kathy Ferrars as lesbians; we cannot know this, and in any case it seems irrelevant. There are aspects of the relationship depicted which, if we were dealing with real people rather than characters in a novel, would tend to suggest it was sexual. It is, however, unlikely that even a sophisticated writer would deliberately depict a lesbian relationship in a book intended for the juvenile market in the mid–1960s; and Brent-Dyer was not, as her biographer has pointed out, a particularly sophisticated writer. In any event, it is doubtful that a girl of the 1960s would have perceived the relationship as lesbian; she would probably not even have known – I certainly didn't – that lesbianism existed.

But a girl would have read this as a picture of love between women – and doubtless Brent-Dyer intended to convey this real love, sufficient unto itself (needing neither men nor children), comfortable, constant, supportive, and accepted. As a model of love it is completely successful – a great deal more successful, it has to be noted, than the idealised marriage of Brent-Dyer's heroine Jo Maynard. The bosom friendship of Kathy Ferrars and Nancy Wilmot is something young girls could both understand from their own experience and aspire to in adulthood. It offers an alternative to marriage as an emotional goal to strive for.

There was strong pressure on girls in the 1960s, as there is today, to shift their affectional focus from girlfriends to boyfriends in adolescence. Many of us girls at that time recognised that most boys, and indeed men, were poorly adapted to meeting our emotional needs. In validating love between women, school stories performed a useful service in presenting an alternative view of a way of living alongside the normative obeisance to marriage and motherhood. They were an inspiration for many girls who came to choose the companionship of other women in adulthood in preference to conventional heterosexuality.

133

6 The Crush

In 1907 Sara Burstall published a book called *English High Schools for Girls*, in the course of which she felt it necessary to mention:

> a phenomenon characteristic of girls' education – the hero-worship, adoration, or *schwarmerei* – there is no exact English word for it – which some girls have felt, and many have seen in others, . . . towards some teacher or leader in school life.[1]

This phenomenon, later to be known as the crush, rave, or pash, provoked educationists to vigorous discussion and analysis throughout most of the twentieth century. The terms of the debate changed over the decades as the distinction between 'healthy' and 'unhealthy' friendships became framed in increasingly sexual terms. Young women of the 1990s unhesitatingly perceive the latter as 'lesbian', and the word is used in a pejorative sense. But it was not always so.

Angela Brazil was the first great writer of girls' school stories, and her early books overflow with examples of unselfconscious love between girls. 'I've simply fallen in love with Catherine Winstanley,' declares the heroine of her first school story, *The Fortunes of Philippa* (1906). Later, Dona in *A Patriotic Schoolgirl* (1918) has an 'immensely hot' friendship with Ailsa. Two of Brazil's novels, published in 1918 and 1920, feature a character called 'Lesbia' who, her biographer argues, is an idealised version of the author herself. But, Gillian Freeman adds:

At the risk of being considered naive, I would swear that the name Lesbia (even when linked with Regina) was chosen by Angela in innocence. . . . The physical contacts and the physical admiration are sexual only to cynical and sophisticated contemporary readers.[2]

Not only was lesbianism not seen as a threat to morality before the 1920s, it was hardly recognised as an idea – by heterosexuals, that is. Close friendships between women, particularly young women, were encouraged in Victorian times. The Criminal Law Amendment Act of 1885 criminalised homosexual acts between males, but no mention was made of women. Since female sexuality was seen, both legally and medically, to be passive, the notion that women could be sexual with each other was not generally entertained. Women were known to be deeply emotional, but few considered that strong female attachments had any sexual component.

For Brazil and other writers of her time, what made friendships between girls or women unhealthy was simply an excess of emotion: 'Foolish, ridiculous, and even injurious forms of this are bad, bad for everyone concerned.'[3] As Janet Montefiore has pointed out, there is a clear historical reason for this condemnation of emotional indulgence: the new girls' boarding schools had modelled themselves on boys' public schools, where emotional reserve and the stiff upper lip were as essential values as the prefect system and compulsory team games.[4] It behoved girls' schools, therefore, to emphasise reason over emotion and to eschew the extravagant forms of feeling with which women had long been associated.

Some school authorities, Sara Burstall tells us, felt so strongly about the subject that they tried to suppress all 'raves'. She herself thought this was the wrong approach; she would not wish to do away with the 'true and noble instinct of hero-worship, of following a leader, which characterises boys as well as girls, and which is the basis of some of our highest values.'

A woman's life is, moreover, largely concerned with emotion; to suppress this would be injurious, to allow it to develop slowly and harmlessly, in respect or even reverence for some one who is older and presumably wiser than a girl herself, is not injurious and may be helpful.

Burstall nevertheless suggested, bowing to the masculine ideal, that teachers should use their influence to ensure a healthy 'tone' in the school, one which deprecated sentimentality and external signs of emotion, and that the curriculum should include 'studies to cultivate the reason' and 'a common-sense way of looking at things'.[5]

THE SEXOLOGISTS

At the end of the nineteenth century a number of men in Germany, France and Britain became interested in what came to be known as sexology, or the scientific study of sexual behaviour. The works of sexologists Havelock Ellis and Edward Carpenter were being read in intellectual circles before the First World War, followed soon after by Freud's theories in translation about normal and abnormal sexual development in childhood.

In the first volume of his *Studies in the Psychology of Sex, Sexual Inversion* (1897), Havelock Ellis expressed the view that the crush which was so common among schoolgirls was a 'rudimentary kind of homosexual relationship'.[6] In order to justify what must have seemed to most late Victorians a shocking observation, he pointed out that girls were more inclined to seek affection than boys; that being more innocent than boys, they usually failed to recognise the sexual nature of their feelings (as indeed did practically everyone else); and that the greater licence – even encouragement – given to physical contact among females (for example, sharing beds) led to lesbian passions flourishing under the guise of female friendship. Single-sex institutions such as boarding schools, he contended, created the ideal conditions for lesbianism to flourish.[7]

Ellis was of the view that there were two sorts of lesbians: those who were born that way ('congenital inverts') and those who became so by circumstance 'due merely to the accidental absence of the natural objects of sexual attraction'.[8] He imagined that the congenital invert or *real* lesbian would first manifest her abnormality at school by forming:

> an ardent attachment for another girl, probably somewhat older than herself, often a school-fellow, sometimes her school-mistress, upon whom she will lavish an astonishing amount of affection and devotion.

The *pseudo*-lesbian would also have these attachments, generally to a real lesbian; but where the latter would go on to repeat the pattern throughout her life, with the former ('the majority') 'it will be forgotten as soon as possible, not without shame, in the presence of the normal object of sexual love'.[9]

Like most Victorian 'scientific' research, Ellis's evidence for these conclusions is insubstantial. His case studies of lesbians apparently comprised his wife, Edith Lees, and three of her friends, none of whom reported a boarding-school initiation. He quotes a letter from a woman who did sleep with another girl at school, but who 'cannot be called inverted'.[10] He claimed that many 'sexually inverted women' were well known 'in literature or otherwise', and conjectured that lesbianism was on the increase – along with female criminality and insanity – as a result of women's greater legal and social freedom.[11]

Ellis was at pains to emphasise that sexuality was diverse and that there were many forms of sexual expression. Like most Victorian men, however, he held the view that heterosexuality was normal and that women were intended by nature to be wives and mothers. In tune with the emerging school of sexual libertarianism he explained women's destiny in biological rather than social terms: women needed to experience sexual activity and childbirth to be physically healthy and psychologically fulfilled.

Among the most prominent sex reformers in the early years of the twentieth century were Marie Stopes, the birth control pioneer, and Stella Browne, who fought to make abortion legal. Following Havelock Ellis, their plea for women's right to sexual pleasure was couched entirely in heterosexual terms. Lesbianism was explicitly attacked as deviant and dangerous.

> Another practical solution which some deprived women find is in lesbian love with their own sex. . . . One of the physical results of such unnatural relations is the gradual accustoming of the system to reactions which are arrived at by a different process from that for which the parts were naturally formed. This tends to unfit women for real union. If a married woman does this unnatural thing, she may find a growing disappointment in her husband and he may lose all natural power to play his proper part.[12]

Like Ellis and other sexologists, Stopes distinguished between 'real' and 'pseudo' lesbians:

> A very *very* few women have strong inborn tendencies of this type; most of those who indulge in the vice drifted into it lazily or out of curiosity and allowed themselves to be corrupted. This corruption spreads as an underground fire spreads in the peaty soil of a dry moorland.[13]

The colourful language betrays the almost hysterical fear which was to characterise discussion of the subject from the 1920s onwards. The knock-on effect was a re-conceptualisation of women's and girls' friendships as potentially lesbian and, therefore, a serious threat to a patriarchal society.

CO-EDUCATION

'Advanced' fiction reflected the new view of women's friendships. Clemence Dane's *Regiment of Women* (1917) is an adult
novel set in a girls' school. Clare Hartill (the surname is
significant) is a teacher who is shown to have a pernicious
influence over devoted pupil Alwynne. The character representing the modern view protests:

> Don't you realize that when you keep Alwynne entangled
> in your apron strings, blind to other interests, when you
> cram her with poetry and emotional literature, when you
> allow yourself to attach herself passionately to her, you are
> feeding, and at the same time deflecting from its natural
> channel, the strongest impulse of her life – of any girl's
> life? Alwynne needs a good strong husband to love, not a
> fantastic ideal that she calls friendship and clothes in your
> figure.[14]

This particularly nasty tale, written by a popular woman
writer who was herself unmarried, goes so far as to accuse
Clare Hartill of 'vampyrism': 'And when she [Alwynne] is
squeezed dry, who will the next victim be? And the next,
and the next? . . .'[15] The image of the predatory lesbian or
vampire thus passed into sexual ideology, to dominate rep-
resentations of lesbians in popular culture up to the present
day.

Regiment of Women ends with a resounding endorsement of
co-education, a novel idea in middle-class circles at the time,
where sex segregation was deeply entrenched. Parents and
teachers who had always believed that boys and girls should
be separated on moral grounds were now being told, confusingly, that the only truly moral arrangement was the mixed
school. The dangers of crowding girls together, with no
outlet for their emotions other than in crushes on their fellow
pupils or mistresses, were emphasised. Educating boys and

girls together was shown to be more 'natural' and 'healthy'; as Alwynne put it after visiting a co-educational school:

> They had room to move. They weren't always rubbing up against each other like apples in a basket. It all seemed so natural and jolly. Fresh air everywhere. And since I've been back I've felt I couldn't breathe.[16]

Clemence Dane was not writing in a vacuum. Annabel Faraday, who has researched this subject, found no fewer than 16 novels published in the first half of the twentieth century which link lesbians with education.[17] Psychiatrists and educational psychologists joined the debate. As Faraday has shown, there was a strong impetus to set up co-educational schools after the First World War. Both wars were followed by an anti-feminist backlash, the desire to force women who had become independent in the 'unnatural', man-free wartime years back into their domestic roles and dependence upon men. And co-educational schools were, and are, good training grounds for 'normal' gender relations in the wider world.

THE SPINSTER TEACHER

Alongside the attack on single-sex schools in the 1920s went a much stronger, more widespread attack on the spinster teacher. This has been documented by Alison Oram, who emphasises that there were economic as well as sexual motives for the campaign. Since women were paid less than men, many male teachers argued resentfully that women undercut their pay, preventing them from earning a family wage (and thus being able to keep a family, including the much-desired wife at home), while ensuring that the status of teaching – as women's work – remained low. Oram also makes it clear that the stereotype embodied in Clemence Dane's Clare Hartill was not uncommonly used to warn of the danger that unmarried women teachers supposedly posed to girls in all-girls schools.[18]

The spinster had long been the perpetual object of condescending pity, disdain, and cheap jokes:

> . . . a woman *is* positively and distinctively created in order that she may become a wife and mother. If she misses this destiny, there is something wrong somewhere . . . You may make an old maid, or a nun, or a nurse all her life of her; but if you do, she is, qua woman, a failure, whatever great and noble things she may do, or whatever she may accomplish to raise the standard of human effort and kindle the lamp of human hope.[19]

But if the Victorian spinster was seen as a sexual failure, she was never criticized as a sexual *danger*. She might be a failure because she had failed to find a husband, because she was forced to depend on other relatives or her own labour for her support. But her failure to experience the delights of heterosexual connection, though perhaps implicit in the description, was never explicitly described as a problem as far as her contacts with other women and girls were concerned; on the contrary, her virginity and innocence were considered to constitute a beneficent influence.

The census of 1921 revealed a higher number of spinsters in Britain than ever before. Many middle-class women were choosing to find their fulfilment not in marriage but in one of the new professional careers which had opened up to them – teaching, nursing, academic work and medicine – or in business. Some chose not to marry for political reasons, as a protest against the enforced social, economic and legal dependence of married women.

To be able to offer the scientific evidence of sexology and psychology to bolster the prevailing social and economic arguments was a great asset to the proponents of the dominant ideology. The attacks on spinsters took on an entirely new tone. The celibate was not a failure because she had not had sex with a man. As Clemence Dane's voice of reason, Elspeth, puts it: 'We both know that an unmated woman – she's a failure – she's unfulfilled.'[20] The pressures on women to marry, or at least demonstrate appropriate heterosexual contact, increased.

Most teachers were female – teaching had always been the most popular career for middle-class women – and of these, 85 per cent were unmarried, according to the censuses of 1921 and 1931.[21] This was in part due to the marriage bar operated by many education authorities, which forced women (though not men) to resign upon marriage. In the nineteenth century teaching had been seen as a particularly suitable career for unmarried women because it offered them an outlet for their maternal feelings, while the school community formed an acceptable substitute for a family of one's own. Twentieth-century critics of the spinster teacher pointed out that neither of these factors made up for the lack of (hetero)sexual fulfilment in the woman's life, and that the teacher's pseudo-maternal influence could, in fact, usurp the real mother's proper role to detrimental effect. The influence of the spinster teacher – sexual failure, neurotic, even deviant – could scarcely be healthy. Girls needed models of truly fulfilled married women to ensure their own normal development and socialisation.

Women teachers could not win. As guardians of children's morality, they could hardly choose to live in sin with men; yet if they married, they lost their jobs. In 1921 there was an attempt in the British parliament to criminalise lesbian acts along the same lines as the 1885 law against homosexual acts between men. This Criminal Law Amendment bill failed on a technicality, but the strongest argument raised against it was that it would be less dangerous to ignore the existence of lesbianism than to 'tell the world that there is such an offence, to bring it to the notice of women who have never heard of it, never thought of it, never dreamed of it.'[22] Even so, there was increasing readiness thereafter to scent perversion in any association of single women, and after the successful prosecution for obscenity of Radclyffe Hall's novel of lesbian love, *The Well of Loneliness*, in 1928, spinsters were subjected to ever more aggressive attacks. The book was banned in the UK (though a similar action in the United States failed), but media publicity ensured that everyone now knew what lesbianism was and, moreover, defined it as dangerous and obscene.

By the 1930s, as Alison Oram demonstrates, the experts did not mince their words in characterising spinster teachers as a danger to girls. Oram quotes a doctor's speech at an educational conference in 1935 on the effect of competitive games on schoolgirls. "The women who have the responsibility for teaching these girls are, many of them themselves embittered, sexless or homosexual hoydens who try to mould the girls into their own pattern. And far too often", the doctor added ominously, "they succeed."[23]

BOARDING SCHOOLS BETWEEN THE WARS

How much of all this filtered through to the girls' schools in the private sector? Lilian Faithfull's *You and I* (1927), based on talks with senior girls at Cheltenham Ladies' College where she was headmistress, included an essay on 'Real and Counterfeit Friendships' which discussed the same phenomenon as that addressed by Sara Burstall before the war. There was no doubt that 'raving' was still widespread, even universal, in Faithfull's school at least, and that she, like Sara Burstall, considered it a problem. But there is no suggestion that this was due to any sexual element. 'The distinctions between a rave and true friendships are many,' she began.

Though a friendship may begin suddenly, it is usually of somewhat slow growth; but this strange devotion sweeps upon you before you can put up any defences. While the true friendship is growing stronger, it weaves itself into

143

your ordinary life without disturbing you very much. . . .
It does not stand beside your bed and lean over you when
you want to sleep. It does not occasion a tremendous flutter
over the post in the holidays. Altogether it keeps you
warm and comfortable, not too hot and feverish.[24]

This is the nearest that Faithfull gets to attributing any sexual
manifestation to the 'rave', and it is hardly explicit. Her
concern, like Burstall's before her, was to discourage excess
and exhibitionism.

In the rave there is extravagant admiration. There is also
a one-sided longing to serve, which looks like unselfish-
ness, but is tangled up with a longing for demonstration,
for some exhibition of affection from the person
served. . . . You are not ready to share her.

Herein lies the problem: 'You are revelling in your own
emotions and are in an unhealthy state of mind.'[25]
Like Burstall, Faithfull clung to her conviction that hero-
worship could be a valuable experience:

A really honest devotion to someone of fine character,
who is however rather remote from you, is healthy and
natural. Its influence may be altogether good, if the person
who experiences it has perception delicate enough to know
that her feeling must be purged of everything silly to be
worthy of so fine an object.

She concluded: 'We would miss a great incentive in life if we
have no capacity for hero-worship.'[26]

THE ANTI-SOPPIST LEAGUE

In 1921 there appeared the first school story response to the
crush discourse: Dorita Fairlie Bruce's *Dimsie Moves Up*, in

which the renowned 'Anti-Soppist League' was founded. The circumstances of its creation reveal its author's total accord with the real headmistresses of her time. Miss Yorke, her fictional head, is chatting about the younger girls with her head girl, Sylvia Drummond. She comments that the recent arrival of Dimsie and her circle in the Third Division will do the others good.

'They need it, too', Sylvia agrees, ' – namby-pamby little wretches those 3rd Div. girls are! Always hanging round somebody older than themselves, and behaving like lovelorn idiots!'

'They're at that very trying stage,' Miss Yorke shrugs.[27]

It's a stage that Dimsie, aged 12, and her chums have not yet reached. When Betty Grey warns them not to hang round Miss Moffatt, because 'We're awfully gone on her, Joan and I, and of course we shall have first claim to talk with her or sit with her,' Dimsie's friends don't understand what she is talking about. Betty and Joan endeavour to explain: 'You musn't [sic] go giving her flowers or sweets, or tidying her desk for her, or carrying her things: it wouldn't be fair to us.'

'You must be quite crazy,' declares Erica, the leader of Dimsie's set.

But Mabs grasps the point. Someone has told her that 'a lot of them were like that in the 3rd Div. just now.'

It isn't only Miss Moffatt, either; some of them are gone on different seniors, like Meg Flynn or Daisy Milne. . . .
I asked mother about it in the holidays. She says it's a sort of complaint girls get, like measles. She thinks they all go through it in time.

'Well, we shan't!' says Erica with decision. 'I won't have that kind of rubbish! We five will form ourselves into an anti-society about it . . .'

So the Anti-Soppists League is born. Erica devises the rules, which are simple and few: not to give flowers to any teacher or senior, not to sleep with any senior's old hair-ribbon under your pillow, and not to kiss anyone 'unless absolutely obliged to'.[28] Bruce treats what she calls 'soppism' with light mockery, but it is significant that she mocks it; Angela Brazil, writing in the same period, is perfectly serious about sentimental friendships and totally accepting of them. Moreover, Bruce locates the crush as a phenomenon which strikes girls at a particular stage in their life, that is, puberty. To a later generation this will be seen as the normal, transitional homosexual stage before the normal, final heterosexual one. Bruce, however, seems to show it as a silly stage before a sensible one; the sexual implications, if indeed she realised there were any, go unmentioned in a book written for girls.

We know that Bruce was interested in the 'new science' of psychology because in a later novel (1938) she offers the girls of St Bride's a course of lectures in the subject.[29] Perhaps, therefore, she did make the link in her own mind between 'soppism' and the age of sexual awakening. Or perhaps she was simply describing what she saw, with no thought to any deeper significance. Martha Vicinus contends that educators would probably not have argued so forcefully for the control of the emotions unleashed by the crush if they had not recognised their sexual force.[30] If Vicinus is to be believed, these manifestations of silliness were themselves aspects of sexual awakening of a pre-Freudian type: the forms that sexuality was most likely to take in girls' boarding schools after the First World War.

The strict rules of the Anti-Soppist League tend to restrict the behaviour of its members, and have to occasionally be broken. When Dimsie and Pam are reconciled after a quarrel, they 'leaned together and kissed'. Fortunately it is dark and no one can see them, otherwise they would 'probably have avoided' doing it.[31] Likewise, when Jean and Dimsie's friendship is renewed after a period of jealousy and resentment, they come together again:

in a tight embrace, which lasted for a second or two, till Dimsie shook herself free and began to dry her eyes.

'Jean!' she said sternly. 'Do at least *try* to remember we are Anti-Soppists!'[32]

For a writer as interested as Bruce is in relationships between younger and older girls, or girls and mistresses, the principles of Anti-Soppism present a constant constraint. Whatever emotions her characters feel for their heroines, they must be carefully distinguished from soppism:

> Hilary was too sane and healthy to indulge in what the school popularly knew as a 'crush', but to her Dimsie had always stood for an ideal, some one to be followed and looked up to.[33]

> Neither the slang term 'crush' nor what it stood for, were encouraged at Jane's where the Anti-Soppist influence had reigned supreme for many years; but Vi had a deep and private feeling that she would willingly follow Dimsie Maitland wherever she led.[34]

Her characters do not have crushes, then; only the healthy sort of hero-worship which Burstall and Faithfull fought to retain as an important stimulus to moral action – as it is shown to be here, through the glowing example of Dimsie Maitland.

SENTIMENTALITY AS A DISEASE

Elinor Brent-Dyer tackled crushes in her second published book, *A Head Girl's Difficulties*, which appeared in 1923. Chapter XV opens with the statement: 'Of all things, sentimentality is almost most to be dreaded in a large school of St Peter's type.' At St Peter's, the author goes on to explain, behaviour was supposed to be 'casual and off-hand to a degree'.

> You might be pals with another girl; you might walk about with her, and lend her your books and pencils and rubbers; you might even sit next to her in form – if you could. But anything further was forbidden. The girls caught walking about with their arms round each other were held up to keen ridicule; while as for those caught kissing, well, they were made to feel themselves pariahs.[35]

This is a very modern school indeed! Occasionally, however, an 'outbreak' of sentimentality may hit even the best-regulated institution, and St Peter's suffers such an 'epidemic' in these pages.

At first the prefects fail to recognise the 'signs'. Then Rosamund and Vivien notice two fourth-form girls with their arms round each other, and Vivien realises what is happening. 'Don't you see? They're turning floppy!'

> A look of disgust came into Rosamund's face. 'How sickening!' she said fervently. 'Well, I did think we were free from rot of that kind!'[36]

The metaphor of disease is relentlessly pursued throughout the account.

> There could be little doubt that sentimentality was beginning to be rampant, especially among the Middle School people, who were just at the age to take it badly. In the Fifth it affected only the three or four who were naturally inclined that way; and in the Sixth the only two who showed any signs of it were Letty Harrison and Adelicia . . . [37]

What is particularly interesting about this description is the suggestion that the two groups most likely to be affected by the 'infection' are the Middle School girls, because of their age, and those who were 'naturally inclined that way'. If Brent-Dyer had in mind any idea approximating to Havelock Ellis's theory of real and pseudo-lesbians, she seems not to have thought very deeply about it. There is an innocence about the description which suggests that it was based largely on hearsay and received opinion, and that the language was chosen for clever effect, not because she was writing for children and needed to mask her real meaning.

Diseases need drastic treatment. Brent-Dyer provides it:

> Letty was easily suppressed; public opinion was too much for her . . . Any attempt at demonstration, whether verbal or active, was sternly suppressed by the others, who were even more guarded than usual, and who, as Letty said resentfully, nearly swallowed her if she ventured on so much as 'my dear'.[38]

Adelicia, however, is more of a problem. She has been only a short time at school among 'normal, healthy-minded schoolgirls who went in for games'; her earlier years have been dominated by her mother, 'a silly, affected woman, who idolised her only child, and who taught the girl to think of little else but clothes and amusements.' A weak, silly governess and an absent father complete the list of bad influences in her background. Plunged into the sensible world of school, Adelicia finds it difficult to make friends among girls of her own age, so turns her attention to the younger ones. 'So the leaders of the Lower School were regaled with chocolates . . . and . . . flattery. . . . The immediate result was the wave of sentimentality which was threatening to engulf the greater part of the school.'[39]

Signed and unsigned letters from admirers change hands. Girls are unable to concentrate on games and work. 'It's got to be stamped out at once!' decide the prefects. A draconian scheme is devised whereby the recipients of fan mail are forced to read them aloud to the whole school. A pretended adorer is devised for Adelicia who persecutes her with false attentions. When the girl, in tears, asks why they all hate her so, they tell her that they are really doing her a favour: 'We're trying to save you from growing into a perfect idiot.' Vivien goes on:

> You quite obviously know that the feeling of the school is against any sentimental rubbish whatsoever. . . . Yet you, a new girl, have the impertinence to come here to St Peter's, and try to corrupt our juniors! You try to teach the children, who are, of course, rather flattered at being taken up by a senior, to hang round each other's necks, to write poisonous rubbish to each other, and to mess up their games and work generally because they can't attend properly to what they're doing. And then, when we try to defend the traditions of St Peter's, which are old and decent traditions, you call us 'beasts'.[40]

This incident occupies nearly a hundred pages in the novel. Seventy years on, it is difficult to know what to make of it. So much of Brent-Dyer's language and imagery echoes those of the sexologists that one is driven to wonder if she had actually read anything by, say, Marie Stopes (whose *Enduring Passion* appeared in the same year). For example, she speaks of the older girl 'corrupting' the juniors, and contrasts her 'poisonous rubbish' with the school's 'old and decent traditions'. Yet she does not seem to be talking about real crushes at all, let alone anything that could be construed as remotely 'lesbian' behaviour. There is an absence of sincere feeling throughout the account and no sensible rationale for the aberrant behaviour. The adorations are exposed as completely fake, which is just as well, as the treatment meted out to the adorers is little short of barbaric. Had any of these girls genuinely loved another, she would have suffered terribly from the cruel humiliation of having her feelings held up to ridicule in front of the whole school.

If readers had been allowed to sympathise with Adelicia,

to feel for her loneliness and understand her reaching out for affection, then how we would have protested at this treatment! If we had identified ourselves with any of these girls, having a crush on a senior, what sort of lesson would we have learnt? But we don't, because Brent-Dyer doesn't seem to be writing about this. 'Sentimentality' in the abstract has nothing to do with love.

Its greatest fault, in Brent-Dyer's account, is that girls get obsessed with it and 'can't attend properly to what they're doing'. It is no more than this. One wonders how much Brent-Dyer understood of the phenomenon she described and whether she ever linked it in her mind to the passionate friendships her biographer tells us she was making at this stage in her life. My view is that she didn't. *A Head Girl's Difficulties* is an illustration of the power of ideology – the ideology that emotional displays between females are wrong – internalised and propounded by a woman who did not realise the significance of what she was doing because she did not understand the reasons and motives behind the ideology and she could not relate it to her own experience.

After I had first formed this conclusion, apparent corroboration emerged in the form of Rachel Davis's real-life tale of her schooldays, *Four Miss Pinkertons* (1936), to which I was referred by a footnote in Martha Vicinus's article on English boarding school friendships.[41] Davis was writing of the period before the First World War but her account of 'gonage' (as the crush was called at Roedean) describes the transition from institutionalised hero-worship ('Sutton Weald [Roedean] was riddled with the brand of worship that youth feels for the heroes of it own species'), through the metaphor of illness ('[The headmistress] presumably considered it one of the unavoidable diseases of maidenhood, like measles, to be cured, like any other epidemic, with drastic disinfectants, with disapproval, and scorn'), to final condemnation.[42] One dramatic evening the games prefect called the whole school together and told them to cease the practice of gonage, as it was silly, wrong, and unhealthy, and gave the school a bad name.

The injunction failed, as Davis points out: 'Gertrude's pluck, the commanding little figure she had cut on the platform, only increased the zeal of her worshippers.'[43] Looking back from the sophistication of the mid–1930s, Davis concluded that the custom was condemned not because of any sexual apprehensions – 'Of course, this was before psychology as such, came into fashion' – but because 'self-control' was prized as 'the greatest of all virtues, particularly in a youthful generation'.[44] Even in 1936, understanding what gonage really meant, she was critical of the attempt to kill raves: 'It was better that the old enthusiasms and devotions should go on than that brutality should have been used to destroy them.' Davis even defended hero-worship:

> In truth the world has always been afraid of love, and until it can be made to realise that here is the one thing that is right and beautiful in all its shapes, persecution followed by distortion is bound to carry on its work.[45]

The character of Tom Gay embodies all the school story's ambivalence, not only about crushes, but about femininity itself. Tom – real name Lucinda Muriel – first appears in a story in a Chalet School Annual of 1948. The only child of a clergyman and his wife, she had been brought up like a boy until the age of 12, when a visiting aunt persuades her parents to send her to a girls' school in the hope that she will become more feminine. She arrives at the Chalet School:

> Tom was standing in a manly way, feet slightly apart, hands shoved deep into her coat pockets, head cocked a little to one side. The Head somehow got the impression that it was only by an effort that her mouth wasn't pursed up into a whistle.

The Chalet School authorities take Tom in their stride:

Such an unusual pupil was of deep interest to Miss Wilson. She gave the girl a keen look, taking in the short, brown hair, cropped and parted at the side, boy-fashion . . . This girl was plain as far as looks went, but she had character. . . . Miss Wilson preferred girls with character, but she had a rooted objection to discussing them before themselves, so she merely said, 'I hope you will be very happy with us.'[46]

Once assured that schoolgirls have as strong a code of honour as the boys she has always emulated, Tom settles down reasonably well, until circumstances arise which lead her to the conclusion that one of the prefects has 'told tales' and got her into trouble with the staff. Unfortunately, this girl – Daisy Venables – is one she has begun to admire a great deal. Her resultant disappointment and confusion makes her ill.

In a chapter entitled 'Growing Pains', Matron tries to take the matter in hand. Tom is critical of the way girls do silly things:

like adoring someone, a senior or some mistress, and giving them flowers and things, and trying to meet them all the time, and wanting to do things for them. Boys aren't like that.

Matron disagrees.

Boys have their heroes, you know, just as girls have their heroines. They don't express what they feel in quite the same way, I grant you, but then, in any decent school, neither do girls – not nowadays.

The usual preroration on sentimental nonsense follows. 'We've never had it here, thank goodness! The outlook has always been too healthy and sane for such rubbish.' But hero-worship is fine:

153

It's a good thing for younger girls to be able to look up to the Seniors; good for them, and good for the Seniors. If an elder girl finds that younger ones are influenced by what she says and does, if she has any decency in her, it makes her careful. As we all need some sort of ideal as soon as we can think for ourselves, it's right that girls should be able to find that ideal among themselves.[47]

Eventually, after an adventure in the snow in which Daisy acquits herself heroically, she and Tom have a showdown. It turns out she did not tell tales at all. Tom apologises for ever thinking so and for behaving so badly: 'When you've thought a chap's a gentleman, and then things happen which made you think she isn't – well, it's a bit of a – a let-down.'

Daisy grasps 'what lay behind all this' – that Tom has a crush on her. She does not condemn it as sentimental nonsense, but reacts exactly as Matron has laid down: 'It strikes me I'd better be careful about what I say or do,' she thinks, for she realises that she is a role model for younger girls like Tom.[48]

Ironically enough, in the following term, Tom herself finds herself the object of a crush when a new girl Rosalie, a very feminine child, is attracted to boyish Tom on their first meeting. Tom is quite unable to sympathise with her, not seeing Rosalie's attachment as resembling in any way her admiration for Daisy Venables. Nor does Elinor Brent-Dyer, who comments:

It was a nasty shock for Tom. She had heard her father speak of the 'silly fashion of schoolgirl sentimentality', and had imbibed from him a strong sense of disgust for anything of the kind. She had been thankful to find that most of her kind had as little use for such things as herself. As a whole the Chalet School was remarkably free of such nonsense, though deep, true friendships were often born there and encouraged . . . [49]

Brent-Dyer is back on her old hobby-horse again.

Tom Gay becomes a Chalet School legend. After leaving school, she takes up missionary work in London, running clubs for working-class boys, and teaching them carpentry. They send regular contributions to the school's annual Sale of Work, and Tom herself returns from time to time. Like all Brent-Dyer's boy-like characters, she grows to a height of six feet and her appearance remains masculine. A description given of her in adulthood to a girl who has never met her is revealing:

> Tom never had any use, either, for what she calls 'Sloppy girlishness'. *You* know – having G.P.s on people and all that sort of rot. We never have gone in for that sort of rubbish here, of course; but Tom's death on the faintest sign of it . . . [50]

Given what we know about Tom's youthful experience, this comment might lead us to suspect in Tom the repression or internalised self-hatred of the closet lesbian. That her surname is 'Gay' is surely an interesting coincidence. Yet she is presented as a Chalet School success and a positive role model for the tomboyish reader. No unlikely heterosexual romance is arranged for her, and she is one of the few important Chalet School characters who never marries. She was also, judging from correspondence in the Chalet Newsletter, one of the most popular with readers.

BLYTON'S TOMBOYS AND MANNISH SPINSTERS

We have seen how Enid Blyton deals in character stereotypes: her tomboy type, one in each of the longer series, has a boy's nickname (Bobby, short for Roberta, at St Clare's; Bill, short for Wilhelmina, at Malory Towers) and boyish ways. Bill, the later version, is an exact contemporary of Brent-Dyer's

Tom Gay – she first appears in a novel of 1948 – and in appearance very like her: 'except for the school tunic', we are told, '[Bill] looked exactly like a boy!'

> Wilhelmina had hair cropped almost as short as a boy's. It curled a little, which she hated. Her face was boyish and square, with a tip-tilted nose, a big mouth, and big, wide-set eyes of hazel-brown. She was covered with freckles from forehead to firm little chin.[51]

Bill's boyishness is explained by the fact that she is an only girl with seven brothers. 'She might have been a boy herself in the way she acted.'[52]

Like Tom, she is keen on carpentry and, at Malory Towers, she can actually attend classes in the craft:

> She had already produced a pipe for her father, a ship for her youngest brother, and a bowl-stand for her mother, and was as proud of these as any of the good embroiderers were of their cushions or the weavers of their scarves.[53]

But her greatest passion is for horses. At Malory Towers, the girls are allowed to bring their horses to school and to tend and ride them outside lesson hours. When Bill is new to the school, she spends most of her time in class day-dreaming about her horse Thunder, to the wrath of her form mistress, Miss Peters.

Miss Peters is another Blyton type: 'tall, mannish, with very soft hair and a deep voice.'

> The girls liked her, but sometimes they wished she would not treat them as though they were boys. She had a hearty laugh, and a hearty manner.

Like Bill, she loves horses. 'In the holidays she rode practically all the time.'[54] In school time, however, she prefers to concentrate on lessons, and eventually forbids Bill to visit her horse at all until her work improves.

Bill's resultant hatred for Miss Peters is swiftly transformed into admiration and gratitude when the mistress saves Thunder's life one night by riding across the fields to fetch the vet. From then on Bill is careful to work in class to repay her, and a good relationship develops between the pair:

> They understood one another, which really wasn't very surprising, because they were very much alike. Miss Peters was mannish, and Bill was boyish. They both loved life out-of-doors and adored horses. They had disliked one another very much indeed – but now they were going to be firm friends. That would be nice for Bill.[55]

And also for Miss Peters, as we learn later: 'So there grew up a real understanding between the form mistress and Bill, delightful to them both.'[56]

The mannish spinster is an instantly recognisable type of schoolteacher – but she is not a type we ever find in novels by Elinor Brent-Dyer, Dorita Fairlie Bruce or Elsie Oxenham. It is interesting that Enid Blyton, writing in 1948, was not daunted by the image of a lesbian, which Miss Peters so clearly resembles, though the other three authors avoid it like the plague. There were plenty of such women to be found in real schools, but the strength of the anti-lesbian campaign tended to put writers off including them in books for girls. Perhaps Blyton was so preoccupied with churning out her 10,000 words a day that all this publicity passed her by.

Miss Peters would seem to sophisticated readers to be an obvious descendant of Radclyffe Hall's heroine Stephen Gordon, the type who was perceived in the interwar years to be a serious threat to young girls. An adult novel featuring a character like this would certainly be understood to represent a lesbian, either caricature or Clemence Dane-style predator. Miss Peters' relationship with Bill would surely arouse the deepest suspicion, for all the worrying elements are there, down to the author's choice of names for her characters.

Blyton might have made a caricature of her, but she chose not to; stereotype is not far removed from caricature and Blyton's Mam'zelles, for example, come perilously close to that. Yet although the girls are initially amused by Miss Peters

'I really wonder she doesn't come to class in riding bree-ches,' Alicia had said often enough to the third form, making them giggle. 'I'm sure she hates wearing a skirt!'[57]

they are obviously fond of her and later, full of respect and admiration. When she comes into the classroom for the first time after her midnight ride, 'three hearty cheers rang out for Miss Peters.'[58] Miss Peters is, in fact, depicted as a posi-tive and popular role model and her influence on Bill as healthy and good for them both.

That Blyton was not describing a crush here is evident from a comparison of this relationship with two others between a girl and a mistress which are very clearly intended to represent crushes and are criticised accordingly. Both con-cern Alison O'Sullivan, the hapless embodiment of girlish silliness in the St Clare's books, of whom Bobby groans, the second time Alison falls, 'Haven't you got over that silly habit yet?'[59]

It is noteworthy that in Blyton's school stories the silliest characters are the most feminine, who are portrayed as vain, affected, over-concerned with their appearance, antipathetic to all sports (especially swimming), and prone to crushes. The sensible characters are all sports-mad, and the tomboys like Bobby and Bill are extreme versions of the fun-loving, sporty, common-sense others.

Alison is always having crushes; the first mistress she falls for is Miss Quentin, the new drama teacher. She begins to copy her 'in everything, from her little tricks of speech to the way she did her hair. . . . She hung on every word the teacher said.'[60] Alison's goal is to take the chief part in the play Miss Quentin is producing, a part which Miss Quentin has given the class to understand will be hers as a reward for her slavish devotion. Then it emerges that another girl, Gladys, is a far better actress than Alison. Miss Quentin therefore switches her allegiance; and Alison, accidentally overhearing an exchange between the drama teacher and the other mistresses, is horrified to hear her say:

> Alison O'Sullivan is going to get a shock. The silly girl thinks she's good enough to play the lead in the second form play! She's been wearing herself out rehearsing – it will do her good to find she's not going to have the part!

Mam'zelle wishes that Alison would work as hard in her classes as in Miss Quentin's. 'Oh, well, she simply adores me,' Miss Quentin laughs. 'I can always make her type work. She'll do anything for a smile or a kind word from me.' Miss Quentin's callousness has no limit. 'Alison bores me to tears with her breathless, "Yes, Miss Quentin! No, Miss Quentin! Oh, *can* I, Miss Quentin!" '

Only Alison's form mistress, Miss Jenks, expresses concern for the effect of Miss Quentin's news on the girl. 'Shocks are not always good for rather weak characters, Miss Quentin,' she says gravely. 'I hope you will break your news kindly to poor Alison . . .' 'Oh, don't worry!' Miss Quentin assures her. 'I'll just pat her curly head and say a few kind words. She'll eat out of my hand. She always does.'[61]

Alison hears all this and is appalled. Blyton writes warmly of her sense of betrayal, her realisation of the teacher's shallowness and disloyalty, her pain and her sudden access of dignity. When Miss Quentin breaks the news in class Alison is able to take it calmly, and she snubs the teacher when she announces, expecting expressions of regret, that she is leaving the school. Blyton's sympathy is clearly with the girl, and Miss Quentin (unlike Miss Peters) is seen as unworthy of her admiration and trust.

A similar situation arises later when Alison, now in the fifth form, has a crush on her English mistress, Miss Willcocks. Again the teacher is shown to be a poser and a fraud and Alison is gently ridiculed by the others not just for her habit of hero-worshipping but because 'You never choose the right people to worship, either!'[62]

An instance of a 'right' person to worship is provided in *First Term at Malory Towers* (1946) where little Mary-Lou admires Darrell who has saved her from Gwendoline's cruel tricks. Darrell finds Mary-Lou's well-meant attentions irritating but Blyton remarks wisely:

> She could not see Mary-Lou's timid reaching-out for a friendship that might help her. Mary-Lou was so weak. She needed someone strong, and to her Darrell was the finest girl she had ever met.[63]

Darrell's impatience leads her to taunt Mary-Lou, to try to shame her into becoming a braver person. 'You've shamed her all right, but not in the way that will make her pluck up her courage,' warns her classmate Jean, who has more insight than Darrell. 'You've given her the kind of shame that puts people into despair!'[64]

Later, however, Mary-Lou's admiration for Darrell leads her to acts of bravery and thus to winning Darrell's friendship on more equal terms. By the end of her schooldays she is seen to have grown to her full stature and is well fitted for her chosen career – in nursing, where she will serve doctors and patients as she once served Darrell.[65]

Blyton is not against crushes as such; she sees them as potentially beneficial to both parties, provided the admired person exercises a good influence over the other and does not misuse her influence or betray her trust. Significantly, however, only her 'weak' characters feel the need to have crushes – though they may grow stronger from the experience, as both Alison and Mary-Lou do. As for the lesbian

160

threat, she seems quite unaware of it; or else, as the sexologists would probably hold, too naive to recognise it.

CELEBRATING HERO WORSHIP

Elsie Oxenham first deals with the subject of hero-worship in a novel of 1916, *The Tuck-Shop Girl*. Drusilla, who is aged 11, is one of several girls who look up to Barbara of the sixth form: 'she was at an age when she wanted not only friends of her own standing but an ideal.'[66] From this point on, for more than 20 years, hero-worship in its various manifestations is central to Oxenham's stories. It is taken for granted. Young people, both boys and girls, are shown to be naturally inclined to idealise a leader or older person. In *The Camp Mystery* (1932) we read that 'John has a pash for Peter, the boys' captain, and Gina adores Guly and Astrid, the head girls of St Mary's.'[67] Not only is this normal, in Oxenham's view, it also serves a useful function, provided the chosen person deserves admiration. When Gard introduces her cousin Ven to her friends:

> Their eyes were devouring her, too, with eager interest and delight. Two or three years older than any of them, she was just at the stage to win their admiration, if not even hero-worship; and, tall and straight and very good to look at, she was worthy of it.[68]

Note that looks as well as character are important!

Sometimes, however, the object is unworthy. In the two novels about Deb, published in 1929 and 1931, Oxenham offers an extended treatment of the crush. Chloe Marlowe 'our foremost music genius *and* tennis champion *and* a prefect' has a crowd of young admirers at St Margaret's.[69] New girl Deb, aged 15 but acting about 10, not having been to school before, has never observed the phenomenon. 'It seemed queer for one girl, among all those hundreds, to be a sort of queen. That was what those looks following Chloe implied.'[70]

But Deb, too, falls under her spell. 'You have got it badly,' her friend Pamela observes scornfully.[71] Her housemistress, Miss Willis, sees what is happening and issues a wise warning:

> The friends you choose during these first few days will make all the difference to you. Be very careful in your choice; don't be in too much hurry to make close friends.

She goes on:

> Above all, you must look up to someone; choose her carefully. Don't give your admiration and loyalty to anyone who is unworthy. Be sporting, and demand true sportsmanship in anyone you try to copy. It matters more than you think what sort of girl you choose for your ideal. . . . Don't follow one who could do an unkind or underhand action.[72]

Here, hero-worship is presented as an institution; just as Deb must choose friends from among her contemporaries, so she is also expected to choose a heroine. Unfortunately, her choice – Chloe – proves to be both unsporting and underhand. She gets Deb to pass a note to a boy at a neighbouring school. Caught, Deb takes the blame. Miss Willis guesses that she is shielding Chloe: 'Are you still going to give your allegiance and admiration where they are not deserved?'[73]

Later Deb confronts Chloe: why has she not taken her share of responsibility? Chloe says: 'Think how it would have let down our dorm!' 'It lets down South Dorm more to have a sneaky head,' Deb replies swiftly. Chloe asks her not to be so hard on her. 'Be sporting,' she begs. 'Sporting! You don't know what the word means,' is Deb's scornful reply. 'I know now that I've been soft all along.'[74]

Deb transfers her affection to Rosemary, her guide patrol-leader. 'I'd rather have Rosemary flung at me than Chloe,' is Pamela's comment. 'Deb being Deb, there must be somebody.'[75]

From this account we learn, first, that Oxenham does not simply accept the crush as a normal and natural part of growing up but regards it as important enough for the plot of an entire novel to turn upon it. And while she indicates that certain girls like Deb are more disposed to hero-worship than others, she also regards the phenomenon as a common and accepted feature of schoolgirl life. It constitutes an important learning experience, not only for the admirer but for the admired. In *Deb at School*, Chloe mends her ways as a result of Deb's influence. As Miss Willis tells Chloe:

You'll never have the same admiration again, but I believe you can still have the friendship, if you're worthy of it. Deb's very loyal. She hasn't ceased to care. . . . If you want her friendship I believe you can still win it, and it is well worth winning. But she must be able to respect you, Chloe.[76]

The truth of Miss Willis's pronouncement is borne out in the sequel to *Deb at School, Deb of Sea House* (1931). Chloe has been deposed from her position of dormitory head and Selina, the school's head girl, has replaced her. All the girls admire and look up to Selina – all but Deb. She is now distrustful of hero-worship: 'all that kind of thing's silly; being soft over seniors, I mean. I've tried it, and it didn't work.'[77] Worse still, two of the juniors look up to Deb herself, who 'loathes' their attentions. She tells one of them:

Don't be a sentimental infant! Being pals is all right, but being sloppy isn't; it's just soft. If you want to go on being pally with me, you'll have to cut out all the silly rot.[78]

Loyal to Chloe, who is having a bad time at school, Deb openly resents the usurper in her dormitory. The juniors copy her rebellious attitude and she finds herself in trouble for using her influence over them badly.

It is Selina herself, a very grown-up head girl of almost 19, who sets Deb right after taking her on Oxenham's favourite long tramp across the Downs. Deb asks how she can stop the juniors from wanting to do things for her. Selina asks: 'But why stop them?' Children, she argues, need help and guidance from older friends.

'I look on that sort of hero-worship as a force to be used, not refused,' Selina declares. 'Used well, it means an enormous thing, both for you and Hild.' Of course, Deb can decide not to use it. 'But you'll have lost for ever the chance of being perhaps the most important person in her life at Margaret's.'

She issues a caveat against 'sentimental silliness' which has no place in this arrangement: 'crush it as hard as you like. But make it quite plain that you're ready to be a grown-up friend and helper, and that you aren't freezing themselves off but only their silly ways.' After her experiences of the previous term, Deb is not sure she wants the responsibility. But the head girl is adamant she must accept it:

> Because in two years' time you'll be one of the leaders of Margaret's, if you learn how to manage girls and what use to make of their love for you. Because in another year you ought to be head of South Dorm, in two years captain of Sea, and perhaps some day head of Margaret's.[79]

Deb therefore is a girl who can choose to be a worthy heroine; the best leaders inevitably attract a following, and it is up to them to influence their admirers for the best.

> You'll always find juniors wanting to look up to some particular senior. It's natural; I see nothing wrong in it. It's a part of their school life. Anyway, it's no use blaming them. They have to do it, and they will do it, whatever we say.

164

This is a far cry from Brent-Dyer's admonitions against crushes and an even further one from the sex reformers'. Oxenham is perfectly clear that, in her view, there is nothing wrong with hero-worship and that even if you do try to stamp on it, 'they will do it, whatever we say'.

INSTITUTIONALISING INFLUENCE

It is plain that Oxenham supports those school and social organisations which institutionalise 'influence'. The trappings of rank impress quite as much as the personal qualities of leadership that go to make school prefects, house captains, dormitory heads and patrol leaders suitable objects of admiration. Oxenham's attitude to leadership is not far removed from her attitude to class, in that she depicts the upper classes as having a responsibility to the lower, who in turn look up to them.

Strong visual elements enhance the appeal of a heroine, and a romantic setting is always an important aspect for Oxenham. Naturally rank and appearance alone are not sufficient grounds for inspiring devotion but, as with wealth and class, they sometimes seem so. Only Oxenham's skill in conveying a difficult but still attractive personality allows us to believe that Mary Devine's crush on Joy Shirley does not depend merely on the latter's riches and beauty.

Mary is one of several Oxenham's adult characters who fall for other women in this way. Her admiration for Joy and Jen, who are both some years younger than herself, is based on a mixture of gratitude and awe. They have so much, she so little. They introduce her to their wider world (in *The Abbey Girls Again*, 1924) and thereby enrich her life. She loves them passionately in return. 'What a lot Mary thinks of these two, Jen and Joy!' her cousin Ruth muses. 'She hardly takes her eyes off them. I wonder if they're good enough? She worships the ground they tread on!'[80]

For the Abbey girls, the obligation both feel towards Mary

mingles *noblesse oblige* with the influence that leaders feel towards their admirers. But Joy inevitably lets Mary down, because for all her good points, Joy has character flaws which are never far from the surface. Mary has to come to terms with this, and does, rising above her disappointment to learn to love Joy all the more because she now loves her realistically.

> I had loved Joy Shirley so, for a year. She had been so good to me. I'd thought her perfect. . . . That night, and for some days afterwards, I felt as if I'd lost her. . . . I found after a while that I was wrong. All I had lost was my picture of her. I still loved the real Joy, although she had faults.[81]

Eventually Mary matures to take her rightful place as equal companion and even adviser to the younger women.

This relationship can be contrasted with that of two other adults, Eve and Fran, in *The Troubles of Tazy* (1926), one of the Swiss books. The language the author uses to characterise it gives us a clue to her attitude; Tazy warns Ven that Eve is likely to 'get up a rave' for her.

> She's always raving about somebody; it lasts for some time, and then she finds some new idol. She's had it for me, but, of course, I soon choked her off. She's quite likely to fix on you, because you're the kind she admires.

> What kind is that?

> Oh, energetic and business-like, and able to do things! The exact opposite of herself, of course. I suppose we all look up to our opposites.[82]

In fact, Eve fixes on Ven's friend Fran, the most sympathetic in the group of young women, who takes an interest in her. Tazy thinks the crush is 'infantile' but Ven says 'Better to look up to Fran than to nothing.' The inference is that Eve is too weak a character to stand alone. 'She's found somebody who's stronger and better, and older in common-sense than she is . . . [I]t's going to be the making of her, if Fran has patience and puts up with her.'[83]

Fran herself doesn't much care for the role she has been thrust into; but, we are told,

> she's leaving her alone and hoping she'll grow out of it. In the meantime she tries to keep her as sensible as she can, and never lets her be sentimental or soft.[84]

Here is the old distinction between 'sentimental softness', which is wrong (though in what way, and why, we are never told) and hero-worship, which can be good. The solution Oxenham finds for Eve, not a character who interests her very much, does not in the end depend on Fran. Instead Eve is provided with a baby to bring up (not her own: she isn't married). It doesn't seem to occur to Oxenham that having someone depend on you does not fulfil one's own dependency needs; many women, however, have been conned into thinking that babies will do just that, and Oxenham always tended to take the traditional line on matters of which she had no personal experience, such as marriage and motherhood. Having a dependant, and work to do, makes Eve grow up and be sensible; now she has no time for silly raves.

Retreat into family relationships became increasingly common as the 1930s progressed as a consequence of the lesbian witchhunt which followed the prosecution of *The Well of Loneliness* in 1928. Certainly Oxenham focuses increasingly on heterosexual relationships in the 1930s, and from the 1940s, very little is said about crushes and hero-worship; she never again builds a novel around these themes.

THE REAL THING

The shift, if reading through the books in chronological order, is so gradual as to be almost imperceptible. But if one is to examine a series such as the Abbey books, produced at the rate of about one a year for 40 years, the difference between the volumes of the decade 1920–29 and those written towards the end of Oxenham's life, in the 1940s and 1950s, is very obvious. To dip into the early stories of this series is to be transported into a world where women's love for women is openly and unselfconsciously avowed on almost every page.

The Abbey books, though clearly intended for the juvenile market, are only loosely linked to the school the girls attended and its customs (in particular, country-dancing and the annual crowning of a May Queen). They really focus on the relations between the various female characters, even after they have left school. Though individuals fall in love with men and marry, these events are seen not as ends in themselves but in terms of their effect upon their women friends.

A necessary lesson the women must learn is that if they really love their friends, they must take second place to male suitors and husbands. Maidlin has always adored Joy, who 'adopted' her, though there are only seven years between them. Now Joy is going to be married.

> She's up against a tragedy, if she hasn't realised that Lady Marchwood's marriage would make a difference. I don't mean necessarily a difference in her feeling for Maidie; it probably won't. But a husband must come first. If Maidie is expecting still to be first with Lady Marchwood, she'll break her heart.[85]

Friendship is seen in terms of mutual support and selfless giving way to the 'real thing': heterosexual love and marriage.

A fortnight ago, Joy had not known she loved Andrew Marchwood; now he was her man, and she was ready to go across the world with him. And her friends who had seen her since her engagement knew that restless Joy was satisfied at last; she had found something for want of which her life had till now been incomplete.[86]

Theoretically, then, the books profess to prioritise heterosexual romance and marriage over friendship. Yet when we read them, we get a different message. This is partly because Oxenham was never very convincing in her attempts to portray men or heterosexual love. More significantly, she was extremely acute at describing a whole range of emotions between women.

When Rosamund seeks to leave the Hall to open a shop with her young aunts-by-marriage, Maidlin wonders anxiously: 'Is Ros going to like these girls better than us?' Joy eventually comes to realise: 'We shall really keep Ros more closely if she goes, feeling we're backing her up, than if we keep her here unwillingly.'[87]

Friends want what is best for each other: Jen admonishes Maidlin, 'You care more that Joy should love you as you wish than that Joy should be happy and have what is best for herself.'[88]

In the 1920s women's loyalty to other women was sufficiently important a subject to absorb Oxenham's sympathetic pen through page after agonising page.

I ought to be thinking about Jen. I've been sorry for her all through, and I've wanted to help her; but I've been thinking about myself, what *I* wanted, how *I* felt. Ann forgot all about herself, and thought only of helping Jen. But almost from the first I was thinking how I'd failed her and how awful it was; and it made me still less able to help . . . I was hardly any use; I just collapsed like a baby – and it was because I was so much upset because she turned from me to Ann . . . [89]

To almost all the major characters (all but Mary and, from the later volumes, Rachel), the prize of marriage is granted. Mary, however, like Oxenham herself a writer of girls' school stories, is made to understand the nature and pitfalls of friendship better, perhaps, than any of the other Abbey women. She exemplifies above all the maxim that true friendship means self-denial. Mary's love for Jen and Joy constitutes the principal subject-matter of three or four books, but her timely intervention secures the marriage of both; and when Kenneth enlists her aid in his courtship of Jen, Oxenham comments without intending irony, 'How was she to give advice on love affairs, she who had dreamt of knights and heroes but had never known love in real life?'[90]

This *is* ironic, for Mary's experience of love comes across far more truthfully and memorably than Oxenham's feeble attempts at depicting heterosexual emotion. Mary has been rescued from a dull and potentially dangerous life of office work and unhealthy daydreams by the glamorous Joy and Jen. Joy and Jen become vitally important to her, so much so that when Jen announces she won't be in London all spring, Mary is devastated.

> 'Not – in London?' Mary looked at her with such blank dismay in her face that Jen's heart smote her suddenly. She had never realised till that moment how much she had counted for in Mary's new life. . . . [Mary], too, had not realised how much she depended on Jen's help, on her visits, on the constant sight of her at classes. . . . It was as if Hyde Park or St Paul's had suddenly announced it was leaving London. The centre of everything would be gone if Jen were not in town.[91]

When the Abbey girls marry, their husbands are bitterly resented by the unmarried women for taking their friends away. When Joy marries for the first time, in *Queen of the Abbey Girls* (1926), Jen moans: 'I daren't face the thought that we've really lost Joy; it doesn't bear thinking about.'[92]

And when Joy returns from her honeymoon leaving her husband game-shooting in Africa, Rosamund declares: 'It's ripping to have Joy come back alone. We like Andrew, of course; but I'm quite content to have him in East Africa.'[93] So, clearly, is Oxenham, who contrives to have him murdered on safari by some 'wild natives' so that Joy may be left free to bring up twin daughters unencumbered by a man, with the help of her women friends.

Another clue to Oxenham's real feelings on the subject of love lies in her unselfconscious descriptions of individuals and groups of women, which often in these books reveal a sensuous pleasure in women's bodies. Consider, for instance, Joan's appreciation of Madam's 'perfect poise and balance' in *The Abbey Girls Go Back To School* (1922): 'her eyes followed Madam, when presently she came down from her perch to demonstrate a movement, with hungry eager delight.'[94]

'Hungry' and 'eager' are favourite words of Oxenham in this context.

Jen's eager eyes widened in delight when Rhoda returned, followed up the drive by a tall, sunny-faced girl in khaki tunic and breeches and big boots, a shady hat covering her yellow hair, which was tied in a bunch of curls behind. Rena was tanned and healthy and straight, strong with a year's work in the moorland garden at Rocklands, and very pleasant to look at. Her gardening outfit was neat and useful, and suited her, and she looked ready for tramping the heather, digging, mowing, tennis, or morris dancing at a moment's notice.

She touched her hat in a boyish salute, as she came up to the couch. Jen stretched out her hands with an eager cry . . . [95]

In 1925, when the novel from which this extract was taken – *Jen of the Abbey School* – was published, Oxenham felt quite free to write appreciatively of women's pleasure in each other's appearance, even – or, perhaps, especially – where the woman described is turned out in trousers and proficient in masculine activities. Ten years later, she seems not to have felt so free to do so, for fear of being accused of writing about sexual perversion, or of herself being 'latently homosexual'.

THE DEATH OF ROMANTIC FRIENDSHIP

When the eleventh book in the series *The Abbey Girls Play Up* appeared in 1930, the characters had moved on a few years. The focus is now very much more domestic: Joan, Joy and Jen all have young families, and a new and even less convincing approach to heterosexual romance is in evidence. Jen introduces Maribel to her husband's cousin and a relationship develops which seems to be entirely based on meaningful looks: 'Mike Marchwood's eyes had been saying something very emphatic, which he might not put into words.' Maribel discusses the phenomenon with her chum, Rosalind, but the subject embarrasses them: 'Oh, I say, Bel, don't let's be idiots! Come and play tennis, and forget all this tosh!' Tosh it may be, but Maribel is engaged by the end of the book.[96]

Already in *The Abbey Girls at Home* (1929) there are signs of the changed approach. Like its predecessors, this book is mainly about love between women. There is plenty of kissing and pages of discussion about feelings: 'I never knew how much I cared about you till I thought you cared more for Betty than for me,' Joy (now widowed) tells Jen (now married). But in this book first Joy and then Mary and Jen realise they are no longer obsessed with folk-dancing. 'At present I feel I've come up against real things too sharply ever to go back to a play thing like country-dancing,' declares Joy.

Mary takes up the theme.

The dancing is all right. It's beautiful, and the music is jolly; the figures are fascinating, and it's a splendidly healthy recreation, some way to let oneself go. . . . But it *is* play. And there are more important things, *real* things.

172

Jen, who is expecting her first baby (though the first we know of this is when it arrives), agrees.

> I used to think country-dancing came first of everything. You've shown me its right place . . . I think perhaps there are adventures ahead of me that are worth-while![97]

Throughout the 1920s the members and activities of the English Folk Dance Society were of central importance to Oxenham; they feature in almost all her novels. But by the end of the decade she seems to have come to feel that her attitude to them was no longer appropriate. It is clear that the Society represented more to her than just a place to enjoy healthy exercise with pleasantly like-minded companions. This may be a far-fetched theory, but I wonder if we can read 'country-dancing' as a symbol for women's friendships? And is it too much of a coincidence that her change in attitude is expressed in a book she was writing in 1928 – the year of the trial of *The Well of Loneliness*?

Take, for example, the ingenuous introduction to Norah and Con in *The Abbey Girls Win Through* (1928):

> They were a recognised couple. Con, who sold gloves in a big West-End establishment, was the wife and home-maker; Norah, the typist, was the husband, who planned little pleasure-trips and kept the accounts and took Con to the pictures.[98]

Descriptions such as these caused critics great amusement in the 1950s and afterwards. How could Oxenham have been so naive – or so explicit? But these words were written before *The Well of Loneliness* trial, before the lesbian scare had made women in couples into objects of suspicion and disgust. I would argue that Oxenham was simply describing a phenomenon which she and her readers were familiar with, which they saw all about them in the male-depleted generation after the First World War and about which they thought nothing.

HETEROSEXUALITY'S TRIUMPH

From the 1930s onwards there is an ever declining ration of expressed love between women, and the books make much more of a feature of heterosexual romance, marriage and motherhood. Perhaps because it was now clear that only adolescent women could safely indulge strong feelings for one another, Oxenham made the interesting decision in 1938 to revert to the pre-marriage years of her original characters. She produced seven books which filled in gaps in the first sequence. The title of the first of these – *Schooldays at the Abbey* – is revealing of the changed approach: though the books continued to be about women's friendships, the relationships described were reduced to the level of schoolgirl passions. Meanwhile, heterosexual love was idealised beyond belief. Here is Joan, aged 18, in *Schooldays at the Abbey* (1938): 'It must be a wonderful thing. I don't suppose it will ever happen to me, but it must be the happiest thing in the world.'[99] (Contrast Jen in *The Abbey Girls in Town* [1925]: 'It's that man. Being in love's a fearful disease. I hope I never catch it.')[100]

In *Tomboys at the Abbey* (1957) which, though written nearly 20 years after *Schooldays at the Abbey*, depicts Joan as only a year older, she expands upon the theme:

> I don't know anything about being in love; I've had no experience. But – I've always imagined that it was a feeling for which one would give up everything and be glad to do it. That if I fell in love, for instance, I'd be willing to go away with – him! – and leave Mother to Joy's tender mercies, and leave my Abbey, that I love so much. . . . And that if I wasn't willing to leave everything, I shouldn't really be in love and it wouldn't be worth while getting married.[101]

(Contrast Jen in *The Abbey Girls Go Back To School* [1922]: 'Isn't this awful? Are Joan and Cicely going to think about

174

these men all the time?'[102] Or Joy, after Joan is married, in *The Abbey Girls Again* [1924]: 'I say it must be such a nuisance having a man round all the time.')[103]

Even the friendships of girlhood, formerly self-sufficient, now look beyond the all-female world. Take the portrayal of 13-year-old Jen and her chum, Jack. We remember the headmistress's laughing acceptance of their 'marriage' in *Girls of the Abbey School* (1921). When Oxenham returned to fill in the gaps in the series from 1938, at first sight the 'marriage' is unchanged:

> Jack's black hair was closely cropped. She was smaller than Jen, and thin and slight, very boyish in her looks and movements. She had been Jen's chum and adopted partner since Jen's first day at school.[104]

But Oxenham was now writing in a different social climate, as we discover when we accompany the girls on their attempt to break into Marchwood Manor next door to the Abbey. The Manor has been lying empty for years because the owners, a dowager and her three unmarried sons, live elsewhere. Jen and Jack have (they believe) very good reasons for breaking in; they want to see if a locket in Jen's possession, found on Abbey territory, belongs to the Marchwood family, so they are looking for portraits of female ancestors kept at the Manor. As they approach the house, Jack is moved to comment that the bachelor attitude of the current generation of Marchwood men is very unsporting: 'How are we girls ever going to get husbands?'

'First time I've heard you say you wanted one!' Jen retorts.

'I don't. It would cut short my career; I'm going in for medicine,' Jack replies. 'But I'd like to see you safely off my hands.'

She goes on:

> You're cut out for getting married, and being properly

domesticated! You'd take care of your husband and house and family beautifully. Of course, you'd boss the lot . . .

Jen does not argue with her. When she muses that she'd like to see the Manor lived in, 'with a jolly family, mostly boys, playing in the garden,'[105] we readers are in the privileged position of knowing that she is the very person who is going to provide all this – by marrying Kenneth Marchwood, as she does in *The Abbey Girls Win Through* (1928), and having nine children, six of them boys.

Oxenham has not changed her story; she has simply changed the focus. Into the world of women has entered a new focus – on men, marriage and motherhood – that was never there in the early books.

The second-generation novels, written at the same time as the retrospective ones after 1938, are very poor. *Song of the Abbey* (1954) resurrects Carry Carter, Joy's antagonist from the very first Abbey book, now 'about thirty-seven, unmarried [clearly intended as a criticism], smart and lively', who spends her life at bridge-parties, dances, and the theatre. To avenge herself upon the school, which 20 years before chose Joy instead of Carry as May Queen, she leads the new Queen astray by taking her to the ballet against her aunt's wishes.[106] Where now is the sisterhood of yesteryear?

If the early Abbey books were about women's friendships, the later ones are about marriage, pure and simple. Nanta has scarcely left school before her thoughts turn to the subject:

But now she was nineteen, and at Kentisbury and at the Abbey she had seen many happily married couples; her mind had grown and broadened and she thought more deeply.[107]

Needless to state, there are no unhappily married couples in the Abbey books.[108] Even Mary, the only spinster among the first generation of Abbey women, and the one who may well have stood for Oxenham's own experiences and aspirations, becomes a mouthpiece for the party line. World-famous ballerina Damaris gives up her career to marry. 'Other people can dance, but only Damaris can marry Brian,' says Mary, incredibly. 'Other people don't dance as she does,' Nanta quite rightly objects. 'You do think she ought to give it up, Mary-Dorothy?' 'To be married – yes, Nanta, I do.'[109]

These books of the 1950s were products of the postwar cult of domesticity, when women were under renewed pressure to return to the home and become full-time housewives and mothers. *Two Queens at the Abbey* (1959), the last in the series, is even more preposterous. With, perhaps, a sense that she had to tie up all loose ends before she died, Oxenham launched every character into frenzied heterosexual activity. Nanta, aged 19, marries and falls pregnant. Littlejan, aged 19, marries and has a baby. Rosamund has her seventh child, Jen her ninth. Jansy, Joan's daughter, talks of marrying Dickon, Cicely's son; both are aged 16. When good old understanding Mary prepares supper for Littlejan (Queen Marigold) whose husband has just gone off to the Antarctic, she remarks, apparently without innuendo, that 'Marigold is hungry for more than sandwiches to-night.'[110] Note that Oxenham still prefers to push the men off-stage so that the action can centre on the women. But they still had to *appear* to focus on the men. In 1924 Mary had been 'hungry' for a sight of Jen!

KILLING OFF THE SCHOOLGIRL STORY

As a source of attitudes to women's friendships over 40 years, the Abbey books are the most revealing of all the school stories under discussion in this book. They show how in the 1920s school story writers had a unique freedom to explore all the dimensions of women's love for women. Not all of them availed themselves of this freedom; both Dorita Fairlie Bruce and Elinor Brent-Dyer clearly felt more inhibited right from the start of their writing careers in this decade. As teachers, these two were probably more *au fait* with modern psychological ideas at an earlier period than either Elsie Oxenham, who remained apparently isolated in her old-fashioned mind-set for much longer, or Enid Blyton, who only wrote for younger children and who has been accused of never growing up herself. As the years passed, however, this freedom was progressively curtailed, with writers becoming ever more confused and restricted by the new heterosexual demands and the negative image of lesbianism. In later decades critics were to look back and sneer at their naivity, or amuse themselves by exposing (or denying) the homosexual tendencies of schoolgirl heroines and their creators.

During the period in which the girls' school story flourished, lesbianism was progressively redefined. From a deviant sexuality caused by abnormal genetic or social development it was extended to encompass all intimate relationships between women, whether explicitly sexual or not (in which case they were categorised as 'latent' or 'unconscious'). This was represented as a newly discovered scientific *fact*, not the man-made invention that it was. A new equation sank into the public mind: close friendships between women equalled lesbianism equalled sexual perversion.

Mary Cadogan and Patricia Craig seize upon the many instances in which Oxenham's heroines share a bed as evidence that the women's intimacy is (however unconsciously) *not* 'healthy' or 'normal'.[111] After the Second World War, sleeping together became a synonym for sexual activity, but it is anachronistic to impose this idea on the social mores of the 1920s. At that time, for Elsie Oxenham and her public, sharing a bed with a girlfriend was a perfectly acceptable sleeping arrangement. When Jen and Jack 'tuck in' together, what is revealed is not unconscious perversion but a very conscious love for one's women friend which in 1923 was fine and after 1928 was increasingly seen as abnormal and unhealthy, representing a female intimacy which was too threatening to a patriarchal society to be allowed to continue.

178

Women were supposed to be putting their energies into men. As the second wave of feminism has shown, marriage, and – since the 'sexual revolution' of the 1960s – heterosexual relationships generally, have been a means by which individual men have been able to keep individual women under their personal control. Hence the sustained attack throughout most of the twentieth century on relationships between women, which, being outside men's control, do not help to sustain patriarchal power.

Censorship of schoolgirl stories was inevitable. From the late 1950s to the early 1970s a handful of Abbey books were reprinted in cheap, condensed editions. Oxenham's prose, often full of tautology, can take a bit of blue-pencilling, but it is not insignificant that the portions excised were frequently the passionate and, to sophisticated eyes, sexually suggestive scenes between women. In the bowdlerised version of *The New Abbey Girls* (1959), Jen no longer suggests that Joy should sleep with Maidlin.[112]

What the Abbey books suffered was also endured by many other school stories. Elinor Brent-Dyer was never so sentimental but even her early Chalet School stories were abridged along similar lines when they appeared in paperback at the end of the 1960s.[113] *Prefects of the Chalet School*, published posthumously in 1970, rushes its heroine Len Maynard into a premature engagement while still head girl. Dorita Fairlie Bruce's last three novels concerned young girls at school, but the romances for young women published immediately before, all four of them, had plots which worked their way inexorably towards love and marriage. And if Enid Blyton avoided this, it was only because she never took her heroines past their schooldays.

By the mid–1970s the Abbey books, along with the majority of schoolgirl stories, had disappeared from the publishers' lists. Readers were told there was 'no demand'. The truth was, however, that these critics had condemned them to death, the later books ostensibly for being ostensibly for being appallingly written (which they often were), the early ones for lack of 'relevance' and 'social realism'. What this meant was that they were *not heterosexual enough*, or, rather, that they were too positive about women's friendship and love for each other.

The destruction of the schoolgirl story is a major piece of evidence for the imposition of compulsory heterosexuality in twentieth-century Britain. The schoolgirl story's resurrection in the 1980s and 1990s is testimony both to the contemporary women's movement – which taught us once again to value women – and to the enduring appeal of these novels for girls and women who want an alternative vision to the patriarchal world we live in.

7 Training to be Wives and Mothers

Whether or not she sought a career, a girl was always seen to be a potential wife and mother. She was therefore exposed to endless debates about the purpose of her education. At different times, different theories dominated. The inspiration for the late Victorian High Schools and public schools for middle-class girls was largely academic, to provide the training which might lead to a professional job, or at least to a more informed and cultured domestic life – something more than 'the button-sewing, soup-making, man-pleasing mission of a woman', as Marie Grey put it.[1] By the 1920s there was a strong feeling in conservative quarters that the academic emphasis had 'gone too far'. Educators colluded with the government's back-to-the-home campaign against working women who they claimed had enjoyed too much independence during the War. Girls' schooling was re-designed to focus more on domestic skills. Even so, many headmistresses resisted, preferring to retain the more masculine curriculum which gave girls the chance to compete on equal terms with boys.

The same happened after the Second World War. John Newsom, author of *The Education of Girls* (1948) and *Half Our Future* (1963), depicted 'woman's mission' as home-making, and wanted education related to 'biological and social function'. Both the Newsom Report and the Crowther Report, *15–18* (1959), sought to give prominence to topics such as personal relationships, dress and appearance in girls' education, at a time when industry was calling on the talents of increasing numbers of married women. Newsom's voice was among the last to call for a scientific approach to housework, a movement which had begun before the First World War and, for some time, enjoyed much popular and official success.[2]

But in the 1960s married women moved into the workforce in droves. That is not to say that they abandoned responsibility for housework and childcare; they became, instead, people with *two* jobs. Their situation was a far cry from that of the middle-class girls of the 1920s or 1930s who did not need to work.

The change in attitudes to women's work and the types of jobs that were open to middle-class girls after leaving school is faithfully recorded in long series of school stories such as the Chalet School books. Brent-Dyer's heroine Jo, for example, leaves school in a book published in 1935 with no expectation of ever working for a living. That she makes a career as a writer, and pursues it even through marriage and motherhood, is incidental; it is not work that she trained for, or needed to do for the money. Yet when her triplet daughters leave school (in a book published in 1970) there is no question but that all three are headed for university and professional careers.

THE RISE OF THE DOMESTIC SCIENCE MOVEMENT

For the young women whose destiny, once schooldays were over, was simply to 'go home', what relevant training did the school provide? In the early days, practically none. The new Victorian schools for middle-class girls were often so concerned to bring their students up to the academic standard of boys that there was no time for education in domestic or social skills. It was assumed that the girls' mothers would provide the latter, while the former would be unnecessary in homes staffed by domestic servants. Practical subjects were in any case associated with elementary and charity schools, where cooking, sewing, cleaning and laundry work played an ever more important role in the curriculum of working-class girls from the 1870s onwards as middle-class advisers sought to turn them into better wives, mothers and, especially, servants for themselves.[3]

Somewhere around the turn of the century this emphasis on the acquisition of practical domestic skills began to be extended to middle-class girls. There are many possible reasons for the shift. The Boer War and, later, the First World War provided the ruling class with an opportunity to note the poor physical condition of its country's manhood. The government's Report on Physical Deterioration (1904) blamed mothers for this as for the high rate of infant mortality; and though the accusations were largely levelled at the working class, the usual generalisations about women's nature and role enabled campaigners to broaden their call for better education in domestic and maternal skills to include middle-class girls. The establishment of state secondary schools under the Education Act of 1902 helped to blur the class distinction between the working-class children who populated the Board schools and the middle class who were almost wholly privately educated, for now some of the former were going on to post-elementary education while some of the latter attended the state secondary schools alongside them. In these schools housewifery became a compulsory subject for girls in 1905. Not all headmistresses welcomed it. Many considered it suitable only for the less intelligent girls or those not intending to take up a career. If the point of secondary education was to fit its students for the professions, then domestic science was often seen as a waste of time and energy.

There were broadly two schools of thought among those who supported the extension of domestic training to all schoolgirls. The eugenists believed that women's only real role in society was motherhood. True conservatives, they held that the drive towards maternity was instinctive but needed to be shaped and trained to meet society's needs. Environmentalists, on the other hand, argued that women's inadequate domestic and maternal skills were due to social deprivation: material, medical, and educational. While the latter group worked to improve the first two factors through legal and practical reforms, they joined with the eugenists to call for training in housewifery and childcare skills. For the eugenists, the push towards 'racial purity' meant particular emphasis on middle-class girls, in their view the most desirable potential mothers. As far as the environmentalists were concerned, educated middle-class women were seen to be able to exercise a beneficial influence on working-class women in their own households (that is, their servants). The increased difficulty in obtaining domestic servants after the First World War gave added impetus to their mission, since it appeared likely that greater numbers of middle-class women would have little or no domestic assistance in the future.[4]

It seems inescapable that the move to impose domestic training on all girls was also an anti-feminist gesture, fuelled by the reaction to women's political, economic and educational gains of the later years of the nineteenth century and early years of the twentieth. Within two decades of the universities' first opening their doors to women, the fair sex had shown that it could perform as well as men in the highest examinations, and by 1900 it was no longer possible to say that the female brain was intellectually inferior to the male (though it was still accused of being less creative, less original, less rational, etc.). Women's history abounds in examples of progress won by women which is almost immediately met by men changing the rules, shifting the goal posts to make it harder for women to compete. See, for example, the history of women's entry into the medical profession.[5] The attempt to impose domestic training on the entire female school population, without adding anything extra to the male curriculum, is another instance. Girls who were often obliged to spend time at home on such activities were now also forced to devote precious school hours to them, while boys remained free both at home and at school to concentrate on getting ahead in their academic studies. Add to that the social and psychological pressure on girls to focus on marriage and motherhood as a career rather than on preparing for a well-paid job, and the patriarchal power structure is guaranteed to reproduce itself very nicely for generations to come.

THE FEMINIST REACTION

The need for domestic training for girls came to be accepted and endorsed by a high proportion of the feminists and female educators in the early part of the twentieth century. It was the older generation, schooled in Emily Davies' insistence on the same curriculum and exams as boys', who resisted longest and hardest; they recognised that if girls had to spend time on domestic studies at school they would have less time for academic work and less chance of competing with men in the workplace. For this reason, if domestic science was offered in their schools, it was either confined to a separate, lower stream (as at Cheltenham Ladies' College) or entirely theoretical, as at Miss Buss' North London Collegiate School, where 'there was neither kitchen nor laundry at our disposal, and I darkly suspected that our teachers had never entered such places.'[6] As a student there in the 1880s, Molly Hughes learned to plan elaborate meals for a family of seven, but not to produce them, and in later years was critical of this aspect of her education. Writing in the 1940s, now a retired school inspector, she observed:

To be deeply pleasing to a husband, and widely pleasing to other men, seems to me as good an ideal as a woman can have. But instead of facing squarely the real needs of future wives and mothers, as the vast majority of girls were to be, Miss Buss seized the tempting instrument at her hand – the stimulus to mental ambition afforded by outside examinations. . . . And thus, for better or worse, the education of girls became a feeble imitation of what the boys were doing . . . [7]

Hughes is an example of someone educated according to the old feminist ideals – the desire to achieve academic and professional equality with men – who came to reject them in favour of a view of woman as equal but different, by virtue of her role as wife and mother. Although she probably owed her own professional status to the feminist campaigns which opened up senior posts to women, she still saw herself as a wife and mother, first and foremost.

In 1911 the Association of Head Mistresses passed a resolution at its Annual Conference that 'Training in Domestic Arts should supplement and not replace the general subjects of a liberal education . . . for girls.'[8] This left the individual headmistress free to confine domestic science teaching to the less academic or non-vocational streams or to ignore it altogether. In some schools this attitude persisted for decades. As Lucy Kinlock wrote, in a novel based on her own childhood (*A World Within a School*, 1937):

Just across the playground was Household Science, where the girls who were not keen about academic careers, exchanged the pen for the delights of domesticity. Nora had already received the distinct impression that this House did not rate very high in public opinion.[9]

Others were inclined to accept eugenic arguments, like Margaret A Gillibrand, headmistress of Haberdashers Aske's Girls' School in London.

Schools that omit all instruction in the preparation for home life, or who, worse still, treat such preparation with hurtful contempt, may, and do, produce fine scholars. But they are doing very little to help our national life, because they are doing nothing to make our girls builders of homes and makers of men.[10]

Sara Burstall at Manchester High School for Girls noted that 'The teaching of cookery and the domestic arts to girls of every class is advocated on national grounds, as is the teaching of military drill and marksmanship to boys'.

> [This proposition] has a scientific, biological basis, the idea that there are specialised functions in practical life for which the sexes should be separately prepared in the school – functions so basic in national existence that the State is not safe unless its young people are specially trained to fulfil them efficiently. It is the natural duty of a man to defend his country in war, and he must be trained as a boy for this natural and inevitable duty; it is the natural duty of a woman to do housework, and she must learn it at school. There is something to be said for this view . . . [11]

By lending her support to this attitude, Burstall might seem to have departed from any feminist views she might once have had on the subject of girls' education. But there *was* a feminist camp which emerged after the First World War which supported domestic education for girls, not on pseudo-scientific grounds like these but in recognition of the practical realities of life. While old-style feminists such as Lady Rhondda and the women who worked on *Time and Tide* and in the Six Point Group fought for equal rights for women with men, the 'new' feminists (of whom Eleanor Rathbone was perhaps the most distinguished) argued for the recognition and special treatment of women's particular position as wife and mother. They campaigned for family allowances to be paid to women, while equal-rights feminists went for equal pay.[12]

Clearly, there were many issues on which both groups were in accord, but domestic science teaching was probably not one of them. Those active women on *Time and Tide* had

187

little interest in housewifery; Vera Brittain recorded that when she and Winifred Holtby moved from their Bloomsbury flat to a spacious Maida Vale apartment, their sole object was 'to acquire space for a housekeeper who would shoulder all domestic obligations, and leave us more time for our ever-increasing work.'[13]

The old feminists' disdain for domestic labour was matched by the new feminists' efforts to have that labour valued and rewarded. They contended that women's work in the home was both socially and economically essential and that as a result the women who did it were entitled to their fair share of society's wealth. This recognition of the importance of domestic work went hand in hand with efforts to give it greater status. The skills involved in housework and childcare were pointed out and their 'scientific' basis emphasised. From here it was but a small step to endorsing domestic education for girls; for if their occupation as adults was to be appreciated as skilled and scientific, it surely required training like any other skilled job. So the dissemination of domestic science knowledge among schoolgirls came on to the feminist agenda and was seen by some (but by no means all) of the leaders of the women's movement as a means of raising the status of women, by raising the status of their work.

AN IDEA THAT FAILED

This was an ingenious idea, but it failed. The status of domestic work may well have risen briefly in the interwar years but it has plummeted since the Second World War and stands now were it did before, at the bottom of the occupational ladder. Gillian Avery recently suggested (hopefully) that 'the inclusion of home economics as a subject at A-level has given it a new status',[14] but no one seriously equates home economics with A levels in more 'academic' subjects, and housework and childcare are still not recognised as work in most quarters – they are certainly not remunerated as such.

There are two reasons why the campaign to upgrade domestic education failed. The most important is that it was only ever seen as women's work. Women's work in a patriarchal society, however skilled in reality, has always been valued as inferior to men's. The other reason is that the move towards co-education and away from women-only studies that gathered momentum in the 1960s has resulted in the steady infiltration of male students and teachers into fields formerly reserved for women, together with the adaptation and transformation of courses intended for women into courses designed to attract both sexes. The upgraded, 'scientific' domestic science was converted into courses in nutrition, craft, food science, and so on; men came to teach the classes, male students took them; and as the years went by, the field came to look less and less like the work that women continued to do in the home, and more and more like any other 'scientific' or technical study dominated by men. Ultimately, it ceased to bear any resemblance to the old domestic science at all.[15]

The belief that domestic studies lent themselves to serious academic work was not held merely by a few cranks or by an unthinking mass who had been hoodwinked by the pseudo-scientific arguments of eugenics. King's College for Women – later Queen Elizabeth College of the University of London – offered degrees in Household and Social Science from 1920 to 1968. The case was arguable, and the results showed, that such endeavours produced important work in areas such as nutrition and social welfare which influenced not only government policy but also the health and well-being of individuals.[16]

The attempt to elevate domestic science to the level of higher education forced public recognition of the value of women's domestic contribution to the social and economic needs of the community. However patronisingly it might be viewed in practice, with the possible implication that women who did not have the benefit of a degree in the subject must be inadequate housekeepers and mothers, at least the discipline remained largely in women's control and provided an acceptable route for women to achieve professional jobs when other scientific and technical strongholds were much more difficult to break into. With the submerging of higher studies in domestic science into the male-dominated general science of the universities, this unique feminine realm was lost.

Its effects were nevertheless felt for some time afterwards. The Education Act of 1944 set up a tripartite system of secondary schools, ostensibly enjoying 'parity of esteem', of which the 'technical' occupied the middle place between the favoured grammar and the despised secondary modern. Prior to this technical schools, though favoured by many industrialists, had been unpopular with the educational authorities whose object was to extend the liberal studies approach of the middle-class schools to increasing numbers of children of all classes. The Spens Report on Secondary Education (1938) broke new ground by presenting the technical school as suitable for children 'whose interests and abilities lie markedly in the field of applied science or applied art'.[17] The fact that for girls, 'technical' meant schools specialising in domestic science, must be attributed to the strength of the movement to promote domestic science teaching, then in its heyday.

The idea of the technical school never really prospered, with numbers declining steadily in the 1950s and 1960s. But many of its functions spilled over into the grammar and secondary modern schools; and with the coming of the comprehensive school, technical subjects were extended to all – at first, of course, along traditional sex lines. This meant that domestic science training was available to all girls, later to all pupils. But for the majority, instruction past the technical level has never been seen as very relevant, and therefore has not been taken very seriously. The same has remained true of the teaching of domestic subjects in adult education classes, where practical courses in cooking and sewing have dominated the provision for women for more than a century.

DOMESTIC SCIENCE AND THE GIRLS' SCHOOL STORY

It must come as no surprise to find that the authors of girls' school stories in general succumbed to the propaganda to introduce domestic science teaching into their fictional schools. The moment of acceptance can be precisely dated in each case. It is important to note that in swallowing the arguments for its extension to middle-class girls, they were not necessarily promoting a reactionary and anti-feminist attempt to put women back in their place (that is, the home). In the 1920s the domestic science movement represented a curious alliance of conservatives, progressives, feminists and anti-feminists, with only a small number of the old guard equal rights reformers standing out against the general tide. As these retired and died off, very few people were left to question the general truism that not only were women in general responsible for domestic work, they were also entitled to proper training and the respect that goes with that – however empty that respect might inevitably be because it was only *women's* work.

Dorita Fairlie Bruce was the first to take domestic science up. In her very first novel, *The Senior Prefect* (later re-titled *Dimsie Goes to School*, 1920), the Jane Willard Foundation undergoes upheaval with the arrival of a new headmistress with radical ideas. Hitherto 'Jane's' has been one of those small private schools which took sport very seriously and study rather less so. Miss Yorke curtails the sport, increases the time available for schoolwork, and introduces 'House-craft'. The story is set in 1919 and accurately reflects the changed circumstances and attitudes of the middle class as a result of the First World War. As Miss Yorke explains to her senior prefect, Daphne Maitland:

After all, you're girls, and you'll grow up in time into the women whom men marry, and on whom they will depend

191

for the happiness of their homes. Oh, I know it isn't usual to talk like this even to the most senior of prefects, but the war has left our country, and our schools, too, very different from what they have been.

Before the War, Miss Yorke goes on, girls 'learnt and played much as boys'.

Games mattered above everything, and then, perhaps, study came next. Now, there is a third thing, which was always important, though very much overlooked, and to-day we can't overlook it any longer. Do you know what that is, Daphne?

Daphne does. 'Cooking,' she replies succinctly.

Miss Yorke laughs. 'I thought "housecraft" would sound more attractive to the cultured ears of Jane's,' she says.[18]

Daphne's response shows the schoolgirl's predictable reluctance to accept change, coupled with the resentful shock felt by middle-class young ladies when they realise they will be expected to occupy themselves with tasks hitherto undertaken only by menials. 'I know it's very sensible and necessary and all that', she exclaims, 'but the girls will simply hate it!'[19]

Bruce's novel shows how great was the mental shift required, quite apart from the need to learn new practical skills. This view is endorsed by a real-life account, that of Winifred Peck who was a student at Wycombe Abbey in its early days at the turn of the century. 'Far, far distant were any ideas of domestic economy or housework,' she writes of that time in her autobiography: 'we felt gravely injured at having to make our own beds on Sunday and count and list our own laundry on Monday morning.'[20]

Elsie Oxenham was the next of our school story writers to respond to the domestic science movement. In *The Abbey Girls in Town* (1925) we learn that 'They're starting a special domestic science course at Wycombe' (the school the Abbey girls go to, a small private affair not to be confused with the real Wycombe Abbey school mentioned above). Jen, who had to leave school at 16, is now returning three years later to take the new course. 'I'm going to learn how to put on patches, and all about washing-up, and upholstering furniture; and cooking and dressmaking and hygiene, of course!'[21]

That exclamation mark at the end of her description is significant: it's all a bit of a joke for wealthy Jen, who will never need to perform her own domestic chores, let alone work for a living. The Abbey girls are in fact supremely incapable of looking after themselves domestically; twice visitors have to come to their assistance when 'Cook' and the maids let them down, otherwise apparently, they would starve to death.

It soon becomes abundantly clear that Jen's commitment to learning domestic science is not strong. Though 'interested in her new pursuit of the science of cookery and domestic labours', we are told she 'did just as much as was required and no more'.[22] This had also been her attitude to her academic work in her earlier years at the school, and for precisely the same reason: it was never going to be any use to her. That Oxenham writes of the 'science' of cookery is revealing, I think, of the widespread social acceptance of the new intellectual approach to the subject, as opposed to the merely technical. Although later generations spoke of 'domestic science' as a matter of course, the noun 'science' lost its force through its association with the adjective 'domestic'; now it is all that remains of the movement to elevate domestic education to a high level.

Jen's real pleasure in her studies lies not in what she is being taught but in 'being back at school again'. She renews old friendships, dresses in short skirts for classes and gym tunic for games and dancing, and throws herself into extra-curricular activities.[23] She is elected Queen of the Hamlet Club. But then, suddenly, her friend Joy decides to get married. Joy is three years older than Jen, and lives with her aunt, but still Jen must leave school to organise the wedding.

School was all very well when I had nothing else to do and would only have been loafing about at home, but in a crisis like this I can't be expected to think about French and cooking, and how you make starch and gravy. Getting Joy married is much more important.[24]

COOKING AND CLASS

Although this presentation of domestic science gives the distinct impression that Oxenham's interest in the subject was, like Jen's, dilettantish and half-hearted, in later books she accords cooking skills, at least, quite serious respect. Rosamund leaves the Abbey to work in a tea-shop and to open her own shop selling hand-crafted goods. When her father discontinues the allowance she has always lived on, his parting gesture to her is to offer to pay for training so that she can support herself in future. She chooses to study to become a first-class cook, going to classes in 'Town', and obtaining the necessary certificates at the highest grade; but has little time to practise her new-found skills before she marries an earl and goes to live in a castle overrun with domestic help. Still, for this brief interlude Oxenham focuses on the busy world of the tea-shop business, and in years to come Rosamund looks back on this stage of her life as one of the happiest – because for once she was doing something useful.[25]

In a later book, Anne Bellanne comes to the Abbey to recuperate after an illness. She too is a trained cook, and will have to find a job when she recovers. 'It won't be difficult; I have good certificates, and cooking is always wanted.' Before her illness Anne had her own cake-shop, in partnership with a friend, but the business failed, and she isn't sure she wants to open another.

Cake-shops are risky; there are so many of them. I could only go as assistant, in any case; I haven't more capital to invest. I can always find good jobs if I'm willing to go as cook in some house, but – there are things to be said for and against that.

Maidlin, listening, understands perfectly. 'It's rather a different life from being owner of a cake-shop. I do see your dilemma.'

'I'm not really snobbish,' Anne insists. 'But if I once go into service as one of the maids in a big house, shall I ever be able to get back to my own place?'

'In the other part of the house,' Maidlin agrees.[26] This is the nub of the matter for Oxenham. All this emphasis on learning domestic skills must not be allowed to blur class distinctions, so immutable in her world-view. Middle-class girls may play at domestic science, may even use it to earn a living; but only in a self-employed capacity, never as mere servants.

The irony is that Anne ends up as Maidlin's housekeeper after the latter's marriage. Like those ex–Hamlet Club nurses, she is content to be absorbed into the service of the Abbey girls, even if it means that the very outcome she feared comes true. Family friend Anne Bellanne may be, but once she becomes an employee we never again meet her in the Abbey circle as an equal.

Oxenham has been here before. When another Ann, Ann Rowney, steps in to cook for the Hall ('I was a cook before I was a typist,' she tells the Abbey girls; 'I mean, I had some domestic science training'), Joy has difficulty in reconciling Ann's two roles as both social equal and servant. 'Ladies can't be cooks' is an axiom perhaps more understandable in 1928, when *The Abbey Girls Win Through* was published, than in 1943 when Anne Bellanne makes her appearance in *Maid of the Abbey*. In the earlier book Joy can only cope by thanking Ann and letting her cook, since no one else can do it, and the Abbey girls must eat. But 'the rest of the work you're to leave to Nelly and Kate [the maids],' she insists. And Ann must have the afternoons free, during which she is expected to execute a swift transformation into family friend and equal:

195

I want you to rest in the garden, or talk to us, or go into the Abbey or the woods, or play tennis with Jen, or drive with me and Mary, or play with the children, as you feel inclined. You're not to work all day, or I shall be unhappy about you.[27]

But Joy has never been unhappy about Cook, or Nelly, or Kate working all day.

Oxenham returns to her old notion of domestic science training when she creates a new school, Wood End, set in the Sussex countryside, for girls 'who aren't going in for professions and don't need to go to college and don't want to pass exams, but do need some special training for the sort of life they're likely to have.' What sort of life is this? Take Tamzine:

> her people have a big place in Cornwall. It will be useful for Tam to know all about gardening and fowls and keeping bees, and household management, and how to preside at the Women's Institute and make speeches and run committees – to say nothing of riding and tennis.[28]

The school is an offshoot of a more conventional school, Cliff End in Brighton, and takes only girls of 15 and over. The uniform consists of khaki breeches and smocks, like the land girls in the (First World) War. But this is 1937, and Oxenham's vision is decidedly backward-looking. By the time of her last book about the school, *New Girls at Wood End* (1957), it seems so remote as to be almost mythical. Yet as a recent television documentary on an English finishing school for girls from abroad showed, such institutions do still exist, the students of which expect to marry and not to work, and where such domestic skills are taught as to enable the students to supervise rather than actually perform the menial work allocated to others lower down the social scale.

Other fictional schools, though not devoted wholly to home management skills, have strong departments in that

196

subject catering to those girls intending to take up a domestic career – that is, to go home. Dorita Fairlie Bruce's *The School in the Woods* (1940) is one such. Speaking on the eve of war, the headmistress tells the assembled sixth formers they should concentrate on subjects likely to be useful to them in their chosen professions.

> 'Because, of course', she added casually, leaning back in the corner of a chintz-covered chesterfield, 'you are each going to have a career of some sort. Even those whose duty lies at home must train for that duty as efficiently as any of the others.'

'That's why I was sent to Thatches,' one girl volunteers. 'Because of the domestic science side. Mummy wants me to learn all there is to know about running a house.'[29]

Thatches sounds a more down-to-earth school than Oxenham's Wood End. The girls do not wear such picturesque costumes, but they do learn about farming and dairy work along with cooking and gardening – skills which are to stand Toby Barrett in good stead when she goes to work on the land during the Second World War.

FUN AND GAMES IN THE KITCHEN

Elinor Brent-Dyer comes late to domestic science, but takes it more seriously – at least in the beginning – than either Dorita Fairlie Bruce or Elsie Oxenham. The Chalet School Middles' attempts at laundry at Guide camp, in a novel published in 1932, prompt the staff to suggest to the proprietors of the school that a 'Domestic Economy' side be introduced, and that each girl should have at least two terms of it. Upon hearing this announcement, one of the prefects, Frieda – a well-brought up Tyrolean – welcomes the idea. 'If we should wed, and have learned housewifery at school as well as what we learn at home, we shall be able to make happy homes for our husbands and children.'[30]

Rather less in character is Miss Wilson's enthusiastic espousal of the scheme.

> Every woman, whether she be peasant or princess, should know how to keep house. It should be a part of every girl's education. I dislike the habit so many English schools have of turning out girls who can construe Horace, but are unable to cook a dinner; who can work out a theorem in Geometry, but cannot patch a shirt; who can read French or German in the original, or know all about the growth of Parliament, or the course of the Trade Winds, and yet who cannot wash a pair of socks or bath a baby.[31]

As so often, Brent-Dyer here appears to be adopting the fashionable critique of the masculine-inspired curriculum of so many of the new girls' schools, which deliberately made no allowances for what were often described as girls' different natures or needs. It sounds a little strange coming from the lips of Miss Wilson, a spinster and a career-woman if ever there was one; but Brent-Dyer has obviously read and accepted the current arguments of those who would return women to the domestic roles, and who did not scruple to justify their views by reference to religious and even biological determinist notions. Thus Miss Wilson, who combines a career in teaching science at the Chalet School with a strong Roman Catholic faith, goes on:

> Eve's first work when she left the Garden of Eden was to be a homemaker. . . . It should be our first work, too. I know that many people talk a lot of nonsense about women being emancipated from such 'drudgery'. [She must mean 'middle-class women'.] Believe me, girls, the woman who is above tending her husband and children or – if God does not give her those – helping other women who need such help, is a poor creature, developed on one

side only. . . . [W]oman, when she tries to ignore the human side of life, is deliberately deforming her nature.[32]

If this reads like propaganda, we should not be surprised, for as we already know Brent-Dyer was a magpie for collecting current fads. Equally, she rarely let them take firm hold on her, so we may often find them as easily and promptly discarded as they were acquired. Brent-Dyer may have believed all this stuff about women deforming their nature if they don't learn domestic skills, but in her books, domestic science – particularly cooking – is treated as an opportunity for a humorous interlude in the plot, generally occasioned by the substitution of one mistaken ingredient for the right one in the recipe under preparation. So in *The Chalet School and the Lintons* (1934) Cornelia wrecks the apple pies by incorporating garlic cloves instead of ordinary cloves in the filling; while in *Jo Returns to the Chalet School* (1936), Joyce flavours her cakes with sulphur rather than saffron.

At the Chalet School, domestic science is more basic than at Oxenham's Wycombe academy, involving tasks such as dusting, cleaning silver and brass, ironing, laying the table and washing up. The food that is cooked is served up to the school, sometimes with amusing results. And although most of the pupils are well-to-do, class does not seem to enter into it. During the War the school grows a lot of the food they eat and the girls carry out many domestic duties. 'Help is short, of course, so we always clear the tables,' Clem explains to new girl Carola.[33] And they *always* make their own beds and do their own mending.

An interesting pot-boiler published in 1953, when the series was well-established, was *The Chalet Girls' Cook Book*. Though the book purports to be the work of Jo and her three friends Frieda, Marie and Simone, it represents them as if they had just left school in the 1950s rather than the late 1930s as in the series. Though all four come from homes with servants, they all appear to be excellent cooks. Much of their knowledge is claimed to have been acquired at school, but some from home: Marie's mother 'the Graefin' (Countess), we are told, wanted all her children to learn about household tasks, just in case; and the coming of the Second World War, when the family have to flee their Nazi-occupied homeland, fully justified her foresight.[34]

The recipes in the cook book are very much dishes of 1950s England, when many foods were unobtainable or rationed. They are of course designed for readers to attempt to make themselves, which tells us volumes about the shift in attitudes towards domestic skills like cooking in the post-war era. A cook book for school story readers of the 1920s would have been unthinkable.

A STUDIED SILENCE

Domestic science does not feature in any of Enid Blyton's school stories. Its absence may be due to artistic reasons; perhaps it did not inspire her to so many good set pieces as French or drama lessons, or games or midnight feasts. A more probable explanation is that domestic science was not a feature of Blyton's own education and, because she was not herself a teacher, like Brent-Dyer, or in touch with many young people (like Bruce and Oxenham) through organisations such as the Girls' Guildry and Camp Fire, she was not particularly aware that by the 1940s and 1950s the subject was common in many girls' schools. It is true that her own daughters went away to boarding school in the 1950s, but one of them has insisted that Blyton based her stories on her own experiences rather than theirs, and Blyton's *The Story of My Life* rather bears this out.

Domestic science was not taught in all girls' schools. In the more academic high schools and grammar schools it was (and still is) deliberately ignored as being suitable only for 'less able' girls. Some of the smaller private academies simply had not the resources to provide the necessary facilities. By the 1940s, when Blyton wrote her first school story, the domestic science movement was beginning to run out of steam. If the intensity of the crusade of the interwar years was waning, Blyton would not have felt it necessary to mention the subject, whatever her personal views as to the pros and cons.

No one seems to have thought domestic skills relevant for boys, and the sexism of the assumption that women will always take responsibility for housework and childcare seems never to have been seriously questioned before the 1960s. This has surely been one of the most powerful barriers to women's ability to challenge patriarchal control. In practical terms domestic work has absorbed their time and energy, while freeing men to pursue ever greater economic, social and political advantage. Ideologically, however much you tried to dignify domestic work and dress it up as a science or an art, as long as it was women's work it would never be seen as important.

That the widespread acceptance of domestic science training for girls (and not boys) represented a major set-back for women during the first two-thirds of the present century – the period betwen the two 'waves' of feminist revolt – is suggested by one of Dorita Fairlie Bruce's novels, published just before the Second World War. The plot revolves around a competition set up by a local celebrity, Miss Peters, among the houses at Springdale School on the west coast of Scotland. The object of the competition is to mark the achievements of girls' education; each house in the school is to demonstrate one aspect of their education, with the house which most impresses the judges receiving the prize.

Miss Peters is an 'eccentric old lady', but in her prime, we are told, she was a militant suffragette, and had even been sent to prison (it was rumoured) for scratching a policeman who tried to stop her shouting 'Votes for Women!' (The use of the verb 'scratch', which has a feminine, ineffectual ring to it, suggests that Bruce sees Miss Peters's suffragette past as a bit of a joke.)[35]

Wistaria, a new house which so far excels at nothing in

particular, decides to go in for domestic science. Their motives are quite canny; as Prim remarks, 'Isn't cooking and housework the dullest and most useful part of a woman's training, and the kind most likely to appeal to grown-ups?' They decide to put on a dinner party for the judges, displaying all the domestic skills they have acquired at school; needless to state, they win the prize. Miss Peters is 'exceedingly pleased to think that the strongest point in the education at Springdale should be how to cook and serve a meal – not forgetting the brooms and dusters that led up to it.'

The former suffragette goes on:

> I haven't a word to say against drill, or science, or languages – or even against business, which is all very well in its place – and music is (as this contest has proved) only second to housewifery. But, when all's said and done, humanity must eat if they're to enjoy music, and acrobatics . . . [36]

One final irony lies in store. The prize for Miss Peters' competition for the best house at Springdale is – a dwarf cedar-tree, 'gnarled into a perfect miniature of its kind'.[37] Of all the images that could have been chosen to symbolise women's position under patriarchy, it would be difficult to find one more apt than this. A bonsai tree is something which is beautiful, certainly, but stunted, reduced to ornamental status to stand on a domestic shelf, certainly not fit to take its place in the mighty forest of real trees. What was Dorita Fairlie Bruce trying to tell us?

We are driven to conclude that her interest in domestic education was not sufficiently strong to allow her to recognise the significance of such a symbol, or else that she was deliberately being cynical about the matter. We know that Bruce espoused conservative ideas, and might well have taken on board eugenist or anti-feminist notions about women's role. On the other hand, there is no avoiding the fact that she did not herself fit too comfortably into that role, and that she had few domestic skills of her own and little interest in acquiring them. Perhaps all this story illustrates, and the same may be true of the work of Elsie Oxenham and Elinor Brent-Dyer, is the power of a dominant ideology to influence the pen of the school story writer.

Although all three authors responded to the domestic science movement by introducing the subject into their fictional schools in the 1920s and 1930s and by voicing its ideals with greater or lesser conviction, ultimately there is a certain half-heartedness about *all* their accounts which makes one question their own commitment to the philosophy. Elsie Oxenham respects cookery skills, but that is the only domestic art she is more than indifferent about, and even that gets her into difficulties with class which she cannot properly resolve. Elinor Brent-Dyer says all the right things about women's nature and role, but reduces domestic science to a device for raising a laugh. Dorita Fairlie Bruce's attitude to domestic science seems fraught with ambiguities. And Enid Blyton simply ignores it.

Conclusion

In three decades of reading girls' school stories I have met
and talked to dozens of women who share my interest in
them. While most had read them as girls, moving on to
other forms of literature at adolescence, some, like myself,
continued to enjoy them into adulthood, and remain ardent
fans. Although a small minority, this group is significant
because its members have usually been happy to articulate
their reasons for reading juvenile fiction long past the apparently appropriate age. Older correspondents to the *Chalet
Club Newsletter* were among Elinor Brent-Dyer's most
enthusiastic fans, and Helen McClelland gathered together a
whole chapter of tributes from

> children, and the whole age-range of adults up to at least
> ninety (the oldest known); people married, unmarried,
> childless, with families large or small . . . They are cer-
> tainly not all middle-aged women seeking to recapture
> their childhood.[1]

As someone who falls into this group, I too have often been
called on by surprised enquirers to consider my reasons for
enjoying this much-criticised genre. Much of what McClelland writes and quotes about the attraction of the settings,
the characterisation, the series factor, I would endorse. But
in the end, I think girls' school stories have been important
for me for two overriding reasons. First, they depict a virtually all-female world of strong role models, close and primary friendships, and community, which I (growing up in

the very different world of the 1960s) found, and still find, appealing.

Second, reading them offered me as a young woman a temporary escape and refuge from the pressures of that profoundly heterosexual society I lived in. Growing up is rarely easy for girls. Adolescence forces on us the conflicting demands of success in masculine terms (at school and work) and in feminine terms (heterosexual attractiveness), and expects us to negotiate confidently in a world which we are fast coming to realise is weighted against us as a sex. For women who see no hope of escaping from the patriarchal milieu in which they live, or of changing it, the stories may continue to function as a retreat throughout their lives.

Other women, on the other hand, have been able to bring their reality more into line with the ideal world of the school stories; in other words, to live in a largely female community. As in the school stories, their circles are but enclaves in the larger patriarchal society, and still subject to its values and pressures; and as in the school stories, men come and go within them, as family, colleagues, acquaintances. But these women's primary links are with *women*, and that suits them. They – and I count myself among them – do not need to read school stories to escape; they do it to *identify* with this aspect of their world view. As one told me, 'I appreciate their women-only nature consciously now.'[2]

The other way in which my perception of girls' school stories has changed since adolescence is in my ability to view them as historical sources, documents which chart the changing social attitudes in Britain to women's communities and women's friendships. The works of the four authors considered in this book span a shift in ideas from the Victorian notion of separate spheres to the present era of what Adrienne Rich has called 'compulsory heterosexuality'.[3] One of the most fascinating aspects for me of re-reading all these novels in the light of this recognition has been in discovering the different ways in which the authors resisted or bowed to increasing pressure to break up the female alliances in their stories and to re-focus their heroines' energies on to men.

With the deaths of the generation of school story writers discussed here, the genre went into eclipse; the critics' efforts to destroy it represented but one of the many attacks on single-sex institutions such as girls' schools and women's colleges that have characterised my lifetime. That many of the old stories have been revived is testimony to a continuing market which economic forces are now happy to exploit.

Another weapon that has been used against the school story is that of parody, which has kept a particular image of girls' school stories before our eyes, and ensured that they are the object of mockery and ridicule. I remember on one occasion asking a group of school story readers what most appealed to them about the books and receiving the reply from one woman that it was because they were so 'camp' and 'twee'. This is a fashionable response to schoolgirl stories, but it is clear to me that these characteristics are not present in the books themselves but in the way we have been encouraged to read them.

Camp is a tradition the roots of which lie in patriarchy's mockery of the institutions it wishes to undermine. It's amusing enough unless you happen to be part of what is being laughed at. That women can read (or see, in the case of films and plays) this kind of attack, and still smile, is testimony to the strength of our indoctrination in patriarchal ideals. Its values become rooted in us and make us view everything from a masculine orientation unless questioned and deliberately reframed. The problem with girls' school stories is that although there is much that we as women would like to criticise, such as their attitudes to class or race, there is much, too, that we would hold dear, particularly their portrayal of female independence and love between and among girls and women. Not surprisingly, these are the very aspects most often singled out for critical scorn and parody.

While I was in process of writing this book, Janet Montefiore kindly sent me the draft of an article she had written entitled 'The Fourth Form Girls Go Camping: Sexual Identity and Ambivalence in Girls' School Stories'. Montefiore was an avid reader of girls' school stories in her youth. In this paper she begins from the perspective of the camp parody of the schoolgirl story, which started in the 1950s and 'flourishes to this day', exemplified by Arthur Marshall, St Trinian's, and *Daisy Pulls it Off*. She notes that there is:

> no comparable camp cult of boys' school stories, the older genre on which the girls' story is based. Arthur Marshall, one of the first people to read girls' school stories for their unintentional comedy, explains that 'I always thought that schoolgirls and schoolmistresses were funny'; schoolboys and schoolmasters didn't apparently, seem so comic.[4]

Of course not. What is being mocked here is, put simply, *women*; and an all-female world, where men are unnecessary and irrelevant, is the most obvious target for patriarchal fear and anger. There are many ways of undermining an institution or idea you don't like, and humour is one of the most powerful, particularly if you can get those associated with the institution or idea laughing with you at themselves. But laugh at *masculine* institutions? Never! Not only is there nothing self-evidently funny about institutions which exclude women, since these are normal under patriarchy, but such institutions cannot be touched, since they are sacred to the patriarchal ruling class: men.

Montefiore, however, interprets the difference not in political but in sexual terms.

> This suggests to me two things: first that the pleasure of these texts, for both kinds of audience [i.e. camp and 'straight'], is tied up with their representations of female identity, and second, that the emphatically feminine identities of the fantasy characters in the all-female world of the stories can actually be construed – and in a camp reading

are so construed – as shifting the norms of gender in ways that bring into question the stability of gender identity.[5]

Montefiore's argument here is, I think, to some extent quite similar to my own in this book, but in some respects quite different. In speaking of school stories 'shifting the norms of gender in ways that bring into question the stability of gender identity', she is drawing attention to the possibility for girls in these stories to be strong and independent, like boys, and to put their emotional energies into other girls instead of boys, as they should do according to the norms of a hetero-sexual society. All this I would agree with. It is when she draws on Freudian concepts to underpin her assumptions about what normal gender and sexual identity are that we part company.

In my view, ideas about what constitutes normal behaviour are historically specific. Freud and the sexologists altered everyone's notions of 'normal' gender and sexual identity. Specifically, they lent new 'scientific' insights to the campaign against female independence of action and they reinterpreted love between women as perversion. As a historian, I see Freud's insights as so clearly a product of his life and times, his class and, above all, his sex, as to find them unreliable and unhelpful descriptions of feminine reality at any period.

School stories came late to psychoanalysis and were, therefore, characterised by pre-Freudian innocence to a much later date than many more intellectually advanced products of Western society. But we have seen how ideas about lesbian deviance caught up with the Abbey books in the 1930s and led Elsie Oxenham to focus with increasing dedication on heterosexual rather than same-sex love. It is this innocence which camp mocks. But it is not necessarily naivety; it may represent girls' and women's actual situation at the time. The sexualisation of women's friendships was a political gesture, intended to reinstate male power at a time when it had been under feminist attack. So-called 'lesbian' behaviour – love between women – is only deviant in a society where hetero-sexuality is made compulsory in the service of patriarchy.

Applying an analysis based on Freudian categories of gender and sexuality to girls' school stories does violence to our understanding of that representation. Take the scene which Montefiore selects from Dorita Fairlie Bruce's *Dimsie, Head Girl* (1925) in which Dimsie burns her hand in rescuing her friend Jean's box of poems from a blazing shed. It is because Jean was always writing these poems instead of attending to her duties as head girl that she was demoted and Dimsie put into her place. This causes a rift between the two, only mended when Jean sees that Dimsie has injured herself for her sake. Jean is then sorry and undertakes to dress the burn herself with healing ointment.

Says Montefiore:

This scene, even more than other rescue melodramas [which are common in girls' school stories], clearly plays out a masochistic revenge fantasy in which the pain of estrangement is represented, as in conversion hysteria, by literal physical damage. . . . [6]

Taking psychoanalysis a step further, Montefiore argues that 'this fantasy of emotional revenge itself both masks and stages another fantasy of lesbian pleasure and punishment.' She compares the incident in Bruce's novel with Freud's famous interpretation of Dora's dream about her jewel-case and the house on fire:

. . . the text mobilizes a cruder version of this dream symbolism whereby the box representing female genitals, together with the fire and its implied opposite, wetness (Jean's ointment) – signifying danger and sexual inflamm-ation – represent the perilous desires of girls who touch one another. [7]

To suggest that Bruce is consciously or unconsciously depicting lesbian behaviour here is misleading and ahistorical. Surely all we have is one girl shown caring for another, natural enough in the circumstances, in a school story written in 1925. Even if we accept the behaviour as lesbian, why should the word be defined in terms of deviance and perversion ('perilous desires')?

Where psychoanalytic theory focuses on sexuality, I prefer to focus on *love* – that emotion we all thought we understood until sophisticates told us it represented unconscious (and in this case, forbidden) desires we never knew we had. It cannot be useful to suggest that we are all unconscious lesbians, given that 'lesbian' is (and must be) a term of abuse in a patriarchal society. But love is a natural human emotion, and most women, whatever our chosen sexual identity, have loved other women. I am sure this would be true of *all* of us if we hadn't been told all our lives that the love of men was paramount above all other loyalties. Millions of women have been actively discouraged from loving women, or have hidden or betrayed their love for women. I would like to be able to celebrate women's love for women affirmatively and joyfully, not shamefully and with an awareness that we are laying ourselves open to the mockery of camp and the patronising superiority of psychoanalysis.

What school stories show us is that this truth – that women can and do love other women – was easier to speak in earlier eras in particular literary genres than it is today or in other literary genres. The reasons for this, as this book has tried to show, are both historical and critical.

Girls' school stories grew out of the first wave of feminism which flourished in the late nineteenth century. Then women banded together to fight for opportunities which a male-dominated society denied them. As masculine institutions were often closed to women, they formed their own. For a long time men left them alone, accustomed as they were to the idea of separate spheres, and content to enjoy the inviolability of their own preserves. But two World Wars shook up their complacency. Both led men to be suspicious and fearful of what women had been up to when the men were away. Both led to attempts to break down women's separate organisations and to re-distribute women into mixed sex groupings where men could keep an eye on them. After the Second World War, these efforts were almost one hundred per cent effective. By the 1990s it must be true to say that there are almost no all-female enclaves left.

Along with girls' schools, women's colleges, adult education institutes, hostels, clubs, trade unions, cafes and single-sex friendships, girls' school stories themselves were ultimately victims of this ruthless heterosexual drive. That Montefiore links camp to psychoanalysis is surely no accident, as it was the psychoanalytic 'insight' into so-called latent homosexuality that justified both the strenuous re-focusing of schoolgirls' affections on to boys rather than older girls or mistresses *and* the audience's knowing laughter at the camp parody of schoolgirl crushes.

In her autobiography, published in 1924, Lilian Faithfull describes a married friend who had studied at Royal Holloway College at the turn of the century. This friend recalled that:

in looking back, the most striking feature of the life seems to her to have been the complete contentment of the whole body of students in each other's society. There was no desire for other than women's companionship.

Faithfull, who taught at Royal Holloway for a time, identified with her friend's experience. 'One revels in the exchange of ideas with older people, and those of one's own sex and age, without any emotion that tends to self-consciousness.'[8]

In that word 'self-consciousness' lies the clue, I think, to the way in which women's experiences of that period should be read, both in real life and in girls' school stories. To read them otherwise is to misread history. As girls most of us were mercifully free of the self-conscious overview provided by psychoanalysis and so were able to enter into the all-

211

female worlds of the stories and identify with the strong, wise female heroines and their friendships and loves. This may no longer be true for young readers today. That is why it is so necessary for us to reclaim the positive message of girls' school stories and to restore to literary criticism an interpretation which does not sneer, collude with the patriarchy, or misrepresent our past.

NOTES

PREFACE

1 Helen McClelland, *Behind the Chalet School*, second edition, 1986, p. 178.

1

1 Marcus Crouch, *Treasure-Seekers and Borrowers*, 1962, p. 163.

2 Grace W Allen, 'To Market, To Market, To buy a fat book', *Junior Bookshelf*, Vol. 1, No. 4, 1937, p. 15.

3 Frank Eyre, *British Children's Books in the Twentieth Century*, 1971, p. 11.

4 Margery Fisher, *Intent Upon Reading*, 1961, p. 170.

5 Q D Leavis, *Fiction and the Reading Public*, 1965, p. 60 (first published 1932)

6 Janice Dohm 'The work of Enid Blyton'. In Boris Ford (ed.), *Young Writers, Young Readers* (revised edition, 1963), p. 106.

7 Ibid, p. 98.

8 'An Aunt', *Junior Bookshelf*, Vol. 2, No. 2, 1937, p. 71.

9 George Orwell, 'Boys' Weeklies', *Horizon* (1940). Reprinted in Sonia Orwell and Ian Angus (eds) *The Collected Essays, Journalism and Letters of George Orwell*, Vol. I, 1968, pp. 464–6 and 473.

10 M J P Lawrence, 'Wanted – Some Good School Stories', *Junior Bookshelf*, 1954, pp. 62 and 61.

11 Mary Cadogan and Patricia Craig, *You're a Brick, Angela!*, 1976, p. 201.

12 Eyre, op. cit., p. 13.

13 Cadogan and Craig, op. cit., p. 200.

14 Charles Hamilton, Letter to *Horizon* (1940). Reprinted in Sonia Orwell and Ian Angus (eds), op. cit., Vol. I, p. 492.

15 A J Jenkinson, *What Do Boys and Girls Read?*, 1940, p. 282.

16 Jan Marsh, Review of *You're a Brick, Angela!*, *New Society*, 26 January 1976, p. 449.

17 James Guthrie, 'Realism and Escapism in Children's Literature', *Junior Bookshelf*, 1958, p. 15.

18 Editorial, *Junior Bookshelf*, Vol. 2, No. 1, October 1937, p. 3.

19 *Junior Bookshelf*, Vol. 7, No. 2, p. 59.

20 Frank Eyre, op. cit., 1952.

21 See *British Books in Print* for the relevant years; Helen McClelland in *Elinor Brent-Dyer's Chalet School*, 1989, pp. 5–6; 'Book and Magazine Collectors' Review of Current Selling Prices: Elinor Brent-Dyer', *Book and Magazine Collectors' Review*, March 1988, p. 10; and check out the stock in bookshops like John Adrian in Charing Cross Road, London.

22 Cadogan and Craig, op. cit., p. 10.

23 Ibid, p. 204.

24 Ibid, p. 194.

25 For example, Rosemary Stones, *Pour out the cocoa, Janet*, 1983.

26 Cadogan and Craig, op. cit. p. 9.

27 Janice Winship, *Inside Women's Magazines*, 1987, p. xiii.

28 Nicola Beauman, *A Very Great Profession*, 1983, p. 5.

29 Winship, op. cit. p. xiii.

30 See Lisa Appignanesi, 'Happily Ever After', *New Statesman*, 13 July 1984, p. 24; Jane Ellison, 'Read Mills & Boon for a Gentle Swoon', *Observer*, 8 February 1981; Sally Beauman, 'When a kiss is worth a million', *Guardian*, 30 June 1982; Peter H Mann, *A New Survey. The Facts about Romantic Fiction*, 1974.

31 Ann Barr Snitow, 'Mass Market Romance: Pornography for Women is Different', in Ann Snitow, Christine Stansell and Sharon Thompson (eds) *Desire. The Politics of Sexuality*, 1984, p. 258; also Gemma Moss, *Un/Popular Fictions*, 1989, Chapter 3.

32 Janice Radway, *Reading the Romance*, second edition, 1987, p. 5.

33 Ibid, p. 16.

34 Ibid, pp. 13–14.

35 Ibid, pp. 54, 77 and 219.

36 jay Dixon, 'Fantasy Unlimited. The World of Mills & Boon', *Women's Review*, Vol. 21, July 1987, p. 19.

37 Jean Radford (ed.) *The Progress of Romance*, 1976, p. 2.

38 Radway, op. cit, p. 88.

39 Ibid, pp. 212, 17 and 217.

40 Northrop Frye, *The Secular Scripture*, 1976, p. 179.

41 Ann Rosalind Jones, 'Mills & Boon Meets Feminism', in Radford (ed.), op. cit., p. 214.

42 Cammilla Nightingale, 'Sex Roles in Children's Literature', in Sandra Allen, Lee Sanders and Jan Wallis (eds), *Conditions of Illusion*, 1974, p. 145.

43 Gill Frith, ' "The time of your life": the meaning of the school story', in Carolyn Steedman, Cathy Unwin and Valerie Walkerdine (eds), *Language, Gender and Childhood*, 1985, pp. 117 and 120.

44 Ibid, p. 121–2.

45 Ibid, p. 123 and 126.

46 Kathleen Adler, 'The Suburban, the Modern and "une Dame de Passy" ', *Oxford Art Journal*, Vol. 12, No. 1, 1989, p. 3.

47 See Rosemary Auchmuty, 'Victorian Spinsters', unpublished Ph.D thesis, Australian National University, Canberra (available in the Fawcett Library, London). Also Philippa Levine, *Victorian Feminism*, 1987; Ray Strachey, *'The Cause'. A Short History of the Women's Movement in Great Britain*, 1928. Reprinted 1978.

48 Nina Auerbach, *Communities of Women*, 1978, p. 5.

49 For example, Francoise Basch, *Relative Creatures*, 1974.

50 Auerbach, op. cit., p. 13. See also, for example, Janet Todd, *Women's Friendship in Literature*, 1980; Lillian Faderman, *Surpassing the Love of Men*, 1981; Liz Stanley, *Feminism and Friendship: Two Essays on Olive Schreiner*, 1985; Rosemary Auchmuty, 'By their friends we shall know them', in Lesbian History Group, *Not a Passing Phase*, 1989, p. 77.

51 Martha Vicinus, *Independent Women. Work and Community for Single Women 1850–1920*, 1985.

2

1 Elinor M Brent-Dyer, *The Chalet School Goes To It*, 1941, pp. 74–5.

2 Erica Oxenham, *'J.O.'*, 1942, p. 97.

3 Dorita Fairlie Bruce, *Dimsie Moves Up Again*, 1922.

4   *Lamp of the Girls' Guildry*, (1933–38).

5   Helen McClelland, *Behind the Chalet School*, second edition, 1986, p. 142.

6   Ibid, p. 164.

7   Ibid, pp. 83 and 96.

8   Sheila G Ray, *The Blyton Phenomenon*, 1982, p. 196.

9   Barbara Stoney, *Enid Blyton*, 1974, p. 20.

10 Enid Blyton, *The Story of My Life*, 1952, p. 117.

11 Ibid.

12 Imogen Smallwood, *A Childhood at Green Hedges*, 1989, p. 35.

13 Stoney, op. cit., p. 120.

14 Ibid; Smallwood, op. cit., pp. 57–8.

15 Smallwood, op. cit., pp. 79 and 18.

16 Stoney, op. cit., p. 172.

17 Ray, op. cit., p. 7.

18 Ibid, p. 27.

19 Ibid, pp. 71–3.

20 Stoney, op. cit., p. 179.

3

1   Elsie Oxenham, *Secrets of the Abbey*, 1939.

2   Emily Davies, 'Special Systems of Education for Women', 1868. Reprinted in Dale Spender (ed.), *The Education Papers*, 1987, p. 107.

3   M V Hughes, *A London Girl of the 1880s*, 1978, p. 10 (first published 1946).

4. See [Charles Hamilton], *The Autobiography of Frank Richards*, 1952 and his entry in the Dictionary of National Biography.

5   Mary Cadogan and Patricia Craig, *You're a Brick, Angela!*, 1976, p. 230.

6   See Gillian Freeman, *The Schoolgirl Ethic: The Life and Work of Angela Brazil*, 1976.

7   See Sheila Fletcher, *Women First. The Female Tradition in English Physical Education 1880–1980*, 1984; and Kathleen E McCrone, *Sport and the Physical Emancipation of English Women 1870–1914*, 1988.

8   *St Leonard's School 1877–1927*, 1927, p. 63.

9   This is the argument of Mary Wollstonecraft in *A Vindication of the Rights of Women*, 1792.

10 Elinor M Brent-Dyer, *Rivals of the Chalet School*, 1929.

11 Enid Blyton, *Upper Fourth at Malory Towers*, 1989 (first published 1949).

12 Enid Blyton, *Second Form at St Clare's*, 1944.

13 See Chapter 7 of this book.

14 Sara A Burstall, *Prospect and Retrospect. 60 Years of Women's Education*, 1933, p. 237.

15 Thomas Hughes, *Tom Brown's School Days*, 1958, pp. 74, 56 and 72, 1857.

16 L T Meade, *A World of Girls*, 1886.

17 Dorita Fairlie Bruce, *Dimsie Goes to School*, 1921.

18 Elinor M Brent-Dyer, *The Feud in the Fifth Remove*, 1931.

19 Ibid, also *Exploits of the Chalet School*, 1933, *Leader in Spite of Herself*, 1956, etc.

20 Enid Blyton, *Claudine at St Clare's*, 1944.

21 For example, Dorita Fairlie Bruce, *Nancy to the Rescue*, 1927; *The New House at Springdale*, 1934.

22 Several times, for example, the point is made that Brent-Dyer's heroines would only go to private schools; see *Three Go to the Chalet School*, 1949.

23 Elinor M Brent-Dyer, *A Problem for the Chalet School*, 1956.

24 Dorita Fairlie Bruce, *The New House at Springdale*, 1934.

25 Ibid, also *Nancy Returns to St Bride's*, 1928.

26 Dorita Fairlie Bruce, *Dimsie Goes to School*, 1921.

27 Dorita Fairlie Bruce, *Sally's Summer Term*, 1961.

28 Dorita Fairlie Bruce, *The School on the Moor*, 1931.

29 Elsie J Oxenham, *The Abbey Girls*, 1920.

30 Elsie J Oxenham, *Captain of the Fifth*, 1922.

31 Elsie J Oxenham, *The Junior Captain*, 1923.

32 Elsie J Oxenham, *The Girls of the Abbey School*, 1921.

33 Elsie J Oxenham, *The School Without a Name*, 1924.

34 Elsie J Oxenham, *The Girls of the Hamlet Club*, 1914.

35 Elsie J Oxenham, *The Abbey Girls Again*, 1924.

36 Elsie J Oxenham, *The Abbey Girls Win Through*, 1928.

37 Elsie J Oxenham, *The Girls of the Hamlet Club*, 1914.

38 Elsie J Oxenham, *The Reformation of Jinty*.

39 Elinor M Brent-Dyer, *The School by the River*, 1930.

40 Elinor M Brent-Dyer, *Heather Leaves School*, 1929.

41   Elinor M Brent-Dyer, *Eustacia Goes to the Chalet School*, 1930.
42   Elinor M Brent-Dyer, *Lavender Laughs in the Chalet School*, 1943.
43   Enid Blyton, *Last Term at Malory Towers*, 1989 (first published 1951).
44   Enid Blyton, *The Story of My Life*, 1952.
45   Enid Blyton, *Claudine at St Clare's*, 1944.
46   Ibid.
47   Ibid.
48   Dorita Fairlie Bruce, *Sally's Summer Term*, 1961.
49   Dorita Fairlie Bruce, *Dimsie Goes to School*, 1921.
50   Elsie J Oxenham, *Schooldays at the Abbey*, 1938.
51   Enid Blyton, *In the Fifth at Malory Towers*, 1950.
52   Enid Blyton, *The O'Sullivan Twins*, 1990.
53   Enid Blyton, *In the Fifth at Malory Towers*, 1950.
54   Burstall, op. cit., p. 60.

4

1   Helen McClelland, *Behind the Chalet School*, 1986, p. 110.
2   For example, Elinor M Brent-Dyer, 'The Mystery at the Chalet School' in *The Chalet Book for Girls*, 1947, p. 18.
3   Elinor M Brent-Dyer, *The Chalet Girls in Camp*, 1932, p. 165. Jo March is the tomboy heroine of Louisa May Alcott's novel *Little Women*, 1868.
4   Elinor M Brent-Dyer, *The Head Girl of the Chalet School*, 1928, p. 236.
5   Helen McClelland, *Elinor M Brent-Dyer's Chalet School*, 1989, p. 47.
6   Elinor M Brent-Dyer, *The Chalet School and Jo*, 1931, p. 261.
7   Elinor M Brent-Dyer, *Eustacia Goes to the Chalet School*, 1930, p. 261.
8   Elinor M Brent-Dyer, *The New House at the Chalet School*, 1935, pp. 29–30.
9   Helen McClelland, *Behind the Chalet School*, p. 111.
10   Elinor M Brent-Dyer, *The Chalet School in Exile*, 1940, p. 191; *A Chalet Girl from Kenya*, 1955, p. 185.
11   McClelland, *Elinor M Brent-Dyer's Chalet School*, p. 11.

12 Nicholas Tucker (ed.), *Suitable for Children? Controversies in Children's Literature*, 1976, p. 21.

13 Elise J Oxenham, *Daring Doranne*, 1945, pp. 80–1.

14 Ibid p. 85.

15 Ibid p. 144.

16 Elsie J Oxenham, *The Girls of the Abbey School*, 1921, p. 53.

17 Elsie J Oxenham, *The Abbey Girls Again*, 1924, p. 195.

18 Ibid, p. 81.

19 Elsie J Oxenham, *Secrets of the Abbey*, 1939, p. 84.

20 Elsie J Oxenham, *The Tuck-Shop Girl*, 1916, p. 202.

21 Janet Hitchman, *Such a Strange Lady. A Biography of Dorothy L Sayers*, 1975, pp. 90 and 98.

22 Mary Cadogan and Patricia Craig, *You're a Brick, Angela!*, 1976, p. 182.

23 Dorita Fairlie Bruce, *Dimsie Moves Up*, 1921, p. 227.

24 Dorita Fairlie Bruce, *Dimsie Among the Prefects*, 1923, p. 109.

25 Dorita Fairlie Bruce, *Dimsie Grows Up*, 1924, p. 143.

26 Dorita Fairlie Bruce, *The New Girl and Nancy*, 1926, p. 128.

27 Dorita Fairlie Bruce, *Nancy Calls the Tune*, 1944, p. 17.

28 Dorita Fairlie Bruce, *Dimsie Goes to School*, 1921, p. 6.

29 Dorita Fairlie Bruce, *Nancy at St Bride's*, 1933, p. 12.

30 Dorita Fairlie Bruce, *The New House Captain*, 1928, p. 14.

31 Mary Cadogan and Patricia Craig, op. cit., p. 181.

32 Dorita Fairlie Bruce, *The School on the Moor*, 1931, p. 26.

33 Dorita Fairlie Bruce, *Dimsie Goes to School*, 1921, p. 233.

34 Dorita Fairlie Bruce, *Dimsie Moves Up*, 1921, p. 20.

35 Ibid, pp. 186 and 43.

36 Dorita Fairlie Bruce, *Dimsie Goes to School*, 1921, p. 249.

37 Dorita Fairlie Bruce, *Dimsie Among the Prefects*, 1923, p. 27.

38 Dorita Fairlie Bruce, *Dimsie Moves Up Again*, 1922, p. 76.

39 Ibid, p. 25.

40 Dorita Fairlie Bruce, *The School on the Moor*, 1931, p. 169.

41 Sheila G Ray, *The Blyton Phenomenon*, 1982, p. 115.

42 Ibid, p. 198.

43 Ibid, p. 196.

44 Ibid, p. 198.

45 Elinor M Brent-Dyer, *Highland Twins at the Chalet School*, 1942, p. 61.

46 Jessie Bernard, *The Future of Marriage*, 1971.

5

1   Dorita Fairlie Bruce, *The New House Captain*, 1928, p. 263.

2   Elinor M Brent-Dyer, *The School at the Chalet*, 1925, p. 134.

3   Elinor M Brent-Dyer, *Three Go To the Chalet School*, 1949, p. 221.

4   Elinor M Brent-Dyer, *Nesta Steps Out*, 1954, p. 54.

5   Elinor M Brent-Dyer, *The Chalet School in the Oberland*, 1952, p. 118.

6   For example, *The Chalet School Goes To It*, 1941, and *Gay From China at the Chalet School*, 1944.

7   Elinor M Brent-Dyer, *Changes for the Chalet School*, 1953, pp. 87–8.

8   Elinor M Brent-Dyer, *Highland Twins at the Chalet School*, 1942, pp. 99 and 266.

9   Dorita Fairlie Bruce, *Dimsie Moves Up Again*, 1922, pp. 183–5.

10 Dorita Fairlie Bruce, *Dimsie Goes To School*, 1921, pp. 28–9.

11 Dorita Fairlie Bruce, *Captain at Springdale*, 1932, p. 224.

12 Dorita Fairlie Bruce, *The Girls of St Bride's*, 1923, p. 102.

13 Ibid, p. 171.

14 Dorita Fairlie Bruce, *Nancy at St Bride's*, 1933, pp. 45–6.

15 Dorita Fairlie Bruce, *The New Girl and Nancy*, 1926, p. 149.

16 Elsie J Oxenham, *Girls of the Abbey School*, 1921, p. 62.

17 Elsie J Oxenham, *The New Abbey Girls*, 1923, p. 175.

18 Elsie J Oxenham, *'Tickles'; or, The School That Was Different*, 1924, p. 75.

19 Elsie J Oxenham, *A Go-Ahead Schoolgirl*, 1919, pp. 122–3.

20 Ibid, p. 237.

21 Elsie J Oxenham, *Rosamund's Victory*, 1933, p. 35.

22 Elsie J Oxenham, *The School Torment*, 1920, p. 301.

23 Elsie J Oxenham, *Patience and her Problems*, 1927, p. 67.

24 Elsie J Oxenham, *The School Without a Name*, 1924, pp. 149–50.

25 Elsie J Oxenham, *The Crisis in Camp Keema*, 1928, p. 189.

26 Elsie J Oxenham, *Rachel in the Abbey*, 1951, pp. 47, 86.

27 Elsie J Oxenham, *The School Torment*, 1920, pp. 15, 17–18.

28 Ibid, p. 206.

29 Enid Blyton, *Second Form at Malory Towers*, Armada edition, 1967, p. 198 (first published 1947).

30 Enid Blyton, *In the Fifth at Malory Towers*, Armada edition 1990, p. 316 (first published 1950).

31 Enid Blyton, *Second Form at St Clare's*, Armada edition 1991, p. 139 (first published 1944).

32 Enid Blyton, *Last Term at Malory Towers*, Armada edition, 1990, p. 467 (first published 1951).

33 Ibid, pp. 470–1.

34 Sheila G Ray, *The Blyton Phenomenon*, 1982, p. 199.

35 Elsie J Oxenham, *The Reformation of Jinty*, 1933, p. 23.

36 Elsie J Oxenham, *The Tuck-Shop Girl*, 1916, p. 301.

37 Elsie J Oxenham, *Dorothy's Dilemma*, 1930, p. 43 and 121.

38 Elinor M Brent-Dyer, *A Leader in the Chalet School*, 1961.

39 Elinor M Brent-Dyer, *The New Mistress at the Chalet School*, 1957.

40 Elinor M Brent-Dyer, *Gay From China at the Chalet School*, 1944, p. 138.

41 Dorita Fairlie Bruce, *The New House Captain*, 1928, pp. 137 and 172.

42 Dorita Fairlie Bruce, *Dimsie Among the Prefects*, 1923, p. 159.

43 Dorita Fairlie Bruce, *The New House Captain*, 1928.

44 Dorita Fairlie Bruce, *Dimsie Moves Up*, 1921; *That Boarding-School Girl*, 1925.

45 Dorita Fairlie Bruce, *The School on the Moor*, 1931, p. 134.

46 Dorita Fairlie Bruce, *Captain Anne*, 1939, p. 51.

47 Elsie J Oxenham, *An Abbey Champion*, 1946, pp. 22 and 27.

48 Martha Vicinus, *Independent Women*, 1984.

49 Dorita Fairlie Bruce, *Captain Anne*, 1939, p. 125.

50 Elinor M Brent-Dyer, *The New Chalet School*, 1938, pp. 28–9, 90 and 199.

51 Elinor M Brent-Dyer, *The Chalet School Goes To It*, 1941, p. 104.

52 Elinor M Brent-Dyer, *The Chalet School and Barbara*, 1954, p. 107.

53 Elinor M Brent-Dyer, *The New Mistress at the Chalet School*, 1957, pp. 9, 24.

54 Ibid, pp. 130 and 204.

55 Elinor M Brent-Dyer, *Excitements at the Chalet School*, 1957, p. 75.

56 Ibid, p. 165.

57 Elinor M Brent-Dyer, *Theodora and the Chalet School*, 1959, pp. 27 and 147.

58 Elinor M Brent-Dyer, *Ruey Richardson, Chaletian*, 1960, pp. 78 and 81.

59 Ibid, pp. 204–5.

60 Elinor M Brent-Dyer, *Leader in the Chalet School*, 1961, p. 36; *The Chalet School Triplets*, 1963, p. 58.

61 Elinor M Brent-Dyer, *Adrienne and the Chalet School*, 1965, p. 165.

62 Elinor M Brent-Dyer, *Ruey Richardson, Chaletian*, 1960, pp. 90, 183; *The Chalet School Wins the Trick*, 1961, p. 90; *The Feud in the Chalet School*, 1962, p. 187.

63 Elinor M Brent-Dyer, *Jane and the Chalet School*, 1964, p. 108.

64 Elinor M Brent-Dyer, *Redheads at the Chalet School*, 1964, p. 26.

65 Elinor M Brent-Dyer, *The Feud in the Chalet School*, 1962, p. 187; *The Chalet School Triplets*, 1963, p. 48.

66 Elinor M Brent-Dyer, *Challenge for the Chalet School*, 1967, p. 84.

67 Elinor M Brent-Dyer, *Jane and the Chalet School*, 1964, pp. 124–5.

68 Elinor M Brent-Dyer, *Adrienne and the Chalet School*, 1965, p. 64.

69 Elinor M Brent-Dyer, *Challenge for the Chalet School*, 1967, pp. 39, 70–1.

70 Ibid, pp. 100–2.

71 Elinor M Brent-Dyer, *Althea Joins the Chalet School*, 1969.

6

1 Sara Burstall, *English High Schools for Girls*, 1907, p. 160.
2 Gillian Freeman, *The Schoolgirl Ethic: The Life and Works of Angela Brazil*, 1976, p. 118.
3 Burstall, op. cit. p. 160.
4 Janet Montefiore, 'The Fourth Form Girls Go Camping: Sexual Identity and Ambivalence in Girls' School Stories', unpublished paper, 1991, p. 18.
5 Burstall, op. cit. pp. 160–1.

6 Havelock Ellis and John Addington Symonds, *Sexual Inversion*, 1987, p. 85.
7 Ibid, p. 82.
8 Ibid, p. 1.
9 Ibid, pp. 83–4.
10 Ibid, p. 85.
11 Ibid, pp. xiv and 100.
12 Marie Stopes, *Enduring Passion*, 1923, p. 29.
13 Ibid.
14 Clemence Dane, *Regiment of Women*, 1919, p. 336.
15 Ibid, p. 337.
16 Ibid, p. 296.
17 See Annabel Faraday, 'Lessoning Lesbians: Girls' Schools, Coeducation and Anti-lesbianism Between the Wars', in Carol Jones and Pat Mahony (eds), *Learning Our Lines*, 1989, p. 23.
18 Alison Oram, ' "Embittered, Sexless or Homosexual": Attacks on Spinster Teachers 1918–1939', in Lesbian History Group, *Not a Passing Phase*, 1989, pp. 104–6.
19 *The Girl of the Period Miscellany*, No. 9, 1869, p. 277.
20 Clemence Dane, *Regiment of Women*, p. 335.
21 Oram, op. cit., p. 100.
22 The Lord Chancellor in the debate on the bill, quoted by Susan Edwards, *Female Sexuality and the Law*, 1981, p. 44.
23 Oram, op. cit., p. 105.
24 Lilian M Faithfull, 'Real and Counterfeit Friendships', in *You and I*, 1927, p. 111.
25 Ibid, p. 113.
26 Ibid, p. 119.
27 Dorita Fairlie Bruce, *Dimsie Moves Up*, 1921, p. 21.
28 Ibid, pp. 24 and 36.
29 Dorita Fairlie Bruce, *Nancy Returns to St Bride's*, 1938.
30 Martha Vicinus, 'Distance and Desire: English Boarding-School Friendships 1870–1920', in Martin Duberman, Martha Vicinus and George Chauncey Jnr (eds), *Hidden From History*, 1991, p. 213.
31 Dorita Fairlie Bruce, *Dimsie Moves Up Again*, 1922, p. 174.
32 Dorita Fairlie Bruce, *Dimsie, Head Girl*, 1925, p. 242.
33 Dorita Fairlie Bruce, *Dimsie Goes Back*, 1927, p. 17.
34 Dorita Fairlie Bruce, *Dimsie, Head Girl*, 1925, p. 189.
35 Elinor M Brent-Dyer, *A Head Girl's Difficulties*, 1923, p. 154.

36 Ibid, pp. 157–8.
37 Ibid, p. 165.
38 Ibid.
39 Ibid, pp. 166, 168–9.
40 Ibid, pp. 177, 224–5 and 249–50.
41 Vicinus, op. cit., p. 212.
42 Rachel Davis, *Four Miss Pinkertons*, 1936, pp. 62–3 and 68.
43 Ibid, p. 80.
44 Ibid, pp. 73–4.
45 Ibid, pp. 80 and 68.
46 Elinor M Brent-Dyer, *Tom Tackles the Chalet School*, Armada edition 1987 (first published 1948, in book form 1955), p. 7.
47 Ibid, pp. 43–4.
48 Ibid, p. 82.
49 Elinor M Brent-Dyer, *The Chalet School and Rosalie*, Armada edition 1987 (first published 1951) p. 33.
50 Elinor M Brent-Dyer, *A Chalet Girl from Kenya*, 1955, p. 46.
51 Enid Blyton, *Third Year at Malory Towers*, Armada edition 1967 (first published 1948), 362–3.
52 Enid Blyton, *Upper Fourth at Malory Towers*, Armada edition 1990 (first published 1949), p. 43.
53 Ibid, p. 44.
54 Enid Blyton, *Third Year at Malory Towers*, Armada edition, 1967 (first published 1948), p. 360.
55 Ibid, p. 463.
56 Ibid, p. 492.
57 Ibid, p. 360.
58 Ibid, p. 462.
59 Enid Blyton, *Fifth Formers at St Clare's*, Armada edition 1991, p. 360, 1945.
60 Enid Blyton, *Second Form at St Clare's*, Armada edition, 1991, p. 29, 1944.
61 Ibid, pp. 148–9.
62 Enid Blyton, *Fifth Formers at St Clare's*, Armada edition, 1991 (first published 1945), p. 360.
63 Enid Blyton, *First Term at Malory Towers*, Armada edition 1967, p. 65, 1946.
64 Ibid, p. 100.
65 Enid Blyton, *Last Term at Malory Towers*, Armada edition 1990, p. 342, 1951.

66 Elsie J Oxenham, *The Tuck-Shop Girl*, 1916, p. 196.

67 Elsie J Oxenham, *The Camp Mystery*, 1932, p. 146.

68 Elsie J Oxenham, *The Junior Captain*, 1923, p. 124.

69 Elsie J Oxenham, *Deb at School*, 1929, p. 19.

70 Ibid, p. 25.

71 Ibid, p. 44.

72 Ibid, p. 60.

73 Ibid, p. 150.

74 Ibid, pp. 159–60.

75 Ibid, p. 195.

76 Ibid, p. 227.

77 Elsie J Oxenham, *Deb of Sea House*, 1931, p. 79.

78 Ibid, p. 166.

79 Ibid, pp. 201–4.

80 Elsie J Oxenham, *The Abbey Girls in Town* 1925, p. 81.

81 Ibid, p. 308.

82 Elsie J Oxenham, *The Troubles of Tazy*, 1926, pp. 45–6.

83 Ibid, pp. 280–1.

84 Ibid, p. 282.

85 Elsie J Oxenham, *The Abbey Girls Win Through*, 1928, pp. 142–3.

86 Elsie J Oxenham, *Queen of the Abbey Girls*, 1926, p. 81.

87 Elsie J Oxenham, *The Abbey Girls on Trial*, 1931, pp. 185–6.

88 Elsie J Oxenham, *The Abbey Girls Win Through*, 1928, p. 145.

89 Ibid, p. 73.

90 Elsie J Oxenham, *Queen of the Abbey Girls*, 1926, p. 284.

91 Elsie J Oxenham, *The Abbey Girls in Town*, 1925, p. 80.

92 Elsie J Oxenham, *Queen of the Abbey Girls*, 1926, p. 129.

93 Elsie J Oxenham, *The Abbey Girls Win Through*, 1928, p. 175.

94 Elsie J Oxenham, *The Abbey Girls Go Back to School*, 1922, p. 110.

95 Elsie J Oxenham, *Jen of the Abbey School*, 1925, pp. 92–3.

96 Elsie J Oxenham, *The Abbey Girls Play Up*, 1930, pp. 163, 166.

97 Elsie J Oxenham, *The Abbey Girls at Home*, 1929, pp. 103, 191, 234, 238.

98 Elsie J Oxenham, *The Abbey Girls Win Through*, 1928, p. 9.

99 Elsie J Oxenham, *Schooldays at the Abbey*, 1938, p. 116.

100 Elsie J Oxenham, *The Abbey Girls in Town*, 1925, p. 299.

101 Elsie J Oxenham, *Tomboys at the Abbey*, 1957, p. 125.

102   Elsie J Oxenham, *The Abbey Girls Go Back to School*, 1922, p. 216.

103   Elsie J Oxenham, *The Abbey Girls Again*, 1924, p. 106.

104   Elsie J Oxenham, *Stowaways in the Abbey*, 1940, p. 86.

105   Ibid, pp. 112–13.

106   Elsie J Oxenham, *The Song of the Abbey*, 1954, p. 14.

107   Ibid, p. 143.

108   Except possibly Biddy Devine, Mary's sister, who is saved from a foolish first marriage by the death of her husband, and who marries Mr Right in the end. See Elsie J Oxenham, *Biddy's Secret* (1932) and *Maidlin to the Rescue* (1934).

109   Elsie J Oxenham, *The Song of the Abbey*, 1954, p. 172.

110   Elsie J Oxenham, *Two Queens at the Abbey*, 1959, p. 65.

111   Ibid, pp. 171–2.

112   Compare Elsie J Oxenham, *The New Abbey Girls*, 1923, p. 175, with *The New Abbey Girls*, 1959, p. 76.

113   For example, this sentence in *The Chalet School and Jo*, 1931, p. 133. The words in brackets were omitted from the abridged edition of 1970 (p. 74). 'Simone Lecoutier [,a French girl of their own age, had a deep adoration for Jo, and] was, unfortunately, inclined to be very jealous [of her].'

7

1   Marie Gray, *Memorials of Emily Shirreff*, 1897, quoted in Carol Dyhouse, 'Towards a "Feminine" Curriculum for English Schoolgirls: the Demands of Ideology 1870–1963', *Women's Studies International Quarterly*, No. I, 1978, p. 300.

2   Dyhouse, op. cit., pp. 300–8.

3   Annmarie Turnbull, 'Learning her Womanly Work: the Elementary School Curriculum, 1870–1914', in Felicity Hunt (ed.), *Lessons for Life. The Schooling of Girls and Women 1850–1950*, 1987, p. 99.

4   Felicity Hunt, 'Divided Aims: the Educational Implications of Opposing Ideologies in Girls' Secondary Schooling, 1850–1914', in Hunt (ed.), *Lessons for Life*, pp. 9–15.

5   See E Moberly Bell, *Storming the Citadel: The Rise of the Woman Doctor*, 1953.

6   M V Hughes, *A London Girl of the 1880s*, 1978 (first published 1946), pp. 42–3.

7   Ibid, p. 35.

8   June Purvis, *A History of Women's Education in England*, 1991, p. 83.

9   Lucy Kinlock, *A World Within a School*, 1937, p. 3.

10 Margaret A Gillibrand, 'Home Arts', in Sara A Burstall and M A Douglas (eds), *Public Schools for Girls*, 1911, p. 194.

11 Sara A Burstall, *English High School for Girls*, 1907, p. 194.

12 The Six-Point Group was founded in 1920 as a non-party pressure group for women to push for parliamentary reform. See Dale Spender (ed.), *Time and Tide Wait for No Man*, 1984; Ruth Adam, *A Woman's Place 1910–75*, 1975; Eleanor Rathbone, *Our Freedom and its Results*, 1936.

13 Vera Brittain, *Testament of Friendship*, 1941, pp. 96–7.

14 Gillian Avery, *The Best Type of Girl. A History of Girls' Independent Schools*, 1991, p. 258.

15 See, for example, the account of the rise and fall of the University of London which granted degrees in Household and Social Science, Neville Marsh, The History of Queen Elizabeth College, 1986.

16 See Helen Sillitoe, *History of the Teaching of Domestic Subjects*, 1933, Chapters XVII, XIX and XX.

17 P W Musgrave, *Society and Education in England Since 1800*, 1968, pp. 83, 90–1, 103 and 114.

18 Dorita Fairlie Bruce, *Dimsie Goes to School*, 1921, p. 42.

19 Ibid, p. 43.

20 Winifred Peck, *A Little Learning*, 1952, p. 127.

21 Elsie J Oxenham, *The Abbey Girls in Town*, 1925, p. 82.

22 Ibid, p. 208.

23 Ibid, p. 209.

24 Elsie J Oxenham, *Queen of the Abbey Girls*, 1926, p. 91.

25 Elsie J Oxenham, *The Abbey Girls on Trial*, 1931.

26 Elsie J Oxenham, *Maid of the Abbey*, 1943, pp. 68–9.

27 Elsie J Oxenham, *The Abbey Girls Win Through*, 1928, pp. 132 and 178–9.

28 Elsie J Oxenham, *Rosamund's Tuck-Shop*, 1937, pp. 12–3.

29 Dorita Fairlie Bruce, *The School in the Woods*, 1940.

30 Elinor M Brent-Dyer, *The Chalet Girls in Camp*, 1932, p. 224.

31 Ibid, p. 225.

32 Ibid, pp. 225–6.
33 Elinor M Brent-Dyer, *Carola Storms the Chalet School*, 1951, pp. 44–5.
34 Elinor M Brent-Dyer, *The Chalet Girls' Cook Book*, 1953, pp. 206–8.
35 Dorita Fairlie Bruce, *Prefects at Springdale*, 1938, pp. 39, 42.
36 Ibid, pp. 50, 223.
37 Ibid, p. 222.

Conclusion

1 Helen McClelland, *Behind the Chalet School*, second edition, 1986, p. 175.
2 Personal communication, Lesbian History Group, 1991.
3 Adrienne Rich, *Compulsory Heterosexuality and Lesbian Existence*, 1981.
4 Janet Montefiore, 'The Fourth Form Girls Go Camping: Sexual Identity and Ambivalence in Girls' School Stories', unpublished paper, 1991, p. 3.
5 Ibid.
6 Ibid, pp. 10–11.
7 Ibid, pp. 11–12.
8 Lilian Faithfull, *In the House of My Pilgrimage*, 1924, p. 97.

Bibliography

(Place of publication is London unless otherwise stated)

GENERAL WORKS ON LITERATURE, POPULAR CULTURE, AND THE ARTS

Adler, Kathleen, 'The Suburban, the Modern, and "une Dame de Passy" ', *Oxford Art Journal*, Vol. 12, No. 1, 1989, p. 3.

Allen, Grace, 'To market, to market, to buy a fat book', *Junior Bookshelf*, 1937, p. 11.

Auerbach, Nina, *Communities of Women. An idea in fiction*, Harvard University Press, Cambridge Mass., 1978.

Avery, Gillian, *Childhood's Pattern. A study of the heroes and heroines of children's fiction 1770–1950*, Hodder & Stoughton, 1975.

Beauman, Nicola, *A Very Great Profession. The women's novel 1914–39*, Virago, 1983.

Brazil, Angela, *My Own Schooldays*, Blackie, 1925.

Cadogan, Mary, and Craig, Patricia, *Women and Children First. The fiction of two world wars*, Gollancz, 1978.

Cadogan, Mary, and Craig, Patricia, *You're a Brick, Angela! A new look at girls' fiction from 1839 to 1975*, Gollancz, 1976.

Crouch, Marcus, *The Nesbit Tradition. The Children's Novel in England 1945–1970*, Rowan & Littlefield, Totowa, 1972.

Crouch, Marcus, *Treasure Seekers and Borrowers. Children's books in Britain 1900–1960*, The Library Association, 1962.

Dixon, Bob, *Catching Them Young 1. Sex, Race and Class in Children's Fiction*, Pluto, 1977.

229

Dixon, Bob, *Catching Them Young 2. Political Ideas in Children's Fiction*, Pluto, 1977.

Eyre, Frank, *British Children's Books in the Twentieth Century*, Longman, 1971.

Eyre, Frank, *Twentieth Century Children's Books*, British Council, Longman, 1952.

Fisher, Margery, *Intent Upon Reading. A critical appraisal of modern fiction for children*, Brockhampton Press, Leicester, 1961.

Fisher, Margery, *Who's Who in Children's Books*, Weidenfeld & Nicolson, 1975.

Ford, Boris (ed.), *Young Writers, Young Readers*, Hutchinson, 1960.

Freeman, Gillian, *The Schoolgirl Ethic. The life and works of Angela Brazil*, Allen Lane, 1976.

Frith, Gill, ' "The Time of your Life": the meaning of the school story', in Steedman, Carolyn, Unwin, Cathy, and Walkerdine, Valerie (eds), *Language, Gender and Childhood*, Routledge & Kegan Paul, 1985.

Gardner, Frank M, *Sequels*, Association of Assistant Librarians, Fifth edition, 1967.

Guthrie, James, 'Realism and escapism in children's literature', *Junior Bookshelf*, 1958, p. 15.

[Hamilton, Charles], *The Autobiography of Frank Richards*, Skilton Memorial ed, 1962.

Harlen, Paul, 'The "Biggles" Books', *Junior Bookshelf*, 1944, pp. 66–7.

Hughes, Thomas, *Tom Brown's School Days*, Macmillan, 1958 (1857).

Lawrence, M J P, 'Wanted – some good school stories', *Junior Bookshelf*, 1954, p. 61.

Marshall, Arthur, *Girls Will Be Girls*, Hamish Hamilton, 1974.

Mason, Bobbie Ann, *The Girl Sleuth: A Feminist Guide*, Feminist Press, New York, 1975.

Montefiore, Janet, The Fourth Form Girls Go Camping:

Sexual Identity and Ambivalence in Girls' School Stories, unpublished paper, 1991.

Nightingale, Cammilla, 'Sex Roles in Children's Literature', in Allen, Sandra, Sanders, Lee and Wallis, Jan (eds), *Conditions of Illusion*, Feminist Books, 1974, p. 141.

Orwell, George, 'Boys' Weeklies', in Orwell, Sonia and Angus, Ian (eds), *The Collected Essays, Journalism and Letters of George Orwell*, Vol. 1, Secker & Warburg, 1968, p. 460. (Originally published in *Horizon* in 1940).

Paxford, Sandra, 'The Happiest Days of Your Life', *Junior Bookshelf*, 1971, p. 153.

Radford, Jean (ed.), *The Progress of Romance: The politics of popular fiction*, Routledge & Kegan Paul, 1986.

Radway, Janice A, *Reading the Romance: Women, patriarchy, and popular literature*, Verso, 1987.

Richards, Frank, 'Reply to George Orwell', in Orwell, Sonia and Angus, Ian (eds), *The Collected Essays, Journalism and Letters of George Orwell*, Vol. 1. Secker and Warburg, 1968, p. 485. (Originally published in *Horizon* in 1940.)

Shaw, Marion, and Vanacker, Sabine, *Reflecting on Miss Marple*, Routledge, 1991.

Tatham, C S, 'Yesterday's Schoolgirl', *Junior Bookshelf*, 1969, p. 349.

Trease, Geoffrey, *Tales Out of School*, Heinemann, 1948.

Winship, Janice, *Inside Women's Magazines*, Pandora, 1987.

SCHOOLS AND SCHOOLGIRLS

St Leonard's School 1877–1927, Oxford University Press, 1927.

Avery, Gillian, *The Best Type of Girl. A History of Girls' Independent Schools*, André Deutsch, 1991.

Burstall, Sara A, *English High School for Girls*, Longmans, 1907.

Burstall, Sara A, *Retrospect and Prospect. 60 years of women's education*, Longmans, 1933.

Burstall, Sara A, *The Story of Manchester High School for Girls 1871–1911*, Manchester University Press, 1911.

Dane, Clemence, *Regiment of Women*, Heinemann, 1917.

Davies, Emily, 'Special Systems of Education for Women', 1868, in Spender, Dale (ed.), *The Education Papers*, Routledge & Kegan Paul, 1987.

Dyhouse, Carol, 'Towards a "Feminine" Curriculum for English Girls: the Demands of Ideology 1870–1963', *Women's Studies International Quarterly* I, 1978, pp. 291–311.

Faithfull, Lilian M, *In the House of My Pilgrimage*, Chatto & Windus, 1924.

Faithfull, Lilian M, *You and I. Saturday Talks at Cheltenham*, Chatto & Windus, 1927.

Faraday, Annabel, 'Lessoning Lesbians: Girls' Schools, Coeducation and Anti-Lesbianism Between the Wars', in Jones, Carol and Mahony, Pat (eds), *Learning Our Lines: Sexuality and Social Control in Education*, The Women's Press, 1989.

Fletcher, Sheila, *Women First: The female tradition in English physical education 1880–1980*, The Athlone Press, 1984.

Gillibrand, Margaret A, 'Home Arts', in Burstall, Sara A and Douglas, M A (eds), *Public Schools for Girls*, Longmans, 1911; also reprinted in Spender, Dale (ed.), *The Education Papers*, Routledge & Kegan Paul, 1987.

Greene, Graham (ed.), *The Old School*, Cape, 1934.

Hunt, Felicity (ed.), *Lessons for Life: The schooling of girls and women 1850–1950*, Blackwell, Oxford, 1987.

Kinlock, Lucy, *A World Within a School*, Warne, 1937.

McCrone, Kathleen E, *Sport and the Physical Emancipation of English Women*, Routledge, 1988.

Marsh, Neville, *The History of Queen Elizabeth College*, King's College London, 1986.

Musgrave, P W, *Society and Education in England Since 1800*, Methuen, 1968.

Oram, Alison, ' "Embittered, Sexless, or Homosexual": Attacks on Spinster Teachers 1918–1939', in Lesbian History Group, *Not a Passing Phase. Reclaiming Lesbians in History 1840–1985*, The Women's Press, 1989.

Oram, Alison, 'Serving Two Masters? The introduction of a marriage bar in teaching in the 1920s', in London Feminist History Group, *The Sexual Dynamics of History*, Pluto, 1989.

Purvis, June, *A History of Girls' Education in England*, Open University Press, 1991.

Sillitoe, Helen, *A History of the Teaching of Domestic Subjects*, Methuen, 1933.

Soulsby, Lucy H M, 'Friendship and Love', in *Stray Thoughts for Girls*, Longmans, 1903.

Turnbull, Annmarie, 'Learning her Womanly Work: the Elementary School Curriculum 1870–1914', in Hunt, Felicity (ed.), *Lessons for Life*, Blackwell, 1987.

Vicinus, Martha, 'Distance and Desire: English Boarding-School Friendships 1870–1920', in Duberman, Martin, Vicinus, Martha and Chauncey, George Jr (eds), *Hidden from History. Reclaiming the Gay and Lesbian Past*, Penguin, 1991.

Vicinus, Martha, *Independent Women: Work and Community for Single Women 1850–1920*, Virago, 1985.

Enid Blyton

Novels, by series, in reading order

Order of publication	Title	Date

Naughtiest Girl series

Originally published in single volumes by Newnes; paperback editions by Beaver 1979, Red Fox 1990

1.	*The Naughtiest Girl in the School*	1940
2.	*The Naughtiest Girl Again*	1942
3.	*The Naughtiest Girl is a Monitor*	1944

St Clare's series

Originally published in single volumes by Methuen; paperback editions by Dragon Books 1967, Armada 1988

1. *The Twins at St Clare's*   1941
2. *The O'Sullivan Twins*   1942
3. *Summer Term at St Clare's*   1943
4. *Claudine at St Clare's*   1944
5. *The Second Form at St Clare's*   1944
6. *Fifth Formers at St Clare's*   1945

Malory Towers series

Originally published in single volumes by Methuen;
paperback editions by Dragon Books 1967, Armada 1988

1. *First Term at Malory Towers*   1946
2. *Second Form at Malory Towers*   1947
3. *Third Year at Malory Towers*   1948
4. *Upper Fourth at Malory Towers*   1949
5. *In the Fifth at Malory Towers*   1950
6. *Last Term at Malory Towers*   1951

Also:

Mischief at St Rollo's. (Originally published under the pseudo-
    nym Mary Pollock) Werner Laurie 1947 (Collins 1976 in
    Adventure Stories; Armada paperback 1982)

Biographical and critical

Blyton, Enid, *The Story of My Life*, Pitkins, 1952.
Dixon, Bob, 'Enid Blyton and Her Sunny Stories', in *Catch-
    ing Them Young 2. Political Ideas in Children's Fiction*, Pluto,
    1977.
Dohm, Janice, 'The Work of Enid Blyton', in Ford, Boris
    ed., *Young Writers, Young Readers*, Hutchinson revised edi-
    tion, 1963.
Ray, Sheila G, *The Blyton Phenomenon*, André Deutsch, 1982.
Smallwood, Imogen, *Childhood at Green Hedges*, Methuen,
    1989.
Stoney, Barbara, *Enid Blyton*, Hodder & Stoughton, 1974.

Elinor M Brent-Dyer

Novels, by series, in reading order

Order of publication	Title	Date

La Rochelle series (published by Chambers, Edinburgh)

1.	*Gerry Goes to School*	1922
2.	*A Head Girl's Difficulties*	1923
3.	*The Maids of La Rochelle*	1924
4.	*Seven Scamps Who Are Not All Boys*	1927
5.	*Heather Leaves School*	1929
6.	*Janie of La Rochelle*	1932
7.	*Janie Steps In*	1953

Chalet School series (published by Chambers, Edinburgh)

1.	*The School at the Chalet*	1925
2.	*Jo of the Chalet School*	1926
3.	*The Princess of the Chalet School*	1927
4.	*The Head Girl of the Chalet School*	1928
5.	*The Rivals of the Chalet School*	1929
6.	*Eustacia Goes to the Chalet School*	1930
7.	*The Chalet School and Jo*	1931
8.	*The Chalet Girls in Camp*	1932
9.	*The Exploits of the Chalet Girls*	1933
10.	*The Chalet School and the Lintons*	1934
11.	*The New House at the Chalet School*	1935
12.	*Jo Returns to the Chalet School*	1936
13.	*The New Chalet School*	1938
14.	*The Chalet School in Exile*	1940
15.	*The Chalet School Goes To It*	1941
16.	*The Highland Twins at the Chalet School*	1942
17.	*Lavender Laughs in the Chalet School*	1943
18.	*Gay From China at the Chalet School*	1944
19.	*Jo to the Rescue*	1945
	The Chalet Book for Girls	1947
	The Second Chalet Book for Girls	1948
	The Third Chalet Book for Girls	1949

53. *Adrienne and the Chalet School*	1965
54. *Summer Term at the Chalet School*	1965
55. *Challenge for the Chalet School*	1966
56. *Two Sams at the Chalet School*	1967
57. *Althea Joins the Chalet School*	1969
58. *Prefects of the Chalet School*	1970

Janeways books

| *A Thrilling Term at Janeways*. Nelson | 1927 |
| *Caroline the Second*. Girls' Own Paper | 1937 |

Lorna books

| *Lorna at Wynyards*. Lutterworth Press | 1947 |
| *Stepsisters for Lorna*. Temple | 1948 |

Fardingales books

| *Fardingales*. Latimer House | 1950 |
| *The 'Susannah' Adventure*. Chambers | 1953 |

Chudleigh Hold books

Chudleigh Hold. Chambers	1954
Condor Crags Adventure. Chambers	1954
Top Secret. Chambers	1955

Schoolgirls Abroad: a series of geography readers published by Chambers 1951
1. *Verena Visits New Zealand*
2. *Bess on her Own in Canada*
3. *Quintette in Queensland*
4. *Sharlie's Kenya Diary*

Skelton Hall books

| *The School at Skelton Hall*. Max Parrish | 1962 |
| *Trouble at Skelton Hall*. Max Parrish | 1963 |

Others

The New Housemistress. Nelson	1928
Judy the Guide. Nelson	1928
The School by the River. Burns Oates & Washbourne	1930
The Feud in the Fifth Remove. Girls' Own Paper	1931

The Little Marie Jose. Burns Oates & Washbourne	1932
Carnation of the Upper Fourth. Girls' Own Paper	1934
Elizabeth the Gallant. Thornton Butterworth	1935
Monica Turns Up Trumps. Girls' Own Paper	1936
The Little Missus. Chambers	1942
The Lost Staircase. Chambers	1946
Nesta Steps Out. Oliphants	1954
Kennelmaid Nan. Lutterworth Press	1954
Beechy of the Harbour School. Oliphants	1955
Leader in Spite of Herself. Oliphants	1956

Biographical and critical

'Book and Magazine Collectors' Review of Current Selling Prices: Elinor Brent-Dyer'. *Book and Magazine Collectors' Review*, March 1988, p. 10.

Chalet Club Newsletter Nos. 14–20, Chambers, Edinburgh, 1966–9.

Elinor M Brent-Dyer's Chalet School, with additional material by Helen McClelland, Armada, 1989.

'Miss Brent-Dyer. Author of Chalet School Tales', *The Times* (obituary), 23 September 1969.

Cadogan, Mary, 'Elinor M Brent-Dyer', in Kirkpatrick D L (ed.), *Twentieth Century Children's Writers*, St Martin's Press, New York, 1983.

Godfrey, Monica, 'Elinor Brent-Dyer and the Chalet School Stories', *Book and Magazine Collectors' Review*, December 1984, p. 40.

McClelland, Helen, *Behind the Chalet School*, New Horizon, Bognor Regis, 1981, 1984.

Dorita Fairlie Bruce

Novels, by series, in reading order

Order of publication	Title	Date
Dimsie series (published by Oxford University Press)		
1. *The Senior Prefect (Dimsie Goes to School)*		1920

| 3. *The Debatable Mound* | 1953 |
| 4. *The Bartle Bequest* | 1955 |

Sally series (published by Oxford University Press)

1. *Sally Scatterbrain*	1956
2. *Sally Again*	1959
3. *Sally's Summer Term*	1961

Others

The King's Curate	1930
Mistress Mariner	1932
A Laverock Lilting	1945
Wild Goose Quest	1945
The Bees on Drumwhinnie	1952

Biographical and critical

Cadogan, Mary, 'Dorita Fairlie Bruce', in Kirkpatrick, D L (ed.), *Twentieth Century Children's Writers*, St Martin's Press, New York, 1983.

Elsie J Oxenham

Novels, by series, in reading order

Order of publication	Title	Date

Abbey books

0. *The Girls of the Hamlet Club*. Chambers (This is not an Abbey book, but the Abbey series is as it were a sequel to it. The book introduces the Wycombe school and the Hamlet club which is central to the Abbey girls' lives.)	1914
1. *The Abbey Girls*. Collins	1920
2. *The Girls of the Abbey School*. Collins	1921
20. *Schooldays at the Abbey*. Collins	1938
21. *Secrets of the Abbey*. Collins	1939
22. *Stowaways in the Abbey*. Collins	1940
30. *Schoolgirl Jen in the Abbey*. Collins	1950

Rocklands books

Kentisbury books

1. *Patch and a Pawn*. Warne   1942
2. *The Secrets of Vairy*. Muller   1944

Rainbows books

1. *Pernel Wins*. Muller   1942
2. *Elsa Puts Things Right*. Muller   1944
3. *Daring Doranne*. Muller   1945
4. *Margery Meets the Roses*. Lutterworth Press   1947

Early books

Set in Scotland

1. *Goblin Island*. Collins   1907
2. *A Princess in Tatters*. Collins   1908
3. *A Holiday Queen*. Collins   1910
4. *Rosaly's New School*. Chambers   1913
5. *Schoolgirls and Scouts*. Collins   1914

Set in Wales

1. *The Conquest of Christina*. Collins   1909
2. *The Girl Who Wouldn't Make Friends*. Nelson   1909

Set in Switzerland

2. *The Twins of Castle Charming*. Swarthmore Press   1920
1. *Expelled from School*. Collins   1919

Others

1. *At School with the Roundheads*. Chambers   1915
2. *Finding Her Family*. Society for Promoting Christian Knowledge   1915
3. *A School Camp Fire*. Chambers   1917
4. *Dorothy's Dilemma*. Chambers   1930
5. *Sylvia of Sarn*. Warne   1937
6. *New Girls at Wood End*. Blackie   1957

Historical novels

1. *Mistress Nanciebel*. Hodder & Stoughton   1910
2. *The Girls of Gwynfa*. Warne   1924

Biographical and critical

Muir, Lynette, 'Fifty Years of the Hamlet Club', *Junior Bookshelf*, 1966, p. 19.

Oxenham, Erica, *'J.O.'*, Longmans, Green and Co, 1942.

Oxenham, Erica, *Scrapbook of J.O.*, Longmans, Green and Co, 1946.